The Symphony of Aging

How to Orchestrate Your Health Maximize Your Life Span Enjoy Your Senior Years

Jean J. Labelle MD

This book is dedicated to my lovely wife Sandy,
who has been very tolerant during this writing.
I love her very much.

DISCLAIMER

This book is the result of a huge amount of reading I have done in the last ten years, but particularly in the last five years since I am retired. My curiosity made me read many medical articles in the *New England Journal of Medicine*, *Journal of the American Medical Association*, *Nature*, *Scientific American*, and so many other publications of my trade. I wanted to know what caused the damage I had in my body, and so I did a lot of literature searching and Web searching.

I have read forty to fifty books on these subjects.

I went to anti-aging meetings and medical meetings yearly.

I have taught senior college courses for six years now and my students urged me to write.

With my medical background, I analyzed all this information and came to the conclusions stated in this book.

Obviously, I have developed strong opinions but they were based on a lot of background studying. They are never fleeting opinions, based on bias from selling a product or advertising one. I do not do that in any form but the teaching.

I do not pretend to know everything, but I can assure the reader that I give these opinions honestly. As the science goes forward, so will I alter my opinions.

My intentions in this book are to inform and educate the public of knowledge relative to the specifics of aging.

I sell no products except this book. If I have made faulty or undue statements or comments about any person or entity, it was done unintentionally and without malice.

ACKNOWLEDGMENTS

Sandi Gelles-Cole who indeed was a book doctor for my first book and with broad strokes of a pen and very appropriate suggestions corrected my first attempt at writing this. She helped me to the very last minute. She is a very dedicated person and dear to me. I am very grateful to her. Kenneth Salzmann was very helpful at the last minute.

Jodi Walukonis, the redactor of my first too verbose and inadequate attempt at writing this book. She was helpful and taught me a lot.

David Merrill, Eric Saunders, Robert Kramer my very dear friends, all supported me and gave me innumerable and invaluable suggestions and constructive criticisms.

Erica Pelton Villnave, Linda Sapakie, Scott Leighton, and many others who have had contact with me about this book in the three years of its inception.

Donna Hunter at Working Words & Graphics skillfully designed the cover.

To my dear deceased Father and Mother who repeatedly said to me" If someone else can do it, so can you can do it."

And finally and very importantly, the constant and total encouragement, support given to me by son Bryan. He designed the web site, thesymphonyofaging.com with Jessica Wittebort, his illustrator-girlfriend. They are special to me.

This book was written at the urging of my many students to whom I taught this course in the last seven years. They sure kept me on my toes. Their questions contributed to the evolution of this book and its author.

ABOUT THE AUTHOR

Jean Labelle, born in Montreal in 1935, is a "retired" plastic surgeon, if you can call retired, a doctor who travels the third world to perform and teach reconstructive and hand surgery. As a member of Interplast (Interplast.org) he has traveled to Nepal, Thailand, India, Vietnam, Myanmar, Peru, Brazil, Honduras, Nicaragua, Haiti and more.

THE SYMPHONY OF AGING was born out of Dr. Labelle's passion for knowledge of his own maturing and turned into an entire change in his thinking and then into a bend in the road in his career. After closing his private practice in Portland, Maine, and his teaching responsibilities at the Lahey clinic in June 2000, Jean could turn his attention to the issue that had been nagging at him, why his own body was deteriorating. Now finally he could find out all the factors responsible for aging, and how he could beat his heredity. That endeavor became a total joy and passion. He started teaching it to the senior college of Southern Maine University and later in Florida at the International College's seniors' classes. Many students wondered why there was no book on the subject that explained the aging process in Labelle's terms, that is, looking at it and as a reversible disease and in all its aspects.

In Labelle's words, "Enter a new profession. I thought it was going to be just writing. Well, it wasn't. I learned to type, to turn my computer on, to use Word, transfer files, research the internet—and I am not even talking about writing, editors, book doctors, agents, publishers, and the list goes on. It all humbled me and invigorated me to be in contact with this new profession of very capable people. But I did find, although I was skeptical at first that we can still learn well in later years, you *can* teach an old dog new tricks."

CONTENTS

Wear and tear theory
Limited cell number of divisions
Exercise, Foods, Damages (toxic agents, radiation, etc)

Their profound effects in the body
The major types of hormones
The various major hormones and their functions
Menopause and hormones
Hormone replacement

Every day of your life
Cells
Free-radicals
Inflammation
Brain-body connections
Tissue damaging agents
    Air pollution
    Dust
    Water contamination
    Radiation
    Toxins in foods and drinks
    Factors from within your own body

Mental Benefits
Advantages to the body
    Reserve
    Brain
    Circulation and lungs
    Muscles, tendons and Joints
    Osteoporosis

Crash diets and anorexia

CHAPTER ONE

Why This Book?

I can understand how you feel at, let's say, the age of fifty to fifty-five. You have had a good life, worked hard, probably raised a family and enjoyed relatively good health, up to now. But now you are seeing different subtle things happening to your body and it brings to mind that, by gosh, "I am aging after all."

"Wow! I must do something to stay in shape, but how in the world can I prevent this aging stuff?"

"I don't want to age if I am going to be sick or mentally unfit."

"I am scared."

That's exactly what I said to myself a few years ago, or at least so it seems. Time goes so fast.

You are an active person with a good job and have been relatively successful in life. You are going to retire one day soon and do not want just to linger around and inevitably get sick. But where do you get the information to continue a decent life, or to help yourself to a healthier older age period. The stuff out there on aging is so scattered that you don't know how to use it with confidence.

Well, I bet these questions and many others like them apply to a lot of you. That is exactly what I asked myself at that age but most particularly at sixty my fears crystallized. At that point,

I went on a quest to see what I could do to help myself to a healthier and less disease-riddled life.

What I soon discovered was that there were no specific publications or centers that would tell me what all the factors of aging were.

There are a lot of them telling you all about diets, exercises, vitamins, growth hormones and whatnot, but none have looked at the big picture and outlined it for you. There was and is a huge body of information out there but it is difficult to sort out. I did not know which was reliable and which wasn't. It all came in bits and pieces and a lot of them from vendors.

Let's go back to my mid life when I was a busy surgeon doing a lot of reconstruction and hand surgery. Of course, I was too busy to exercise except occasionally on weekends. I was thirty pounds overweight, always hungry--like one hundred percent of the time hungry—and constantly eating anything I could put my hand on, which of course meant mostly carbs.

Although I loved what I was doing as a surgeon, I knew that one day I would end up like my Dad and all of his male siblings, dying of heart disease around fifty. I stopped smoking at forty, and that was a start, but I gained more weight. I could not understand why I was so hungry, since I was following the low fat diet that was "so healthy for me," with my high cholesterol and the hereditary heart condition.

Guess what! At sixty, I had heart symptoms but knew not to be in denial about it. I was intelligent enough not to yield to my instinct to procrastinate, so immediately I saw my cardiologist who did an angiogram to look at the inside of my heart vessels.

Paul said, "Jean, your main heart artery is blocked ninety-four percent and the next attack could be fatal." Two days later, I had an open-heart operation done by my closest friend, Dr. Robert Kramer, who did seven bypass vessels on me. You can imagine that I, the busy surgeon, didn't have time to be sick and I knew from long surgical experience that the sooner you get your butt out of bed and exercising, the sooner you recuperate.

Six weeks later I was back to work, but a different man: now I really had to answer that question that had consumed me then and is doing so to this day, and hopefully until I die twenty, thirty or forty years from now:

"Why am I deteriorating? Why do my vessels have this killing arteriosclerosis? And why can't anybody give me straight answers about aging?"

That was ten years ago and a great many books, articles, Internet research sessions, and anti-aging meetings later, I am still researching today. I discovered a lot of causative factors that we can positively alter to change our aging years very favorably.

I stopped looking at aging with tunnel vision. I started seeing it from an overall view and realized that it is a mistake to blame aging only on one or two factors. It is purely the outcome of many vectors converging to cause destruction on the body— relentlessly, minutely, day by day over the years.

I answered a lot of questions: What causes arteriosclerosis? Why was I always hungry? Why was I gaining weight? Why was I always feeling sluggish?

In short, why was my body slowly disintegrating? And I started seeing a much bigger picture and gaining understanding. I eventually started teaching these answers in colleges in Maine and Florida, and my teaching stimulated me to more research.

Of course, everyone who ever took my courses asked me why I did not write a book. You know, it turned out I wasn't too old to do that after all. I knew that at that age one should never shut the door to new hobbies, new avocations or new sports.

So I learned to type, use computers, write in Word, to become a schoolteacher, to become a writer and come to understand the ABCs of the writing world, and here I am today.

I still have a lot to learn, but at least I am trying. I have not thrown in the towel. Besides, I am having great satisfaction knowing I can do it. What a rush!

I was seventy a few months ago. Does that tell you something? Sure, we can all do it at this age! No, you are not too old to start, and to reverse the process. Of course, if you have shut the door to your brain and will power, you will never begin to help yourself.

Well, I am very frustrated by the "lie down and let the steamroller go over me" attitude of most people. I see all these people aging poorly with no energy and often just coasting, backaching, slow, depressed, forgetting, cantankerous, osteoporotic and sick. I know that if they had known, they would not have gotten to this point. I know they could be so much better if they just knew how and gave themselves the benefit of the effort.

They actually can do something to improve themselves, to slow or prevent the aging process, to be better and healthier next year and in the years afterward. I hate that defeatist attitude of our population, of the whole world for that matter. I'd love to reverse that attitude. I just want everyone to realize that there is a major priority in life and it is: *me, myself and I,* first and foremost. We all tend to put that aside. I failed on this one badly until the heart condition shocked me back to reality.

Let me give you a very common example in our lives of our misplaced priorities: We mostly all own cars, and look at all the fuss we make about them. You mostly know how that car functions. You know what a carburetor is, what pistons do, what axle joints are, what kind of gasoline your vehicle needs, what specific oil and grease it takes and when, what happens if you no longer have water in the cooling system, and so on.

When that car wore out or got damaged in an accident, you took metal, rubber, paint and plastic to replace or repair the injury. Each car you have owned has cost you between $500 and $1000 a month (according to AAA), including depreciation, gas and oil, maintenance, insurance and all that stuff.

You ran that car for 80,000 miles and it started breaking down, yet you had that baby in the garage for repairs at the earliest possible signs of problems. Eventually, it required too much maintenance, so you sold it and bought a new one. You loved that car and you did everything for it. But when you stopped using it and left it in unused in the field, it started to rust very fast and gradually died.

Why for heaven's sake don't we know the anatomy and functioning of our most precious car, our own body and mind? Why don't we learn what a heart, vessels, hormones, muscles, and so on, are and do? Why they break down. How to repair them. How to maintain them. How to feed them the right fuel. How to avoid inappropriate wear and tear.

Why do we procrastinate on maintenance when our knee joints are worn, when our heart vessels are obstructed, when we have a bad back …? Why for heaven's sake don't we want to spend $500 to $1000 a month on this most precious body and mind of ours? Yet we do just that for our cars without even giving it a second thought. Why is that? Why do we listen to vendors trying to sell us a bill of goods to magically cure or prevent aging? We all know they can't be right. We know inside our hearts that these magic pills, five minutes-a-day exercisers and terrific, foolproof crash diets won't work.

Incidentally, we will not be able to exchange that body of ours for a new model when we have worn it down. We are stuck with it. So we must either maintain it or ultimately end up in the junk yard… graveyard?

Disuse is the same for cars as it is for our precious bodies. When autos are being used actively, they are much less likely to break down. Look at how many early twentieth century cars are still functioning because their owners took care of them. Imagine if we did the same for our bodies. We'd live one hundred years plus, and remain healthy.

Of course, we will have to do maintenance to our bodies as we grow older. So what? It's an old body, but can keep functioning for a long time, like the old cars.

I decided to write this book to share my experiences and acquired knowledge with you. I enjoy pursuing knowledge. I always have. So this book is *Your Body 101*---just the basic concepts of what your body is and what to do to maintain it.

I must warn you, a lot of the concepts are going to irritate you. You will think them wrong, but persist on reading, as you will also learn many tricks and principles that will complete your knowledge. Of course, you won't agree with me on everything, and that is good. I want to rattle your knowledge cage so that what you believe in today either will re-affirm itself or you'll find my concepts better and adopt them. I believe in them after all that research. Maybe you will, too.

Notice I didn't say it was going to be easy. But if you follow the advice, you will feel better, more alert and vigorous later, next year, and you will get better and better as you age. Please don't expect immediate gratification and immediate results. That is one of the major failures of our society—fast cars, crash diets, magic anti-aging pills, magic surgery or ointments for wrinkles, and they all yield short-term results and, as a matter of fact, in the long run often severely harm mind and body.

By the way, I am not selling any products and I am giving you this knowledge, analyzed with a solid medical foundation and keen interest in teaching. I am not perfect, nor is the knowledge of aging so far, but I will try my best I assure you.

I love life and what it gives me. I take the most advantage of it. My wife and I play tennis, bike, swim, kayak, walk most evenings, ski, go camping, and we love all of it. Most of our trips are activity trips since activity is an intrinsic part of our life. These trips are always more fun anyway. I still do my third world surgery trips and try to take long daily walks on all of them. By having that emphasis of exercise in life and somewhat proper eating—at least my wife's cooking—both of us are able to be very fulfilled and happy. I am sure that my heredity will catch up with me at some point, but I sure will make it run after me, rather than lying down and letting it bowl me over.

Incidentally, heredity is not inevitable. I was born with the genes for gout, elevated homocysteine, severe arteriosclerosis and allergies and so far have managed to beat all of them. Just remember that many genetic problems can be overcome. You must never think that they are inevitable.

This concept is not about committing your life to drudgery. Totally the contrary. I am having a lot of fun, being with friends, exploring, exercising, being fulfilled and not aching constantly, thus making life so much more enjoyable in all aspects. This concept is all about making a strong commitment to *Numero Uno*, signing a contract with yourself to follow the advice and particularly to do something positive on a daily basis to reverse the damage, so that you can be a lot better next year and thereafter. It really is a modest commitment that will yield the great result of a happy, energetic, and very satisfying life.

You will reverse or forestall the brain damage that we so fear, the arthritis, osteoporosis, fat, heart disease, achy-breaky feeling of so many aging people, and above all the downward slope of the aging degradation of our minds and bodies.

It will not stop that process but it will reduce it by seventy to seventy-five percent and give you an enjoyable life as a side benefit. So please bear with me and follow the logic and advice. It will work to your favor. If it doesn't, at least you can always say, "I tried," and feel good that you did. You never will say "I should've, could've, would've."

It is interesting how as a "know-it-all" physician I had to set aside many preconceived ideas about various aspects of everything concerning ourselves. For instance, the fat free diet was the best thing for cholesterol and the heart.

What a shock it was to find out what a fallacy that was. But the fact I was on that diet and got severe heart vessel damage made me research and seriously question it, and eventually find out what food was all about. From that, many other cast-in-stone concepts were questioned and some were quite good, although some were equally bad or false. *Start with a fresh mind.*

You'll cringe at a lot of things I say, as I did myself at the beginning of this quest. *My mind had been biased.* You may have to dispel some of your preconceived ideas, but try it—you have nothing to lose. I did ten years of reading, thinking, discovering and sorting out before I wrote this book. I am very aware that I do not know everything, and I hope that that very factor leaves my mind opened for more growth.

First, you have to want to do it.
Then learn the basics of Body 101
Then challenge my advice
Then follow the advice.
Then continue reading and growing.

I guarantee you will be happy you have done it.

CHAPTER TWO

Mind Over the Matter of Aging

Why is attitude so important?

Simply because if you do not have a positive attitude and do not *want* to live longer or better, you'll never do what is necessary to attain a long and healthful life. If you are depressed, bored, unhappy for any reasons, hate your mate or are lonesome, why would you want to live much longer? Conversely, if you are not stressed and you feel fulfilled and positive about yourself, life will certainly be worth pursuing in health and longevity.

Controlling every aspect of your life *and* influencing the lives of people around you, your attitude sanctions you to live a happy life or an unhappy life. It really is that simple. You can choose to be lazy and inactive, sustain a negative disposition, rejecting those around you as inadequate and inferior; however, in the end you will be the one who feels inadequate, inferior and rejected. Your other choice is to remain positive, take actions to attain goals, and participate in life. At the end of this path are pride, dignity and peace.

I admire Dr. Phil McGraw's philosophies, especially his slogan "Get with it!" That is how easy changing a negative attitude into a positive attitude is--just get with it.

At age twenty, I moved away from my parents' houses and hometown to take my first pre-medical year. I enjoyed the newfound freedom and had a wonderful time, but unfortunately failed the year and my dream of becoming a doctor faltered severely. I knew I had played too much, not studied enough.

I was devastated, as I knew I would never be a doctor. My father encouraged me to fight the adversity that I myself had created and become resolute in my goal to become a doctor. He told me I had only two choices. I could either fight and attain my goal or do nothing and start coasting downhill. He taught me that once adversity has occurred, you can no longer stay on the same course. You must take action.

I never forgot that conversation with my father, and adversity became a positive force in my life after that episode. Life can be a tortuous road and adversity happens to everybody. You can either let it make you, or let it break you.

Priorities

Priorities must determine your life's choices so make sure you have them right. You must take care of yourself first and then— in this order—your mate, kids, family, friends and security. The story below (a brief message I got in a mass mailing and do not know the author) painted a vivid picture of where priorities should be for me.

The professor of philosophy walked into his classroom one day. He had a clear jar filled to the top with golf balls and asked his class if the jar was full. They all agreed it was full. Next, he poured pebbles into the jar and asked the same question, which resulted in the same answer. Next, he poured sand into the jar that filled all the crevices and asked the same question which resulted in the same answer. Next, he poured two bottles of beer into the jar and then it was completely full.

The professor explained that the golf balls were the first priorities and signified yourself, your health, your partner, kids, family and friends. If you lost everything else in life, you could still have a happy and full life. The pebbles are the next level of priorities and include your work, your house, and your retirement. The sand signifies your cars, boats, toys, and your accumulated money. If you were to put the pebbles or the sand in first, there would be no space for the golf balls.

The same goes for your life. Take care of the golf balls first and you'll find everything else takes care of itself. As for the beer, there should always be space for relaxation.

Do not forget that the absolute number one priority is you. If you're not healthy and alive, nothing else counts and nobody else can enjoy you.

Maintaining a Positive Attitude

- o It will make you enjoy life
- o It will make you want to live
- o It will improve your relationship with your mate
- o It will attract friends and family
- o It will have a major positive influence on your body
- o It will dissipate fear and stress.

A negative attitude **can** defeat all the positive aspects of life. If you consistently believe the worst will be true in any situation, person, event or object, then it most likely will turn out to be the worst-case scenario.

Behaving honorably in a conflict is important. Honesty is essential. You can always defer an opinion if you need time to think about it, but honesty or sharing what you need to think about is essential.

It is also important not to engage in gossip about anyone. If you speak meanly about one person to another, why wouldn't the first person think that you would talk meanly about them to someone else? What you do with one, you most likely will do with everyone. Be honorable when you speak of others.

Remember to concentrate on behaviors, not people. Everyone has both redeeming qualities and unfavorable qualities. Prejudice is an awful prejudgment usually based on inappropriate superficial knowledge of the other person. Negative attitudes are a huge problem in our society. So why not accept other people for what they are? The Golden Rule always applies.

Moving elsewhere will not change a life of negativism. Unless you change your outlook and attitude, you will create the same environment in a new location. You will have changed places but not your attitude. Your attitude is what you must correct.

What you do as work in life is an important consideration. The best advice I have heard on careers is to go where your passion is and then make money doing *something* in that field. If you do not like your work, there are two alternatives. Either change your work and do something that stimulates you more or change your attitude about your present work and coworkers. Look for positive aspects about your job. Create your own enthusiasm for the job you have, working even harder to do an excellent job. Notice how your attitude shifts and how proud you feel about the job you are doing. Reversing your thoughts and attitude can be that easy.

In medical school, I failed a biochemistry examination. I hated biochemistry. I had to take the exam over during the summertime and my wise professor, Doctor Etori, said to me, "The more you hate biochemistry, the less pleasant it will be and the more chance you will have to fail again. If you make an effort to enjoy it, you will start loving it." I changed my attitude and I did pass the exam with high marks. To this day, I love biochemistry.

Dr. Phil calls negative thinking "the hurdle of our minds." You can clear those hurdles. Nothing improves your life quality unless you want improvement. Your mind's attitude regulates your longevity and welfare. A positive attitude will help you grow and learn, enjoy life, and be more satisfied with your accomplishments.

Staying Happy: Keeping Really Alive

We are not happy when we are not fulfilled. The brain is an extraordinary organ with amazing capabilities that must be stimulated and used often to remain at its highest performance level. If the mind is not kept busy and inspired, it quickly lags into boredom, depression and irritability. The brain needs stimulation and activity to continue its growth. You are the only one able to provide this service to your brain.

The "I can do it!" attitude is one you have to generate. You must get out on that morning walk or bike ride whether a partner or friend joins you or not. It's great when you have someone to chat with as you walk, but the walk is for *you*, and that is where it must begin, with you, where all healing starts.

Both mental and physical hobbies and interests are good to have. Imagination, resourcefulness, intelligence, creativity and judgment are all part of one's brain. There are unlimited amounts of things in a world that can make each and every one happy. Find yours!

Above all, you must climb out of bad moods. Eventually you will not have any bad moods to climb out of.

Denial: The Silent Killer

Denial is an impediment to beneficial behavior. I believe emphatically that denial is our worst enemy and contributes the most to human deaths. Ignoring important signs from your body and mind can destroy your health and environment. This denial occurs on a daily basis when ignoring damaging cumulative habits, and it can gradually contribute to a premature demise.

When you justify behavior, you tell yourself that you will do it better—different, the right way—later or tomorrow. That is a denial by itself. Tomorrow does not exist. Well, today *is* yesterday's tomorrow and a *very* good time to stop denying anything you are denying. Once again, honesty—in this case, *being honest with yourself*—is essential to review and determine what denial behaviors you might be practicing.

13

Once these behaviors have been acknowledged, you can begin to eradicate them with sheer willpower, constant self-correction and immediate action. In those cases, such as when I had medical problems that required my researching what habits needed to be changed, you can fight denial with research like reading this book, going on the internet, taking classes. We live in an informed age.

Daily life offers opportunities for denial on a regular basis. Not using a seatbelt is denying that you might get hurt in an accident. Ignoring a small lump in the breast and saying it will go away is denying you might have a tumor. Ignoring stomach pains is denying that you may be having a gallbladder attack. Ignoring the need to exercise is denying that your body requires consistent, dedicated time to exercise in order to keep operating at prime efficiency.

Three years ago, my brother had a fairly severe heart attack in the early morning hours. He told his wife not to summon an ambulance. Thankfully, she overcame his denial and made the call, despite his wishes otherwise. He had a cardiac arrest just as he was arriving in the ER and he would not have survived that attack had he still been at home denying that it was occurring. He is alive and well six years later. Sticking your head in the sand and pretending things are not happening is not beneficial. When things happen, one must respond actively.

Another frequent denial tactic was evidenced to me by a friend when I inquired about his cholesterol level. He said it was okay. When I pressed him for a number he didn't know what it actually was, but replied that his doctor was monitoring it for him. *It is imperative to be active in your own health care.* Some doctors have more than seven thousand patients and it is impossible for them to know all the details of each of us. You must monitor your own situation and thus be active in managing your own health. Having a partner or friend with you during appointments, exams or procedures is also helpful. Learning as much as you can about any medical problem you have is essential. Often information received from medical staff is not within everyday experience, so besides a medical problem happening to you it is also foreign material and requires a learning curve to understand.

At the core of this aging symphony is the fact that aging happens gradually, the daily accumulative effects are either added to your good health or subtracted from your good health. Doing nothing to facilitate good health will actually take you backwards. Denial plays a large part in what one does or does not do. Daily denials build over time and eventually shorten healthy living.

A teacher whom I greatly admired during my college years repeatedly said "ignorancia crasssa," which means ignorance is crass. I still remember it today as a very important lesson in my life.

Sometimes in denial you read an article or two on an expansive subject and consider yourself an expert. Make sure you learn all the aspects of that subject. Otherwise, you create opinions based on very little knowledge. *The most categorical statements I have heard were from people who had very little knowledge of that particular subject.* It is really another form of denial and I have seen it many times in people making comments about diets, exercises, antioxidants and other such subjects.

Beware that you don't fashion your lifestyle on inadequate knowledge. Please do not fashion your life and health on inadequate knowledge.

Because everyone is different, allowing for personal beliefs is also important. Your beliefs will start to form from those around you, professionals, family and friends. Make sure you research thoroughly your beliefs and any others you are attracted to outside your circle. Make choices that are healthy and are best for you. You are generally in denial if you feel uncomfortable about a choice you made. If you are doing the right physical and mental exercises to extend and improve the quality of your life, then you are in a better position to feel comfortable about your choices.

Have a good Partner

Perhaps the most important influence in your life other than your parents is your partner. In an ideal scenario, one chooses a partner and the two continue through a life of children, careers and passages together.

When things are not smooth in a relationship, it can be due to either one or both of the partners. If your relationship is not satisfying, you must look honestly to determine who contributes what to the tension. If your attitude and behavior contribute to the stress in your partnership, you should find ways to communicate differently. Think about why your partner might not like to be around you. If your attitude is nasty most of the time, or erratic, you might remember how you feel about being around people who are negative or complaining. *It doesn't hurt to be nice, and it always hurts to be mean, or have someone be mean to you.* It is so easy to be nice to a nice person, but it is so difficult to be nice to an un-nice person.

Honesty, truth and integrity are important factors in a partnership. Although no one in your life will ever know *everything* you think and feel, let your partner know how you feel about all-important issues. Lies of omission are just as damaging as lies of exaggeration, or making up lies. If there is no trust, a relationship is never real. When someone lies to you, they essentially take away your ability to trust them. That is also true of you.

Even if you are already very good about being nice to your partner, start some new traditions or one-time surprises. If met by a negative response at first, which may be the pattern you two have developed to communicate, just keep "killing them with kindness" and eventually kindness will become your new pattern.

Really! It works!

Whatever it is that is wrong about your relationship, do something to change it. Being passive, procrastinating and denying the problem will just make things worse. Seek help.

Sometimes a couple will reach a place when dissolving a partnership seems the best and only thing to do for all concerned. Those instances should be rare, I believe, and *every* positive effort should be made before this solution is executed. Although extreme cases do exist, I believe many relationships that break up could have persevered. One reason this might happen is that one or both partner's irritability, impatience and need for self-gratification creates a shield to the big picture. Once you are in a union, that partnership should have priority in your life. If you work hard at resolving your problems, your relationship will be that much stronger since you both gave up some ground. Sometimes picking and choosing your battles may win the war and allow you to reach the Golden Anniversary.

Changing partners, neighborhoods, or situations in life rarely solves a problem if your attitude hasn't changed. Professional counseling may be helpful in this situation. If a negative attitude contributed to a lifestyle that is not fulfilling, that negative attitude will be present wherever you go. Changing your *attitude* and not everything around you is a clear path to becoming a happier partner.

Cultivating Friends and Relatives
Friends are the family you give yourself, and family is the foundation of life. A strong support system is appreciated during an unfortunate crisis, and is a pleasure to have around during the good times. "No man is an island," wrote John Donne.

Friendships encompass many attributes and one should consciously work at being a good friend. In friendships, humility is important as pride keeps many a situation from being resolved. Accomplishments shared are celebrated and act as catalysts to inspire each other. Keep an open mind. No one in the world will share your exact opinion on everything, and sometimes even like-minded friends will have a different opinion. Be curious about others' thoughts, experiences and feelings.

A good friend, Dick, a wonderful psychiatrist, was involved in research on biofeedback and various behaviors. He took a twelve-month sabbatical in Southern California, and came back seven months later with interesting observations. Dick saw neurotic behavior in residents who otherwise had great advantages, money and opportunities in life. He surmised that these people were insecure, nervous and anxious because most had extracted themselves from their roots, their families and lifelong friends to move elsewhere. They lost the important psychological stability that the support and strength of being surrounded by family provided. This sudden loss of support caused their erratic behavior. It was an instructive insight for me. It amplified my priorities in life.

Families are the "unchosen friends" life gives. No one who meets us in later life will have the same perception of us that our family does, simply because family watched our growth and development.

The support of family contributes to psychological wholeness. As beneficial and essential to our mental health as family members are, they are also sometimes participants in huge feuds. There will always be differences, but conflicts in relationships help you grow, and resolving those conflicts is an important part of growth. Even though you may have different opinions, practice tolerance for family member's opinions and be grateful when they tolerate your opinions. And be tolerant of theirs.

Relieving Boredom

Boredom is a lack of function of the brain. The brain naturally needs activity to be stimulated and to relieve boredom. If the brain is not active, not only does a person become bored but also the normal traffic pathways of brain transmission will not occur and the brain eventually atrophies. And the most amazing thing about this process is that we each have the ability to eliminate boredom.

Multitudes of ways exist to eliminate boredom. Start with friends and relatives who might be looking for someone to join them in a favorite hobby or pastime. You could also develop a new hobby or pastime. Think of all the things you've wanted to try or do throughout your life, pick one, and do it. Look in newspapers, local publications and hobby magazines for ideas on activities you might not have thought of on your own. Make an effort to go to plays, festivals, and include musical events in your agenda. Music is an international language and some musical events can lift spirits.

As you may change your behavior and time schedule with new activities and hobbies, it is especially important to include your spouse in your exploration for new things to do. There may be some new activities that you can do together. There may be others you do alone or with friends that won't include your partner, but you should always advise and update them of your search for new interests.

Remember that you are able do *anything* you want as a new interest. With over five billion brain cells, humans have ample resources to grasp concepts and learn new physical abilities. Using your creativity and determination can allow an active participation in any field that you can imagine.

Once you start practicing something new, your brain engages and remains more alert and open to other new ventures. You can become very good at whatever you choose to tackle. If you do not, *you have shut the door to your brain* not permitting it to be used. You are saying "I can't do it," and automatically you will never do it unless you empower yourself and say "I *can* do it." At that point, you will be the proudest person in the world to find all that available brain power. Mental and physical exercises are the most consequential actions in aging healthfully. It is the most important deterrent to the aging process. As a matter of a fact it can very positively reverse the mental and physical processes and very substantially.

Here are a few suggestions for keeping your brain active:

Cultivate your curiosity: Curiosity is probably the most important quality a human being can utilize to develop, grow, learn, or research. Curiosity maintains interest and eventually you will end up doing what your curiosity dictates you to do.

If you start reading about an interest and that interest grows, you will continue research and may go quickly from one topic to another. Curiosity always moves fast. It will create a chain reaction that is the fun aspect of curiosity.

Stop fearing memory loss: It will just stress you into thinking you have Alzheimer's when you just have a lapse of memory as when you were younger and then called it "on the tip of my tongue".

Go to lectures: The ideas and the information that you encounter will open new vistas and interests.

Reading: You'll find it will constantly replenish your memory banks and stimulate your mind.

Crossword puzzles: They are wonderful tools allowing you to practice actually retrieving memory from your brain.

Hobbies: They do increase your interests and develop new skills, besides showing you that you *can* do it. It will not be perfect at the beginning but see yourself growing more and more capable and dexterous.

Computers: I know they involve some mental hurdles to tackle, but go slowly, do not get frustrated, and soon you will have a skill and a tool that will open the sky to you.

Restrict time spent watching TV: We do not do a lot of thinking looking at the television. Sometimes you are only brainwashed by psychological terrorism as in soaps. Please control what goes into your so-precious brain and you will be so much better off. Ads are by necessity biased, and thus give you an awful lot of misinformation. Much of this misinformation stores in your brain and can lead you to make faulty purchasing decisions. Much of the media is misleading.

Music and art: They are the relaxation and enjoyment your mind needs. It is also a wonderful meditation form.

Meditate: This is a generic word I use to describe calming your stress and you can do it by listening to music, concentrating on relaxation, doing yoga, or stopping during the day to "take ten." It is a wonderful stress reliever, and I have used it all my working life to calm down the churning inside that my profession stimulates. It works. So, boredom is brain apathy and both mental and physical exercise is important to keep the brain active and learning.

Taking charge of your time and starting each day with both a physical activity and a mental pastime is important. These brain exercises will help to get you out of a slump. If you do so, next year you will be *much* better. It will not happen overnight. Remember that it took years to get where you are now, so if you are somewhat negative in your thinking or physical shape, you will need time to get back to the positive side of the scale.

Empower yourself: No one does things well the first time. There is a learning curve in every endeavor, sometimes several learning curves. Be patient and the rewards will be endless. That is one of the reasons it is exciting to take on new hobbies and interests. Remember, challenge is positive! Keep practicing and you will master anything, whether it is carving, knitting, woodworking, collecting rare documents, creating stained glass or learning to ride a bike. Start by simply reading magazines on these subject and they will springboard you to wonderful achievements.

Sometimes one can have a little fun encouraging others to be more positive. After being retired for a few years my brother complained of boredom. I suggested he try woodworking, a hobby that I enjoy passionately. He told me he couldn't do it because he had never done it before.

With a good-humored dose of sibling rivalry, I suggested that perhaps he was correct; he couldn't do woodworking if he wasn't as intelligent as I was, since I did it so well. All of a sudden, he was reading woodworking magazines and trying to make things from wood. Today his children and grandchildren have cherished many beautiful pieces of furniture he crafted for them. From my encouraging him to help himself, his family and friends also gained.

The best outcomes happen when you consider what you enjoy and stick with whatever that is until you've learned it. If you have always wanted to do a hobby or job, you will likely enjoy it once mastered.

Overcoming Fear of Disease

If you do not want to age because you do not want to live to be sick like an old person, you have already defeated yourself. Keep a positive attitude and do not think that you will have disease or a serious illness. What is thought often becomes our reality, as your mind will certainly affect your body detrimentally if you think negative. Of course, your body deteriorates as it grows older but *just think of it as need for maintenance*. You will be much better afterward if you have repaired it.

Different degrees of adversity may be encountered and they may be small, large, destructive or absolutely terrifying. *That* there will be adversity in life is not the issue, what you *do* with that adversity is the real issue. Fear does not help, but doing something about it does. And remember to be grateful that you *have* an opportunity to reverse or eliminate a poor medical condition. My heart blockage discovery could have been a massive heart attack. I am grateful I was given, and listened to, early detection signs. I had no denial about what was happening to me. Being grateful is an important part of many things but especially useful in conquering adversity.

Another antidote to fear is to research your specific problem. The sources listed throughout this book and in the Resource Reference section in the back of the book, Internet Quick References, are very good starting points for much of this research.

The more familiar you are with your body and its reactions to external and internal assaults, the better you will manage your own health. Unfortunately, some of the material currently available is not accurate or does not compare apples to apples. The media sensationalizes stories at times. One instance is the controversial Hormone Therapy Treatment (HRT) debates when media offered findings from several different studies. Some studies may not have offered additional information, which had relevance in the study. Read everything you can and ask every question you have. Question your findings, in every area, and look for confirming sources. Utilize the medical community around you and consult with your doctors for advice and direction. Participate with your doctors in your preventive health.

Never say "I am too old"

It is an automatic defeatism when you actually say, "I can't do it anymore." Therefore, you put yourself on the slippery slope. Now, not everyone may want to be a marathon runner or fly her own plane, but they *can* and have. *Discrimination against yourself is the worst form of prejudice, and "I am too old"* is throwing in the towel. *If you do not play the basketball game, you sure will never win it.* However if you do try it and try hard you have a good chance of winning it. The "poor me" attitude, or the entitlement attitude, is very destructive. You will never do anything for yourself if you stay stuck in that attitude.

Subduing Anger, Stress and Negative Moods

The turbulent emotions of stress and anger can consume and control each of us if allowed. Less intense forms of anger include impatience, irritability, intolerance, blaming and criticizing others or being mean. Anger in all its forms is a constant stress reaction in our bodies that releases damaging hormones, adrenalines and cortisol, which persist until the anger is resolved.

The secretion of these hormones is normal and good on a short-term basis but not for extended periods. If anger is not resolved, stress will remain in the body, and will slowly deteriorate it.

There is a strong brain to body connection. When the brain has a sustained stress reaction, the autonomic, automatic, nervous system is affected, damaging many organs in our body, particularly our vessels and heart, often although not solely by triggering high blood pressure.

Stress is present in other situations, acutely during mortalities, adversity or accidents. If there is closure with these situations, the stress disappears naturally. Stress is found in relationships with a partner, family members, colleagues, and even strangers. Court cases, arguments and other adversarial situations create especially high levels of stress and tension.

Stress can cause a perpetual bad mood that becomes a chronic problem, destructive to one's physiology, until there is **closure** from a situation. Reducing and eliminating stress is important so its effects do not become long term and damaging. During times of stress, priorities can get out of order, but this is when priorities need to be the most basic in your life. Your golf balls are far more important than pebbles or sand.

Mood

Mood is an up and down reaction one has that is most often mediated by hormones, but not always. Irritability before meals can be caused by low levels of insulin associated with low blood sugars. When you eat, the insulin and glucose levels are raised and normal bodily functions resume. Some people are cranky when they first awaken in the morning, and this is due to accumulated water on the brain (edema). Other variables that contribute to bad moods are using alcohol, extremely hot weather, common colds or flus.

But, more often than not, mood is mediated by hormonal variations in our bodies, such as male and female menopause, around menstruations, the advent of teen-age estrogens and/or testosterone, and so on. The mood is nevertheless controllable, either by willpower or by seeing a physician to regulate the imbalance.

Bad moods can be altered into good moods in a variety of ways and mental exercises. You must use strong will power; determining that you *will* have a pleasant mood is the first step to having one. You will get used to being in a good mood and you'll like it.

Another part of orchestrating one's body is to calm the brain that is constantly firing damaging impulses to the body. The mind and body connection is powerful and can be very destructive in negative and stressed minds but conversely very beneficial in positive attitude.

If you see that mood is the result of hormones or other secretions, and that you can control the mood, perhaps you can begin to grasp that controlling the mood might also regulate the secretions. Such is the power we have over the mind/body connection. If we can will the secretions to subside, how else does our mind control our body? The ramifications are mind-boggling. That is why I have a passion for you to understand how your body works, how we age it and how we can slow the process down.

Sleep

Sleep is very important for the well-being of your psyche and, for that matter, for your whole body. There is no question that those who are sleep deprived have a much harder time getting through the day. Both body and mind revolt with sluggish, inattentive behavior. Good decisions are more difficult to make. There is no question that some people manage better than others with insufficient sleep. Everyone has a level of required sleep, which becomes your standard.

During sleep, you experience cycles of more-asleep and less-asleep periods. This is a gentle waxing and waning of sleep during the whole night. During the light periods, you are subconsciously awake and this is when you have dreams.

Problems are often resolved in dreams. It is possible to solve problems while sleeping. It is then that we are unimpaired by all the conscious garbage we may have to consider during waking hours. During sleep, you can develop an idea or come to a decision that is usually far better than a thought you come upon while awake. Your subconscious will work on a problem, analyze all the pros and cons and usually the answer is much clearer in the morning.

There is a reason people encourage those wrestling with a problem to "sleep on it." Usually everything looks better in the morning.

Try this experiment. Go to bed with a thought and let it grow during the night. If you give your brain a question to answer, a decision to make, or a dilemma to solve before you go to sleep many times you will awaken in the morning with the problem totally solved to your great satisfaction. Intuitive reasoning leads to growth of ideas during sleep. This is an enormously beneficial asset for you to use. You may also feel much better by having slept more soundly because problems are usually solved at the beginning of the night. Your mind is then more peaceful you awaken in the morning far more refreshed. If a problem causes fear or anxiety, sleep on it and the problem is often no longer one.

For example, I was canoeing with a group on a river in Maine. We were facing a class four rapid the next morning. We scanned the river that night, but I was frightened since I could not find the right channel or pathway to follow. I went to sleep and subconsciously I solved the problem of which pathways to navigate and slept soundly thereafter. The next morning I was calm. We navigated it without incident.

Sleep is when your body replenishes cells, immunity, energies, hormones, enzymes, oxygen saturation, and adjusts all the chemical reactions that occur. We know that growth hormones and particularly melatonin along with other endocrines hormones are produced at night. During that process, all body functions slow down. The metabolic rate, which is all the functions of your chemical reactions in your body, slows down substantially and has time to recreate what has been lost during the previous day. Your heart, blood pressure and lungs slow down to a very slow rate to recuperate and in the process some fluids accumulate in your tissues. So you may have some swelling of your brain and body. This quickly disappears as you awaken. This may be the reason you wake up with a foggy brain, and, as you become active and circulation comes back to normal, you reabsorb it and the process is repeated.

Sleep is mediated by a hormone called melatonin that is secreted by a tiny gland in your brain called the pineal gland. Melatonin is secreted when your eyes tell your brain darkness is occurring. As it secretes, it starts the cycle of other hormonal glands' productions. Melatonin is the major orchestra leader of the hormonal symphony and signals the brain to slow down the excitatory part of your brain so that the calming part can take over to relax you. As people grow older, the pineal gland naturally atrophies, its secretion of melatonin is reduced thus the sleep cycle is not as good. Melatonin is also a natural product and can be taken when insomnia occurs.

There are other things that you can do to induce sleep. Of course the darker your room is the more melatonin you will secrete and thus sleep better. For example, if there is light in the room you will not secrete as much melatonin and sleep will be restless. So turn off all the lights and use heavy or dark drapes. You'll find that total darkness makes a huge difference in the quality of your sleep.

Sleeping well requires adhering to a regular schedule. Melatonin secretion is on a regular cycle, called a circadian cycle, which is the normal cycle of sleep, wakefulness, hunger and any other pattern of life that you created for yourself, such as the amount of exercise your body needs every day. That cycle changes with the seasons. If you can sleep when it is dark and wake up when it is light, your cycles will likely be more consistent and restful. Your body adjusts to a regular cycle and thus can predict sleep time.

Never work at falling asleep. The harder you try to sleep the less you will. You are actually keeping your brain active by pushing your body to sleep. Get out of bed and do something else for a while. Return when you are slightly drowsy. That way you will not create anxiety of trying to fall asleep which is doing the opposite, keeping you awake. Reduce all noises. Create a peaceful and serene sleeping environment with no distractions. Some people find certain music lulls them to sleep. The more sounds you can eliminate the better you will rest.

Keep your bedroom at a temperature that is comfortable for you. Too warm or too cold can disturb or interrupt your sleep pattern. Eliminate or decrease beverage intake with liquids containing caffeine like coffee, tea, cola, or chocolate before bedtime, as they will definitely disturb sleep cycles. Sleep as much as your body needs to feel rested. Oversleeping can cause you more trouble sleeping the next night and may make you foggy during the day because of edema on the brain. The right amount of sleep for you is what makes you perform at your peak after an appropriate amount of resting time.

Eating before you go to bed will keep your body's digestion functions going and sometimes keep you awake. Sleep after eating may only be temporary and your sleep cycle will be interrupted. You should not eat for about two hours before you go to sleep.

Do not exercise just before bedtime. You will start secreting hormones for your 'second wind,' and these are activity hormones not sleep hormones. You probably should not exercise for a couple of hours before going to sleep.

Surviving Depression

During especially stressful times in life, one can fall into a groove that could include boredom, loneliness or depression. These periods are natural if temporary. Work yourself out of them as soon as possible. The longer you are in them the more you produce cortisol and the more it harms you.

If the depression is mild, try to work yourself out of it. If it is severe, get help. If it is a result of grief, try very hard to work yourself out of it and to have closure. Be with friends and support. That will prevent this stress and depression from becoming chronic and life threatening.

Slight mood changes are normal experiences and can roll up and down. Depression is a common and transient affliction and transient bouts of depression so don't get all stressed out about it.

You can take positive actions to help you climb out of that groove. Find things to do that are enjoyable. Look up old friends. Be nice to strangers. Volunteer. Learn a new hobby. You will find that time passes faster and more pleasantly when you become active and all these actions are good to keep the brain active. Partners and friends often encourage new activities and interests. Take their good advice.

Deep depression however can make you feel incapable, negative, sad, inactive or gloomy, and can interfere with performing daily activities and making good decisions. Maintaining a healthy relationship is very, very difficult when one is experiencing depression.

Only when the downs occur more frequently than the ups should one seek medical advice. But be aware you should do so immediately if life has become more—or all—down moods. Depression can lead to suicidal thoughts and it should be arrested immediately in that situation.

Suicidal thoughts are a life-threatening situation and must never be taken lightly. An emergency room visit is essential if you ever entertain the idea of suicide. There are always much better alternatives, which you will learn once you treat deep depression and feel like your old self again. Depression is a severe physical disease of the brain and can kill as easily as any other disease such as pneumonia. You are not "crazy" when depressed; you are physically sick and need attention.

Depression is caused either by biological, genetic or environmental factors. Biological factors such as hormone variations occur in the body and the brain. Genetic factors often are a factor. Environmental factors are also called emotional factors and result from traumatic events like a death of a loved one, lack of love from a parent or a partner, or some other environmental element. More severe situations like bipolar depression do exist and need professional help.

The path out of depression consists of a group effort between you, your circle of support and any medical staff or medication required. Any and all of these resources can be used in escaping depression. As in all cases, early awareness and diagnosis is best. Depression can lead to serious consequences like suicidal thoughts so take action immediately and see someone.

Body Image and Growing Older

Appreciating one's body is one of the most fascinating aspects of human behavior that I have encountered as a plastic surgeon. Of course being happy with your physical body is important but remember that it *is* just a shell. Body image has far less to do with appearance than it does with perception.

The most important part of my evaluation was determining if surgery was requested for physical or psychological problems.

People who had bad scars, severe congenital deformities had bad images of themselves and felt less confident in themselves. Repairing these defects was very productive in resorting self-confidence. But for example, one patient requested cosmetic surgery while she was going through a divorce. At consultation, I dissuaded her and she decided to defer the surgery. Years later, she wrote and told me that not having the surgery, but following some other options we discussed, was the best advice I could have given her. Her emotional situation had distorted her view of herself.

On the other hand, we see a child with a cleft lip defect and repair it, the personality transformation is quite dramatic and the attitude of the people around him/her is very positive.

If changing an aspect of your body will make you personally happier then this is a good option. If you are considering cosmetic surgery for any other reason than your own well-being, you are considering it for the wrong reasons. *Do not ever have cosmetic surgery to please anyone else.*

There is no question that body image is a psychological perception. What you perceive your body to look like can be a very positive or negative influence in your life.

I was amazed to learn that even animals have a body image. I was given a pair of swans once that I kept in a pond behind my cottage. I built a small enclosure for them and fed them weekly as one would a pet. The male was aggressive and territorial, always attacking me when I came to feed them. I used the cover of the garbage can as a shield to protect myself from his assaults. When the female laid a few eggs, a raccoon found and ate them, killing the male swan in that pursuit.

I was devastated and purchased a new male swan that had a broken wing tip causing its feathers to flare out. He was not a pretty sight. During the first few months together, the male swan stayed in his corner, not going near the female swan nor attacking me.

As a plastic surgeon, I grew impatient of his jutting feathers and one day performed surgery removing the male's wing tip with the flared feathers. His appearance improved. The very next morning the male swan attacked me as I came with food. The next day I observed the two swans snuggling together.

They were partners from then on. Obviously, the male swan had been hampered by his poor self-image! The ungainly feathers destroyed his male ego, and the moment they were removed he acted like a beautiful swan again, able to court and become a proper mate to the female. Self-image is important in all the kingdoms.

The first breast augmentation was done by the Indus two thousand years ago, and they implanted sea sponges. Just imagine the tragedy that must have been. Our modern society has not invented plastic surgery; they have just popularized it and enhanced it.

If you have not come to terms with your body image, growing older will become more of a problem as normal aging occurs. As wrinkles and sagging muscles overtake your body you will rely even more on a strong secure self-concept. You must know throughout every day of your life that there is value in a well-functioning body and mind and do everything you can to ensure you have both.

Self-image motivates or depresses. Your responsibility is to take advantage of the great benefits that come from feeling good about yourself by constantly enhancing your mind and body, which are also part of this body image.

My mother, who was a bright very active woman, became slightly depressed as aging occurred. One day she went and got a facelift and didn't even consult me, her plastic surgeon son. She later said to me that I would have told her it was ridiculous. But I would have been wrong. All of a sudden, she was everywhere, alert, alive, going to symphonies, shopping, traveling, and essentially my Mom again.

Taking care of yourself throughout your entire life gives you a better opportunity to grow old with a sound mind and body. A healthy mind is always a beautiful mind. A healthy body is always a beautiful body.

Keep your mind and body healthy and your attitude will *always* be positive! If you feel comfortable in your body due to your persistence in exercising mind and body, you will not pay attention to wrinkles, as you are secure in your skin. Aging then is a comfortable natural progression.

Retirement

Of course you should not retire. If you insist on quitting your job, especially if you love it, then don't retire, **recycle instead.**

Focus on Priorities

When you recycle, remember first the golf balls in your life. To be well surrounded by partner, family and friends is by far the most important priority and luxury. Don't ever forget that, for fear you will become very lonesome. You can have all the money, all the toys in the world, but your life will be artificial and mostly empty.

Remember what my friend Dick, the psychiatrist, learned in Los Angeles: We are adrift without family, and made neurotic when cut off from those who love us, no matter how rich or successful we are in material terms.

Find new skills or recycle the ones you have

If you have loved your craft or profession, why not continue in the same or a parallel field? I loved every minute of my surgery and left it only to avoid the continued stress of insurances, malpractice, inner medical politics, daily scheduling, etc. Now I practice my skills as a volunteer, helping people and still doing my coveted surgery. I also have used my medical background to research what caused the aging deterioration and here it is: this book, and hopefully others. However, if you want to do something else, then prepare yourself with new skills. Learn a new craft or hobby that you always wanted to do. Now is the

33

perfect opportunity. Don't tell me you can't do it because if you say so even to yourself, you have shut the door to development, growth, learning and curiosity. Your brain has ample database ready to be fulfilled. I always thought I could not do computers, but I hated myself for closing the door to a new skill.

Now I can type, do many tasks on this machine, internet research, electronic transfers and I am still growing. I am no longer afraid of the computer. If I can do it, so can you.

Volunteerism
Altruism is magically rewarding. You will never get paid so highly.

There are a million ways to volunteer. Additional help is always needed and appreciated at non-profit organizations, schools, libraries, medical facilities, nursing centers, theaters, religious associations and community foundations. You can volunteer at Habitat for Humanity, social clubs like the Lions, Rotary, Knights of Columbus, Kiwanis, Masons, etc. You can create chapters of organizations such as Ronald McDonald House, The Gift of Life, Fill a Dream, soup kitchens, and more.

There is always something to do to help people locally, or you could travel abroad to volunteer. You can go and do surgery if you are a surgeon, or be support staff. There are many organizations that have programs in plastic surgery, orthopedic surgery, dental surgery, eye surgery, and teaching. Many countries on our globe are suffering enormous tragedies and can use help. Religious organizations build facilities and provide support while building clinics in third world countries. The Peace Corps has to be one of the best organizations in the world and the most wonderful example of what an American truly is. To meet, converse and see the Peace Corps in action in the Third World has been the most elating experience I have witnessed. These are universally the most uplifting people I have ever met and I will always honor this compassionate group of young and not so young people and they do this despite all adversities.

Giving blood or donating your organs is another way to give. Giving your body or organs after death to teach young medical students and help professionals learn their craft is enormously important. This will benefit many future generations. There are fifty-two thousand potential organ recipients waiting for donors at all times in the United States, and that number is growing. Your body is simply a shell that contains the organs that keep it alive. When your body dies, it no longer has use for these organs and they return to ashes, either by cremation or through natural decomposition. The essence or spirit of a body lives forever, not the physical body. You will no longer need these organs, and if the miracles of medicine create an opportunity for other lives to continue because of the donation of your organs, I believe that is a valuable service to mankind.

Also, medical students are sometimes allowed to conduct research on donated bodies, and this not only provides an excellent learning venue for new doctors but is also valuable in researching diseases. Transplantation saves lives and you can donate your organs simply by obtaining a donor card. Each day about sixty-three people receive an organ transplant; however, another sixteen people on the waiting list die because not enough organs are available.

I encourage you to contact organizations (two are listed below) that can assist in the formal donation of your body and organs after your death. As with all choices you have about your body and belongings after your death, make sure your family knows your wishes.

http://www.organdonor.gov
http://www.livingorgandonor.org

In general, giving is about sacrifice, taking some time from your day or making an effort to organize something that will be of benefit to your community. Financial resources are always needed and appreciated, but there is something extraordinary about giving time, effort, and skills to an organization that aids people. My son volunteers time with Special Olympics and takes disabled children sailing during the summertime. He is very proud and fulfilled by his participation. He puts a *lot* of effort into this endeavor, but he glows when he talks to me about his experiences on the water with the kids. I am grateful that I have also had those experiences in my life, so I both understand and am proud of his feelings about his giving.

To those who might guard resources and time to conserve them for themselves, be reminded that giving and volunteering is for oneself—and everyone else benefits. That is the miracle of volunteering. Give freely, in whatever way you are able, every day.

Our country is particularly special about devotion and giving and we can be very proud of it. Just join the club. Your very selfishness of giving is the best of all worlds. *I have always felt that I want to do what I enjoy the most, but if I happen to help someone in the process, everybody wins.*

Prepare for the proper exercises
There is no factor more powerful in affecting your beneficial aging process than exercise. Without mental and physical exercises, there is relentless atrophy, aging degeneration. Exercise is the most crucial part of aging.

Even if you are a "human mess," physically, you actually can turn your situation completely around. Don't tell yourself that you are too busy at work to exercise. That statement means that your priorities are money over your health. That statement means you will retire with a lot of money but are likely to die early . . . with a lot of money.

Performing exercise regularly is *essential*. Even at the beginning of retirement, when you might be resting and planning your new life, develop good daily exercise habits. Create your own schedule so you will enjoy following it. If you feel you do not have time to perform physical exercise, remind yourself of the golf balls and take care of priorities.

Do friendly exercises. Biking, swimming, weightlifting, cross-country skiing, core body exercises, kayaking, canoeing, yoga, and speed walking are activities, which will keep you physically fit. You will feel much better and secrete endorphins and other hormones in your body that will provide a great sense of well-being. Exercising will make you better and better every year. Of course, it will be tough to begin with. But once you've taken the step, you will never stop because you will see the benefits. It will be the most important part of your thorough enjoyment of this recycling period of your life.

Attitude
Charles Swindoll

The longer I live the more I realize the impact of attitude on life. Attitude, to me, is more important than facts.
It is more important than the past, than the education, than the money, than the circumstances, than failures, than success, than what other people think, say or do.
It is more important than appearance, giftedness or skill.
It will make or break a company, a church, or a home.
The remarkable thing is that we have a choice every day regarding the attitude we embrace for that day.
We can not change our past.
We can not change the fact that people will act in a certain way.
We can not change the inevitable.
The only thing we can do is play on the one string we have,
that is our attitude.
I am convinced that life is ten percent of what happens to me
and ninety percent how I react to it.
And so, it is with you.

CHAPTER THREE

Aging is a Disease, and is Curable

I suppose that the first thing we need to understand is what makes us age. It is much easier to solve a problem when we know what we are solving rather than stabbing in the dark. That is the concept I talked about when I described this book as *Knowing Your Body 101*. So here goes.

I read a lot of theories on this subject and most of them offered just small portions of the whole picture. The more I reflected over this, the more I came to the conclusion that cumulative micro-damage encompasses everything, not just a slice of the whole picture. This is true in the mind as much as in the body physiology. Aging is the relentless result of continual mini daily deteriorations that accumulate with time in our bodies. It is the accumulation of tiny injuries over a long period of time that affect molecules, cells, organs, systems or the entire body, as Dr. Vincent Giampapga has stated.

Look at it this way: add a grain of sand, a minute injury, every day of your life and eventually it will become a huge pile. That is when you start seeing the aging symptoms. If these mini-injuries are tackled individually and preventively on a daily basis, much less cell damage or death will occur. Therefore, extending the life span of these components by preventing mini-injuries will improve your health, and in the process extend your life.

In our younger years, our cells sustain the same daily mini-damages, but at that point they have a tremendous capacity of regenerating or replacing themselves, and at a very high pace, if injured, worn out or too old. As aging occurs, the replacement of these cells gradually becomes less vigorous and eventually becomes outright sluggish, ultimately ceasing completely. That is, unless you do something about it. So you already can see that a part of the aging process is a slow-down in the inner repair mechanism.

In our youth we have up to ten times the reserve necessary for each organ. For example as a medical student I spent a few months in a tuberculosis sanatorium and repeatedly witnessed surgery that involved taking a large portion of the TB infected lung out in young patients without affecting the body. The young patients came out of surgery and in general did not suffer ancillary affects. However the older the patients were, the more their bodies suffered from surgery.

The other concept of aging that we must sink in our brains is that *aging is a disease.* Our organs, the heart, lungs, endocrine glands, brain, blood, all break down as time passes, creating a domino effect. One breakdown leads to another. This vicious cycle ultimately and gradually starts deteriorating the body at a more and more expedient rate. The word disease actually means an abnormality in a body and the lack of normal processes. Isn't that what aging is all about? One reason the word disease is used for aging is that we now know more about this disease and are now finding cures for these problems. Thus, aging is not totally irremediable.

If you look at it as a disease that is not inevitable, you will also recognize that you can do something about it. You can either prevent it or cure it.

Consider these major factors that cause aging, roughly in order of importance. I do think that all of these are working in cooperation with each other, not as isolated agents.

Atrophy: If you do not use a cell, an organ, or a system, the body will get rid of it, thus the deterioration of old people. *So exercise, both physical and mental, is paramount.*

Hormonal reduction: Without the CEO of the company, none of its systems work well. Similarly, hormones are the major orchestrators of all of the systems in the body. Without them, everything comes to a halt.

Free-radicals: These are necessary oxidizers supporting combustion in the body, but the excesses become damaging just like rust on a bridge.

Proper nutrition: We need to feed the cells all the proper ingredients to keep them healthy.

Avoiding poisons and radiation: These damage cells

Our heredity: Often curable.

Atrophy

Many researchers are recognizing that not using our body structures is probably one of the *more important lacks of stimulus that starts the avalanche of tissue destruction.* Your body is created so that if you use a part actively, it rises to the occasion and develops to the level of the challenge. It is just like the corporation that will shrink the size of its staff when business is slow but will gear up if the need occurs.

So, if not used, the body gets rid of tissue (atrophy) as a useless resource. Muscles are a very evident example of atrophy as there is a distressing difference in muscles that have not been used and have weakened and those used that are strong and responsive. That incidentally includes the heart muscle.

The most consequential part of the aging process is to use your body every day. If you use your mind, it will stay active and alert. If you use your body, it will not atrophy but will stay functional and actually grow stronger and stronger, in proportion to the usage. It will heal better as these resources are also kept and very active. That is not restricted to muscles only, but to all organs and systems. It takes a lot longer to rebuild than it does to atrophy. If you do not use a muscle for two weeks, it will take four to six weeks of good exercise to bring it back to its original state.

Being in a surgical practice for thirty years, I had a lot of experience with postoperative patients in that regard. Early on it became very evident that the wimpy, "Oh poor me" patients, or the workman's compensation patients, took much longer to heal from their surgeries, had a lot more pain and subsequently had poorer results.

The others who were positive in their recuperation did far better on all counts. That is exactly why I exercised very actively after my heart surgery, as I knew this phenomenon too well and did not want that to happen to me. It was interesting to me that within two days I controlled pain strictly with Tylenol, since I had less pain and it did not impair my mind to be active, like narcotics would.

Inevitably the patients playing the "poor me " game all had difficult and long recuperations.

My most profound experiences with atrophy have come from treating paraplegic patients over the years. Some of these were patients paralyzed below the waist from severe spinal injuries. The denervated lower portion of their bodies was totally atrophied and osteoporotic. Of course, their bodies have the same hormones, immunity, heart, lung, circulation and nutrition access as the rest of the body. Therefore, the only factor causing the atrophy is inactivity, no functional use, i.e. total disuse.

The nerves were severed and that made a difference. This experience taught me the effect of atrophy and I later applied it to the deterioration of aging. Of course, I personally witnessed my body aging but exercise reversed it well. Exercise will boost all functions in the body and its cells, including the hormonal system. Aging not only can be prevented but greatly improved just by doing very active exercises, not wimpy or "I am kidding myself" exercises.

Hormone Reduction

Don't forget that in the normal depletion theory of aging, cells losing their function are not restricted to only a few cells but the loss can happen to *all* cells. This includes the endocrine glands and the other cell systems that secrete hormones. Naturally, if they are minimally or totally non-functional they won't secrete hormones.

Hormones are the catalysts of all chemical reactions of body functions. They are the master orchestrators, the CEOs of all that occurs in your body's function and metabolism. They are the stimulus for weak cells to be replaced (Growth hormones and their precursors).Without hormones all normal activities relative to metabolism, body reconstruction, and especially all chemical interactions between the cells either start slowing down or may come to a total rest.

These hormones are major orchestrators of mind as well as body functions, and as they decrease so will the functions of the body follow suit. The flagrant example in the human life cycle is, of course, menopause, when the hormone levels crash and it becomes the turning point of our lives toward the aging phase. So it goes without saying that when hormones are depleted the body automatically goes into the aging phase.

Free-Radicals

In 1954, Dr. Harman developed the theory that molecules are naturally neutral electrically. If inappropriate outside influences cause a cell to have an extra electron, thereby becoming negatively charged, they are called free-radicals and are no longer in balance or neutral. When this occurs, the molecules. become unstable and, like scavengers, try to steal electrons from other molecules to neutralize themselves, thus creating havoc in the molecular environment. The other molecules themselves become damaged, and they in turn become free-radicals, creating a dangerous chain reaction. This process is called oxidation. An excess of free-radicals will prevent normal chemical interaction within the cells and thus will create diseases, such as cancer or birth defects, or abnormal chemical interactions in the cells.

Of course, oxidation is in general a normal phenomenon, since we need oxygen transfers everywhere. But if it is produced abnormally, such as by a transfate or toxins like pesticides, or there is an excess of it, then it becomes a damaging free-radical. It is like everything in life, moderation is good, and excess is bad.

There are a whole bunch of categories of these free-radicals and each is caused by different influences. Let's simplify it for you: *it's the rust of our bodies*. A car rusts because it is exposed to oxygen and water and it oxidizes (iron oxide): rust.

Proper Foods and Supplements

Just think of a cell, made of mostly proteins, fewer fats, and *very little* carbohydrates. Cells also need enzymes in the form of supplements and vitamins to coordinate functions properly. You sure give your car the right ingredients to function well, but think of the junk you feed your body. For instance, your brain is eighty percent fat, so why would you expect good healthy neurons with a fat-free diet? You will also see in our heredity that we all need different nutrition. So why not feed the body a broad spectrum of food so it can pick what it needs?

Years ago, Dr. Hayflick did some research and found that a human cell could divide about fifty times in its life cycle before it died. End of life. However, if he fed the *right ingredients* to these cells growing in an agar plate, they could live much longer and healthier. Need I say more?

Avoiding Poisons and Mechanical Injuries

If you pour nitric acid on your skin, that skin will simply be destroyed. If you dilute the acid or put just a little bit on the skin every day, it will do the same damage but over a longer period of time. That damage can be just a partial impairment, such as the formation of free-radicals, which at first will create only small alterations to the cells' chemicals. That damage will accumulate with time. Or it can destroy the cell completely.

What I am trying to say is that you absorb or ingest toxic substances all the time. Large or concentrated quantities will do a lot of harm to you body and the damage will be immediately evident. But small quantities or diluted quantities will accumulate the damage over a long time. The damage is cumulative. Some of it heals as it occurs, but most of it doesn't. It heals less and less every day, and this is particularly true in the aging period when there is less regeneration.

It then becomes a vicious cycle; the more you damage the systems the less they can heal themselves. There will be proportional damage to your body's cells, depending on the toxicity of the agent and its quantity. And if you absorb some every day, there will be an accumulation of these damages

In essence, the more deleterious agents enter our bodies, the more cells are impaired, thus we experience additive destruction or a gradual micro-accumulation of damage. That is the reason why *we start seeing the damage—or aging—only later in life.* This is the point at which accumulated deterioration becomes evident. This is when you have finally accumulated a ton of sand and the body feels its weight. Some of these categories of bad agents are smoking, pesticides, radiation, air pollution, bad bacteria, heavy metals, and so on. They will be discussed later, so you should know to avoid them as much as possible.

Our Heredity

I know that everyone is quite concerned with genes or heredity or chromosomes, and this consideration is a real factor. But it also is a factor that in many instances is surmountable. Let's say that your dad had heart disease like mine did. There are probably a number of genes that can be involved in contributing to this heart condition.

For example, I had high cholesterol, a high homocysteine, and slightly high blood pressure. All three will be factors in heart disease. I managed to correct the high cholesterol I experienced with statins, the high homocysteine with folic acid, but did not know about the dangerous effect of the *moderate* blood pressure elevation, although today I would. Ultimately, I ended up with an open-heart operation.

Another example that obviously I am very familiar with is children born with cleft lips and palates. Some are hereditary. Here in the U.S.A., we repair them immediately so they are not psychologically a lifelong destructive mechanism. However, in third world countries, where I travel to perform these surgeries, the children are quite often left with the deformities until well into their childhood years. The psychological damage can scar them way beyond the correction of the cosmetic problem.

People who have longevity happen to have *many of the "good" genes* well lined up, thus their healthy long life. It is not just one gene that brings it about. The assumption can be also dangerous. If your parents are dying old, let's say age one hundred, it is very important not to assume that you will live a long life automatically. Your parents' longevity may blind you to the fact that you have some bad genes, and these can kill you unless you realize that you have them and you do something to avert the problem.

A moment's insight is sometimes worth a life's experience.

-Oliver Wendell Holmes

CHAPTER FOUR

Hormones, the Great Communicators

Hormones are by far the most important regulators of body chemistry whether in humans or animals. Even plants are controlled by hormones. In this orchestration of our physiology, hormones are the sheet music that is distributed to all of the musicians so that they may stage this absolutely wonderful melody called the symphony of aging. Without them, no well-orchestrated harmonics can occur.

What are hormones?

They are chemical communicators of the whole body secreted by cells to instruct other cells concerning their systems and chemistry to engage predetermined activity. They are mostly highly specialized proteins and lipoproteins created for the specific purpose of sending a command to start a function, either within the cell itself or in one that influences a whole organ system, a whole body, or for that matter a whole species.

For example, food enters the stomach and stimulates a series of cells to secrete the hormone gastrin, which then commands adjacent cells to secrete gastric digestive juices to prepare the food for absorption.

Another instance is exercise that encourages the release of growth hormone from the adrenal glands and the brain to start expansion and division of muscles cells, so they can meet the demand imposed on them.

Nighttime, that is darkness, triggers the manufacturing of the hormone melatonin in order to aid sleep. This is because our body produces most of our hormones during sleep.

There are also hormones secreted outside our bodies to influence others to react to us. These are called pheromones. They signal our availability for procreation, thus continuing the growth of our species, or of any other animal species for that matter.

There are major hormones and minor hormones; that is, some communicate to whole systems and some to individual cells only. Medical science knows today that there are a lot more of these chemicals than we ever imagined involved in this communication system. At first only endocrine hormones, such as adrenalin, estrogen, testosterone, those that affect whole systems, were recognized. But research has uncovered many other hormones, even inside the cell communicators, such as eiconasoids, which are as important in the whole picture as those chemicals that govern entire systems.

Please realize that hormones are not drugs, but a natural product of our body. When administered by pill or otherwise, they are used as imitators of the natural product. These are not all alike, and some are synthetic products that could and do have side effects.

Hormones control all interaction: behavior; sexual activities from attraction to having babies; all body responses to external stimuli, including stress, fright, depression and crazy behavior such as a young man has with excess testosterone level.

They control the body's development and growth; mood; bowel and bladder function; daily and monthly life cycles; electrolyte balances; sugar balances and fat deposition. They are responsible for aging when they become deficient. As soon as we are born we need growth, so our glands emit many hormones. During our teenaged years, the glands emit profuse quantities of them, mostly testosterone or estrogen and hence the stereotypical moody teenager. As we age, the production levels out until about thirty to thirty-five years of age. But a few years later, as we have lost our reserves, the body starts atrophying and its production of hormones is reduced inexorably. That is the menopause phase.

What Comes First, the Chicken or the Egg?

Is it the damage that has resulted from multiple micro-injuries to our cells, including the hormone producing cells, that causes the aging process? Or is it primarily the reduction of hormones that stop stimulating the normal cellular orchestration? Some advocate that the deterioration of our body is inevitable and the body's reduction and ultimate cessation of hormone production causes its ultimate demise.

Recently I heard Dr. Dean Adel on his radio commentary argue that aging is a natural process, wherein all the cells in the body degenerate. Giving hormones at this stage is useless, Dr. Adel said, since they would not affect these degenerated cells. This is the first time I ever disagreed with one of his statements.

The alternative is: As the cells that produce these hormones are damaged by all the environmental factors and micro-accumulation, like all of our other cells they stop secreting these hormones. Their reduction greatly aggravates the downward slope of damage to the rest of the body. In this case, replacing hormones would substantially alter beneficially the downward slope, and thus improve health in these later years.

I am a strong believer in the latter theory, as witnessed by the dramatic reversal of the aging and deterioration process through the supplementation of hormones such as estrogen, progesterone, testosterone, and growth hormone. I have seen too many instances in my life of very striking favorable changes after menopause, when hormonal replacement therapy was given.

I am *not* supporting in any way taking growth hormones to enhance sports performance. By doing this, you offset the fine *normal* push-pull mechanism of the endocrine system, and in the long run create imbalances that are greatly detrimental to the body's refined controls and that ultimately cause serious disease. For the sake of performance, using growth hormones, in essence, causes the secreting gland to find that it no longer needs to give off that particular hormone and it just atrophies. It thus is quite difficult to restart it all over again. One of my young patients who had seen me for a physical complication resulting from taking growth hormones despite my advice to the contrary, died from taking them.

On the other hand, I do advocate the replacement of hormones when the body no longer produces them, and thus is bound to the ultimate deterioration of aging. What possible harm can you do here? There are no hormones and there are no push-pull mechanisms to destroy. As a matter of a fact, gonadotropins are secreted in excess trying to stimulate the other hormones. They could be the cause of Alzheimer's. The glands are mostly or totally atrophied already. You can only reverse the body's descent and bring it back to "normal" or at least closer to it. You cannot harm a gland that is already non-functional. You however can reverse the severe, relentless damage that is the ultimate product of the loss of hormones.

I know that many health professionals say that this will stimulate cancer. In the first place, this is not proven beyond the shadow of a doubt. And secondly, don't you think if you live longer you will statistically have a greater chance of acquiring a cancer simply by the virtue that whatever has caused that cancer has a much longer time to develop?

Furthermore, the fact is that the percentage of increase in cancer is way lower than the high percentage of health in aging and possibly longer life gained by taking replacement hormones. In the beginning of the twentieth century, our ancestors died at the age of forty-five or forty-six. They had very few cancers. We die on average at seventy-five to eighty today, and of course we will have more. But then too, we may have more resistance to them due to better immunity. Or the cancers are caused by gonadotropins.

If we take no hormonal replacement, our bodies will necessarily deteriorate and die. Having problems such as bad knees, cancer, heart disease or Alzheimer's sooner or later all result from hormonal imbalance. If, on the other hand, we add hormones, we will delay the inevitable and be a lot more comfortable and vigorous in the process. Isn't this our goal?

Just look at that curve below, and see that if you improve that descending curve you more likely will be better off. You'll live a better life, at least, instead of feeling awful, pain-ridden, crippled by disabilities and unhappy.

Of course, this whole book is about trying to keep your body cell groups healthy. By living healthy, the hormone secreting cells also stay active longer. And while exercise will not be as dramatic as hormonal replacement therapy, it is nonetheless very good.

When we are born, we have high levels of hormones but toward menopause they dwindle down dramatically. That is precisely when we begin to experience aging. Exercise and hormone replacement therapy help at least enough to keep us vigorous. Without them, comes the inexorable decline into aging and ultimately demise. But worse than that is the decline in health, vigor and satisfaction of life most individuals fear will haunt them before death.

Menopause, both in males and females, is the dramatic entrance to this process in the aging years. You can see this by the descending curve at this period. That is when hot flashes, loss of energy, depression, burnout, osteoporosis, loss of sexual drive, foggy brains, and so on become evident. There is a wealth of experience with hormonal replacement indicating how much more energy, vigor, stamina, strength, positive attitude, joie de vivre, sexuality, alertness and memory we have if we take hormone replacement therapy.

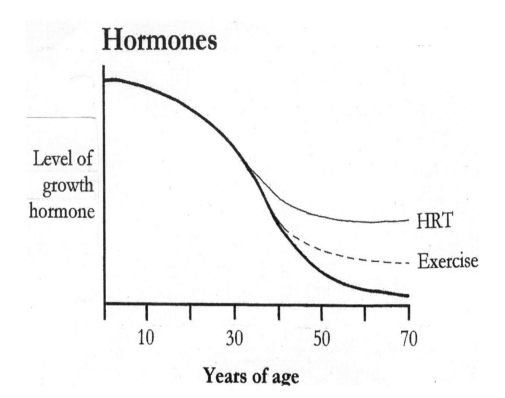

So at their heights the systems function well and healthily. All these hormones are the reason for our bodies' fine balance between all the systems, from the cellular levels all the way to the interaction between members of a species. As we have noted, precise and true communication is the key to all well-functioning corporations and the body is no exception.

If this interaction starts depleting or fails altogether the ultimate results is failure and eventual demise of the whole corporation of cells. Just think what would happen if all the members of a corporation stop communicating. Or what would happen if it were to stop advertising or interacting with other corporations, or interchanging research or selling. How can it survive?

Aging no longer looks benign at this point. The inevitable

decline has removed all ambitions and left us with no hope. All we have to do is wait. Now we are out of tune. The orchestration of the body is gone.

Menopause is actually the acute period when we all of a sudden the body undergoes massive changes due to the lack of hormones and we experience the aging process. It is an insipient process occurring within a variable period, between two and ten years. It is usually a waxing and waning effect on us, subject to much variation caused by many factors. Ultimately, the body no longer has these hormones and gets into the downwards aging slope. It is entirely preventable.

Why the controversy is beyond me.

"Hormonal decline is of course normal, but so is heart disease," says E. Shippen M.D. in his book *Testosterone Syndrome*. If you do not want to replace hormones, you are automatically saying, "now I want to die and let myself go down the tube".

Of course, you are not trying to kill yourself by not replacing hormones, but the end result is the same isn't it? If you suffer side effects, you can always stop.

Here is another argument for taking hormones: As we speak, there is research going on that shows very convincingly that as the sexual hormones decline, gonadotropins increase dramatically. This phenomenon is more accentuated in women than in men. Gonadotropins that are secreted by the brain are the stimulating hormones that tell the gonads to secrete their sexual hormones. After menopause when the glands atrophy, they just secrete more to try and over-stimulate these now nearly nonfunctional gonads. The net result is they attain very high levels. The higher these levels are, the higher the occurrence of cancer of the prostate and of Alzheimer's.

The conjecture is to either take hormonal therapy, which would quite naturally stop the high production of gonadotropins, or alternatively give a drug-hormone, like Luprolide, that would stop the production of these gonadotropins. If this theory is indeed true it would be the discovery of the century as it would get rid of these two diseases.

Male Menopause

Menopause occurs as much in men as it is in women, although it is less evident simply because its ultimate arrival is more insipient over years, instead of within months as in women. It takes years for both to happen, but the curve is more acute in women than in men, where in many instances they don't even know it has happened because the bleeding indicator is not there.

Not very many people know men do have menopause (the event is less conspicuous, so not recognized as strongly as women's) but it ultimately often has the same effects. The symptoms can be psychological: irritability, nervousness, impatience, insomnia, inability to concentrate, foggy brain and even outright depression. Hot flashes, headaches, sweating, and palpitations might be experienced along with weakness, fatigue, muscle pains, nausea and vomiting, constipation and abdominal pain, weight gain, decreased force of urination, urinary frequency or hesitancy of urination, along with diminished libido and erections.

More and more we recognize that cancer of the prostate occurs in *men with no or much reduced testosterone secretion* and therefore it is a post-menopausal problem. I suppose that I would not give testosterone to a man with diagnosed prostate cancer, simply because we do not know if it would stimulate the cancer cells. It is scary at best to experiment on this.

But more and more data indicate that cancer of the prostate may be prevented or at least abated if not cured by giving testosterone replacement therapy. I am aware that some European countries treat it with depot testosterone. We also know that if we withhold the testosterone subsequently, the symptoms of cancer will recur. So I am suggesting that menopause for men, as well as women, is not aging but rather the sequel of an event brought about by the loss of male or female hormones. If hormone replacement is taken early, aging is reversible. Aging is reversible, but not at that rate and with so much facility, after the onslaught of deterioration has set in. It is not as easily reversible as menopause is with just hormonal therapy. So the earlier you take the hormone replacement the better the alleviation of the symptoms.

If men could just recognize this, they could easily avert the symptoms by taking hormonal therapy via a good physician.

Female menopause

Of course, we hear more about it than men's, but essentially it is only an episode in life. There are varied way it occurs. Dr. Christiane Northrup describes *natural menopause* as occurring gradually between forty-five and fifty-five years of age. Then, there is *premature menopause,* occurring earlier around thirty-five and of shorter duration, one to three years. Thirdly, *artificial menopause* is an abrupt onset due to surgical removal of the ovaries. This could be also be induced by radiation, chemotherapy, certain drugs or disruption of the blood supply to the ovaries.

The symptoms are hot flashes, night sweats, palpitations of the heart, migraine headaches, swelling and tenderness in the breasts, heavy or irregular menstrual periods, loss of sexual drive, fibroids of the uterus, vaginal dryness, urinary symptoms such as recurrent infections of the urinary tract, dryness, and wrinkling of the skin, osteoporosis, mood swings, insomnia and lack of mental concentration. These symptoms may last five to ten years. But the deterioration does persist thereafter. Again, we can likely add Alzheimer's to these symptoms.

We have a huge amount of experience in hormonal replacement and have seen wonderful responses alleviating these symptoms. The question is, does hormonal replacement have such side effects or complications as increasing the rate of breast cancer or the incidence of heart diseases? There are many articles touting both, one that it increases breast cancer, although maybe only by a small percentage. On the other hand, many medical literatures praise hormonal replacement therapy as alleviating symptoms and continuing the body on a healthier course for less deterioration in aging.

The Various Groups of Hormones

Major Hormones

These control the body's systems. Many of them are produced primarily by the endocrine glands, although they also can be produced by fat cells, skin and hair follicles, the liver, breast or pineal gland, to name a few. In essence, the mechanism of hormones is to be secreted by one cell or gland in order to stimulate other glands to start secreting and affect an organ system.

For instance, the pituitary gland at the base of the brain emits TSH (thyroid stimulating hormone) that sends a message to the thyroid gland that it is not producing enough thyroid hormone. The thyroid then ups the production and this shuts off the TSH message by telling the pituitary, "We are now in production and thank you for the message." It is the boss telling a worker to start a project and, when started, the boss goes on to other tasks.

There are many such major hormones; growth hormone; estrogen; testosterone; progesterone; adrenalin etc. all of which have the same push-pull balance. As they circulate in the blood stream, they actually affect many organs, not the least of which is the brain. Look at the effect of estrogen on women's cycles or testosterone on an adolescent male's psyche and you'll get a flavor of their functions. They are responsible for the cycles of life.

Moderate Affect Hormones

Cell secretions throughout the body that mediate many mostly "local" functions such as serotonin that affect the brain and vessels' actions, endorphins that alter pain patterns in exercise, and cholinesterase that permits transport of impulses in between nerve cells are what I consider moderate in impact. They affect more localized systems instead of the whole body.

Minor Hormones

These are emitted inside the cells by the cells themselves to affect either their own inner sanctums or the immediate neighboring cells for interaction between them.

It took us a long time to find these, since they do not circulate in the body but stay at the cellular levels. Our micro bioassays, analysis at the microscopic levels, have become sophisticated enough to find and recognize their presences and there functions. These are the paracrine hormones or eicosanoids.

Outside Hormones

We also secrete hormones outside the body. They are called pheromones and they communicate between individuals. We often call them "Musk."

This is how a flock of birds flies together in coordination, the form of communication they use. It is how animals and humans attract each other to procreate. They are powerful hormones responsible for six billion humans on this earth and countless animals.

Replacement Hormones

I am referring to Hormonal Replacement Therapy, or HRT. These are pseudo-hormones that, obviously, come from other sources. For example, Pempro is an estrogen derived from the urine of a mare plus the progesterone that is synthetic.

How do we preserve our levels of hormones?

- By preventing as much as possible damage to our body, in such ways as avoiding toxins, **not** *smoking*, avoiding preservatives, radiation etc. By doing so, the cells of the hormone secreting glands, the endocrine glands, will stay healthy and produce more.

- By keeping the body functioning at peak performance through mental and physical exercise.
- By not gaining weight. Fat cells produce estrogen in inordinate quantities offsetting the normal balance of the normal hormones.
- By replacing deficient hormones after the glands no longer produce them.
- By having a very positive attitude to keep all these mechanisms active. A negative outlook causes the adrenals to secrete hormones like cortisol and adrenalin, which causes undue damage such as hypertension and chronic stress.
- By choosing foods well. Soy for example has a molecule that mimics estrogen and can influence the balance in the body.

Description of various hormones:

I will try to give you the most important major and minor ones. Many are discussed elsewhere in the book, but for a global understanding I will give you the rough guidelines of what specific hormones do.

Obviously, I cannot discuss all hormones, as it would take the whole book to do so. Just understand the rough line of what they are, what they do and their importance.

The Hormonal System

Melatonin

Is the orchestra leader of all hormones and is produced by the pineal gland in the brain. Among other things, it starts the night cycles just like the manufacturing whistle starts the work shift.

- It slows the body by putting it to sleep. This is recuperation or replenishing time. This is the time orchestrated by melatonin for the brain to replenish all the hormones in the body. Thus, sleep is very important.

- It then signals the pituitary, a small gland in the brain to secrete growth hormone and many like hormones.
- Meanwhile it cleanses the body with its powerful antioxidant capacity.

As we grow older, the pineal gland atrophies. So, gradually we have less and less melatonin available and sleep less and thus have less recuperation time. For that reason, melatonin pills are the best sleeping pills. They are nature's way to sleep. See dosages in chapter eleven, the Ten Commandments.

Sexual Hormones

The first thing you must understand is that both males and females do have all three hormones: estrogen, progesterone and testosterone. Men have a much higher level of testosterone relative to estrogen and progesterone, whereas women have the reverse. Testosterone tends not to be as cyclical as the female hormones, since males do not have the menstrual cycle.

In general, *the menstrual cycle* is regulated by a higher amount of estrogen at the first half of the cycle; then comes the progesterone that promotes endometrial growth to accept the fertilized ova, if such is the case. If the ova are embedded into the endometrium, the cycle is stopped; thus the start of pregnancy. If it is not, both estrogen and progesterone are withdrawn and the endometrium sloughs off the menses. This is all regulated by the pituitary gland that sends its messengers to trigger estrogen and in turn progesterone.

During pregnancy however it secretes LH, gonadotropins that promote all the necessary mechanisms for the embryonic growth.

Testosterone

It is one of the most important hormones in men, and this becomes quite evident when male menopause begins. We know that its levels decrease about one-and-a-half percent yearly, and so when a man reaches sixty - seventy he likely has very little left. Thus, the signs of aging become more evident: that is male menopause. Dr. Eugene Shippen even goes on to say, "Testosterone may in fact be the single factor that links all age-related diseases."

As the testosterone levels decline causing skeletal muscles to atrophy, males gain weight since they have lost that muscle bulk and thus reduced the ability to burn calories.

So the increase in fat mass particularly is in the midriff. There has been a reversal in muscle-fat ratio. The skeletal muscles are not the only ones affected, as the heart and vessels' muscles are also part of this loss of stimulus from testosterone.

From that, the higher the amount of fat cells the more the production of an enzyme called aromatase, which converts testosterone into estrogen. It in turn suppresses the pituitary to simulate the production of testosterone, thus the vicious cycle.

Let's look at the effects of testosterone deficiency. These are reversed when testosterone therapy is instituted. This therapy should never be undertaken unless monitored by a physician and appropriate blood tests.

In testosterone deficiency

Psychological symptoms:
- Nervousness and irritability.
- Insomnia
- Depression
- Foggy brain
- Lack of concentration
- Poor memory

Sexual symptoms:
- Diminution or loss of libido
- Decreased erections
- Decreased semen

Vascular symptoms
- Hot flashes
- Sweating
- The heart muscle becomes weaker and weaker.
- Heart palpitations
- Increased pulse rate and maybe irregular heart rate.
- Headaches, migraine like.
- Higher blood pressure.

Urinary symptoms
- Decreased force
- Frequency, mostly at night
- Slow starting, hesitancy

Systemic symptoms
- Weakness
- Fatigue
- Muscle aching
- Constipation
- Weight gain of the abdominal fat
- Lower growth hormone production

While testosterone decreases, estrogen stays at the same levels or even rises precipitously, since no longer checked by it. That may be the reason for increase in heart disease and gynecomastia, male breasts, in the male post-menopausal years.

If testosterone is replaced:

- There is increasing evidence that there is a lower cardiovascular disease rate.
- All of the above testosterone deficiency symptoms are reversed for as long as the hormone is taken.

A naturally occurring in-the-body by-product of testosterone is dihydrotestosterone (DHT), which is the cause of baldness— not testosterone itself. DHT is the potential stimulus of prostatic cancer once it has developed.

Today there is controversy about this, as doctors feel that prostate cancer is most likely caused by the excessive rise of gonadotropins. This rise is inversely proportional to the reduction in testosterone production.

DHT however can by suppressed by either Proscar or the more commonly used Saw Palmetto. I noticed that once I started taking Saw Palmetto, my hair loss stopped. I just wish I had taken that drug way before. However, it happened that way and I don't really mind.

Estrogen

This extraordinary hormone has been responsible for all the cycles of a woman, including the gift of childbirth.

All the symptoms mentioned in menopause are present. It can:

- Improve memory lapses and sharpen memory
- Improve the ability to learn
- Thwart the advent of Alzheimer's
- Improve depression
- Prevent hot flashes
- And essentially have the same effects as growth hormone increase muscle, immunity, etc, heart, but to a lesser degree.

The cancer issue:

I have read many books and articles and am more and more baffled by the present attitude of not wanting to do HRT, hormonal replacement therapy. The only factor that has impressed me in all the literature I have read is that there is no consistency in any of them.

For example, the type and quality or source of estrogen used for replacement is rarely mentioned. Today, more and more, we understand that there are three types of estrogens and a higher level of one of them, estradiol, may be to blame for the higher cancer risk. Altering the percentages relationship in HRT with the other two, estrin and estriol, may alter the whole picture about cancer.

All of this issue is based on one particular NIH-funded study called the Women's Health Initiative (WHI). The study reviewed ten thousand women for five years taking one 'drug' called Pempro. They found that eight more women would develop breast cancer (one in twelve-hundred-and-fifty women), seven more developed heart disease (one in fifteen hundred), eight more would have strokes and eight would develop blood clots (or, one in twelve-hundred-and-fifty for both strokes and blood clots).

But they did not tell you that normally 9.7 percent of women develop breast cancer (nine-hundred-and-seventy out of ten thousand) over a period of twenty to twenty-five years, that is during the active cancer period.

Also they did not tell you that six fewer colorectal cancer and five fewer hip fractures developed during this study.

Cancers in general develop within long periods, ten to twenty years. The five-year period of the WHI thus was too short to produce full-blown cancers, making their conclusions invalid or making their drug, Pempro, a particular stimulus. It could accentuate the already present cancers in that short period, but not develop from the inception.

We also know that Pempro is mare estrogen that is not quite similar to human estrogen, and the progesterone was synthetic hormone not found in the female human body.

Natural or bio-identical hormones do not have the pro-inflammatory effect that synthetic hormones have.
Other factors that are important and are seldom considered:
- Whether the patient was on any forms of estrogen before
- Smoking

- Genetics: estrogen sensitive breast cancers. Today the more we know the more we find genes or alleles that could be a factor.
- Obesity: fat cells produce estrogen even after menopause and could be a major stimulus.
- Age: the older the person, the more time to develop a cancer
- The various combinations of estrogen, progesterone and testosterone.
- The protective effect of testosterone that may thwart breast cancer
- Diet: soy for example has an estrogen like molecule and in good quantities may be a real factor in the stimulation of cancer.
- Marijuana: mimics estrogen. Men do develop breasts if they smoke three to five times a day. Women increase estrogen levels by smoking it.
- DHEA: does produce estrogen as one of its by-products. It is an early production of the adrenals.

By the way, there is a recent study that showed Tamoxifen, as a cancer prevention in patients who were cured of their cancer of the breast, as lowering the chance of recurrence by thirty-five percent.

The heart disease issue:
Estrogen has the following effects, and they must also be considered in the possibility of causing heart disease

Pros
- We know that estrogen elevates the good cholesterol HDL and reduces the bad one LDL
- Reduces arteriosclerosis
- Physical shape and conditioning

Cons
- The synthetic estrogens cause inflammation. The natural ones do not.
- As it keeps women alive and older , they of course

have more susceptibility of heart disease
- Increase clotting and thrombosis
- Family genetics can be pros and cons depending on the gene you inherit
- Homocysteine elevation
- Obesity
- Type of diet consumed: elevated saturated fats, excess soy, high carbohydrates
- Medications that could increase heart disease susceptibility
- Smoking

Other issues such as the many varied symptoms of taking HRT are most often resolved by altering the hormone, taking more or less, as the case may be, taking "natural hormones," taking combination hormones, and so on. A good physician will be able to titrate your hormones to suit your needs. There are three books worth reading for all women: *The Schwartzbein Principle*, *The Wisdom of Menopause* and *The 30- day Natural Hormone Plan*, all listed in the bibliography. It is your life, your aging, your well-being, and it is imperative that you not regulate it haphazardly. So read, or at least see a gynecologist specialized in this therapy.

Progesterone

Progesterone tends to be a balancing hormone for estrogen. It is used extensively during the normal female cycles to reverse the effects of estrogen and trigger the onset of menstruation. It probably offers protection against some cancers such as endometrial and colon.

It is the yin and the yang with estrogen.

Adrenal secretions

Cortisones: Are mostly concerned with the regulation of inflammation in the body.

- Some control the electrolytes balances in the blood

and are called Mineralocorticoids. For example, in pregnancy they permit the accumulation of fluid to form amniotic fluid and the excessive swelling that woman often experience.

- Some control the sugar distribution and are linked with insulin. They are called Glucocorticoids.

Cortisols: Are the stress hormones closely interrelated with adrenalin and the sympathetic nervous system in the body. Both are the stimulants that increase the speed of everything in the body, such as heart rate, high blood pressure, etc.

- They are mostly present in stress and helpful only if in acute situations but quite harmful in long run events such as unresolved stress.
- They are present in chronic inflammation of any causes.
- They sure facilitate obesity.
- They create free-radicals.
- They are mostly produced at night.
- They dissipate with closure in stress.

Insulin: Is secreted by the pancreas. The secretion is triggered by the absorption of foods by the intestine into the blood. Sugars and pastas are by far are the strongest stimulators of insulin secretion.

Other carbohydrates in vegetables do not raise insulin levels as much, nor do proteins and fats. See the Graph on pages 193 and 194. It is predominantly a storage hormone that disposes of the carbohydrates appropriately. I will discuss this hormone in more detail in Nutrition.

Thyroid Hormone: The thyroid hormone's function is as a regulatory mechanism that raises or lowers the basal metabolic rate of the body, that is, the speed at which all the body functions perform, ranging from such functions as higher body temperature to faster heart rate, and so on.

Thyroid hormone:
- Regulates body temperature
- Enhances Cerebral function; faster clearer thinking.
- Fat breakdown
- Decreases appetite
- Increases heart rate
- Sleeplessness
- Fine tremors of the hands

So the more hormones secreted the higher the metabolic rate is. It is incumbent on another hormone from the pituitary called thyroid stimulating hormone, or TSH, to regulate this proper level. Too much causes hyperthyroidism, which is the excess of the above. Too little causes deficiency.

Deficiencies:
- Apathy
- Weight gain
- Lack of sleep
- Dry skin
- Constipation
- Sluggishness
- Heat and cold intolerance
- Fatigue
- Sore muscles
- High cholesterol

Thyroid Hormonal Therapy or replacement is relatively easy and, in general, is administered in pill form. The therapy must be monitored by a physician to titrate the level precisely.

Growth hormone is one of the major factors in keeping the body in good repair and function. Experimental growth hormones have been given to people with excellent and surprising results. These results are among the reasons that I strongly believe that these hormones, which include the sex hormones, are a fundamental key to slowing the aging process. Here are some of the results of trials of experimental growth hormones.

- Fat loss of fourteen percent without diet in six months.
- Muscles strength; gain of nine percent without exercise after six months.
- Elevated exercise performance
- Increased memory
- Improved cardiac output
- Stronger bones
- Better cholesterol levels; higher HDL lower LDL
- Mood elevation
- reduced fatigue and depression
- Improved sleep
- Improved immunity
- Enhanced sexual activity and performance
- Improved vigor, energy levels and satisfaction with life.
- Faster wound healing
- Eliminate cellulites
- Promotes regrowth of heart kidneys, liver and lungs that have shrunk or atrophied with age. In other words, it reverses the aging of these organs.
- Removes wrinkles and replaces them with younger and thicker skin with better elasticity
- Promotes hair regrowth

So far, growth hormone replacement is expensive and a physician must control its therapy However, despite the drawbacks it is what many doctors say is the ultimate anti-aging hormone. Remember that after menopause we produce little or no growth hormone. Therefore we are not harming our normal balance; rather, we are bringing it back to normal. Once in the body, it will branch out to produce sex hormones.

Adrenal Fatigue

We tend to forget about the adrenal glands that secrete all of the cortisones, including cortisol. They actually secrete fifty hormones. In men, the adrenal glands are the only source of estrogen, and in women they are the only source of testosterone.

This gland is depleted when there is chronic stress to the body, like alcoholism, sleep deprivation, chronic fatigue syndrome, many prescription drugs, mental stress such as accompanies job loss and marital problems, and such chronic illnesses as fibromyalgia and auto-immune diseases. Typically a patient will say, "I have never felt the same since" that severe illness or event.

The symptoms include sleeping later, awakening later and tired, feeling at your best in the day after lunch and between six and eight o'clock.

People with adrenal fatigue crave salt; become hypoglycemic easily; suffer from mild depression, lethargy, decreased memory; want to lie down after a stress episode.

If they have allergies, the allergies get worse; their chronic fatigue episodes grow more severe; they are apathetic; they frequently have swollen ankles, chronic constipation or the reverse, mild diarrhea. They experience chronic cough and repeated respiratory infections; crave food high in fat but are unable to handle carbohydrates or high potassium foods like fruit salad or molasses.

How to diagnose:
- Twenty-four hours salivary cortisol testing for four days: low cortisol levels
- Blood sugars may follow suit.

- Low blood pressure
- Pupil fatigue: can't focus and the irises flutter open and shut.
- Pressure over kidney area is painful.

Treatment:
- Resting from *mental and emotional stress*
- A night out with friends and laughter
- Early to bed
- Regular balanced meals:
    - Carbs: whole grain breads and vegetables
    - proteins and fats combined and in good proportion
    - Eat by 10 a.m.—In other words, have a good breakfast
    - No junk foods
    - No caffeine or other stimulants
    - Vitamin C since adrenal gland needs a lot of it.
    - Vitamin E
    - B complex
    - Magnesium 400mg/day
    - Calcium 800mg/day and do not take magnesium and calcium together, but about two to three hours apart.
    - Mild exercise. Too much is bad.
    - Multiple glandular extract (ask physician)
    - DHEA: 25-150mg/a day for men 25-50mg /day for women.
    - Cortisone treatment, if severe (MD will prescribe)

It is being recognized that adrenal fatigue is very common and quite unrecognized in our high-speed society. See The Schwartzbein Principle in the bibliography.

Take a risk. Not taking a risk is the biggest risk of all. You stand to lose much more if you do not take hormone replacement therapy. Be flexible with change and stay on top of your situation at all times.

The Paralysis of Analysis
Don't be directed by the one percent chance of failure.
Be directed by the ninety-nine percent chance of success.
Doing nothing Is inevitably going downhill

CHAPTER FIVE

Aging Happens a Day at a Time

It doesn't occur all at once

The key to understanding aging is to know that it does not occur all at once. It is a constant, daily accumulation of tiny injuries to your cells. It is like adding a grain of sand in your body everyday of you life One day you wake up and you have accumulated a ton of that sand. That is your aging process that occurred bit by bit, damaging the seventy-five trillion cells in your body. The good news is that it is never too late to stop, or at least slow down, the injuries.

There are many sources that cause that relentless damage Let's explore first of all what a cell is and what harms it. Then a short story on free-radicals, as I have tried to summarize this complicated issue. After that, let's look at the important consequences of the interactions between the brain and the body.

The Cell

The first concept you must understand is that cells are the basic units from which you are made. They are tiny, individual living organisms that have a whole physiology of their own, and each of those cells has a specific function in the body. We have estimated that there are seventy-five trillion cells in the body and twenty-five trillion of these are red blood cells transporting oxygen in the blood. The rest are divided into various organ cells all having their own specialty.

Thus, every individual cell is associated in a society or "town," the organs. These organs are composed of many cells having various functions. Some of them secrete hormones and enzymes and some of them promote chemical reactions. Some of them will transport nerve impulses while some will transport oxygen, information or immune cells. They all come from *stem cells, which are totipotent*, meaning they can differentiate into any form of cell given the proper stimulus. Once all of these structures have developed and all organs have differentiated, then you are whole and can be a living human being. Your body is made up of all these little cells and their inter-cooperation and orchestration permit the existence of these wonderful bodies of mine and yours.

I am amazed at the brilliance of the Being who created humans. I cannot see evolution as a haphazard creation; this marvelous vessel is endlessly complex and extraordinarily put together.

The whole body is seventy-six percent water, which is the means of transport of everything from one cell to the other. That is why we cannot go without fluid for more than four or five days. The water content of the entire body, however, is less than that of the individual cells because the bones have little water.

Each cell, however, is eighty-five percent water, a level that permits chemical reactions to occur, allowing substances to diffuse and to be transported, and distribute electrolytes such as potassium, magnesium, sodium, calcium, phosphate and bicarbonate. The cell is like a nice swimming pool into which all the organelles and molecules swim and in which they can readily interact with each other.

Usually inside the cell is rich in potassium and magnesium, which contribute to the inner sanctum of the cell. Calcium and sodium are more concentrated in the outside the cells.

Proteins
Twenty percent of the whole cell is protein, or sixty-six percent of its solid matter. There are two types of protein. Some

proteins are structural with fibers that support the cell and also support the body in a structural mechanism. Helping in muscle contraction mechanisms is an example. The second kind are called the globular proteins, responsible for all chemical reactions. They are enzymes, catalysts for chemical reactions, hormones, DNA and RNA, which are the genes inside the nucleus of the cell and part of the cell membrane.

Lipids

Lipids, also called fats, are about fifteen percent of our cells but up to fifty percent of nerve cells, particularly in the brain. They form the cell membrane, mitochondrial membrane—the cell's batteries—and the nucleus' membrane. The nerve cells are often surrounded by an insulator called myelin, which is a specialized fat. This is destroyed in multiple sclerosis. Other fats are used to manufacture certain products in the cell such as cholesterol to make hormones. Low fat diets do not seem a good idea when you look at these facts.

Carbohydrate

Carbohydrates comprise about two percent of the cell and have very little function in cells except to supply the cells energy and fuel. It is the fuel for the cell's battery, to heat and produce energy for the chemical reactions in cells. Muscle and brain cells need more energy than other cells. The liver will store carbohydrates as glycogen. There is a little bit of carbohydrate in the cell membrane that makes up the docking stations to which all vendors attach themselves.

Cell Structure

The cell is a unit that can live on its own. It has *a cell membrane*; the envelope that isolates, protects, and controls what comes in and out of the cell. It is actually a very specific organ permitting certain electrolytes, proteins, lipids and water to come in and regulate the inner cell environment very carefully. It also prevents the same materials from going out, so there is always a good balance between the outside fluids and tissues (extra cellular fluids) and the inside. For instance, it has a *potassium pump* that will let specific amounts of potassium in and out depending on immediate needs. Muscle contraction needs that exchange of ions across the cell membrane to activate its inner mechanism. The pump is the very active part of the cell membrane and needs to be kept very well regulated. The cell membrane also has docking stations that will permit hormones such as insulin to attach to the cell and affect its behavior.

The material inside the cells called *cytoplasm* is like a gel that contains multiple little organs called *organelles*, each of which are specialized organs. Some secrete hormones and some create material for the cell function.

One in particular is the *mitochondria*, the cell's batteries, which produce the energy necessary to permit all the cell functions. This battery is especially important in more active cells like muscle cells (heart, vessels, bowel and skeletal muscles) and brain cells. Remember how important it is to change the batteries in your cell phone, clock and radio. It is just as important to keep your mitochondria charged and in good working order. The mitochondria have a chemical reaction called the ADP-ATP system that liberates energy when they are properly maintained. If they are not properly maintained, they will slow down or prevent the chemical reactions so important to the cell's functions. Most cells have between two and five mitochondria, but muscle cells have up to thirty, brain cells about twenty, and heart muscle cells seven hundred.

At the center of a cell is a *nucleus* which specializes in DNA and RNA, the proteins in the chromosome, the reproductive genes. The nucleus' function is to control the whole cell division, making new cells either to grow or to replace damaged or old cells. If another cell dies and needs to be replaced, then a signal is given to the *chromosomes* to make the cell divide and create another cell to replace it. This is controlled by *telomeres*. In a normal cell, thirteen percent of the chromosome is a telomere and its function is to regulate whether a cell will divide or not divide. It is regulated by an enzyme called *telomerase* controlled by hormones, particularly growth hormones. As you grow older, the telomeres will gradually get smaller and smaller. The smaller they are, the less cell divisions. Ultimately, there will be no more cell replacement when the cells are sick or dying. They have been damage by time and its constant invasion of offending agents.

Chromosomes are proteins that can be and often are damaged by genetics, free-radicals, radiation or poor nutrition. The result is called a mutation. So instead of having a normal duplication, the new DNA molecules are defective and will reproduce abnormal proteins and subsequently abnormal cells. This can create a hereditary defect if the abnormal gene was inherited or transmitted to siblings. This can be a gradual, cumulative change that occurs over a lifetime. If micro-damage accumulates over a long period, some of these damaged genes may start the cells dividing totally unregulated and uncontrolled, which is expressed as cancer.

Cells must be given the right nutrients. Proper proteins, fats of the appropriate type, proper electrolytes, proper quality and quantity of water and *a small amount of carbohydrates.* On the other hand, if the cell is fed inappropriately, it is likely to become sick and diseased or simply perform sluggishly.

Every cell has a different function. For instance the liver acts as a chemical plant to process the food that comes in, rearrange the food, break it down into building blocks and then send these through the blood to each of the cells in the body in order to feed cells the proper nutrients. The liver also detoxifies various chemicals or abnormal foods. Many times it will alter or reject these foods. The majority of fat coming into the liver will be processed to form cholesterol. Eighty percent of the cholesterol will become cholic acid, which becomes bile. The remaining cholesterol circulates in the body, and part of that cholesterol will be utilized for hormone production, cell membranes, and particularly nerves for cell construction. Chapter seven, beginning on page 173, covers cholesterol in nutrition in more detail.

The nerve cell provides many functions. One of these is to transfer electric impulses from one cell to another particularly in the master computer called the brain. The electric impulses may go from a distal organ to the brain to communicate what's going on in the body to the brain. It is the telephone system to and from the brain. For example, food comes into your mouth and the sensory cells of your tongue will tell the brain if you think the food is good, pleasant, not pleasant, or not acceptable. With that information, the brain will either enjoy and process the food into the stomach or reject the food. Another example would be if you touched a hot plate with your finger. The fast pain nerves called C fibers immediately tell the brain that there is an acute emergency. At that point, the brain sends immediate impulses to a whole series of muscles that will immediately withdraw your whole arm back away from the hot plate.

Muscle cells are also a very important unit in the body and, except for the bone, constitute the biggest bulk of cells in the body. The muscle is a contractile mechanism with little combs that inter-digitate when given electric stimuli from the brain. These combs can close completely to produce the contraction. It is also true of heart muscle fibers. As the nerve potential relaxes, the muscle fiber stretches out. Much energy and a very important balance between electrolytes outside (sodium and calcium) and inside (potassium, pages 160 and 302) .

Endocrine cells are different types of cells that perform a manufacturing process of hormones by the organelles. Upon stimuli from other hormones, these cells will start secreting the hormone regulatory mechanism of the body.

These are just a few examples of what cells are, what functions they have, and how they create and affect the whole structure of your body.

Free-radicals

Free-radicals are destructive molecules, mostly proteins that have lost an electron and become unstable. Molecules are usually neutral in their electrical charge, but if they lose an electron there is an extra electron present that essentially makes them negatively charged, thus the instability.

Because these molecules are abnormal and because they lack an electron, they scavenge surrounding molecules that then also become deficient, creating a chain reaction. These abnormal molecules prevent normal chemical interaction and promote more abnormal molecular products. Naturally, the various functions depending on these defective molecules will produce abnormal cell functions and irregular cell divisions. They disturb DNA and RNA, the important gene molecules, and can create mutations in chromosomes that could result in cancer or other abnormalities like hereditary defects and some diseases.

Free-radicals are not all bad. The highest percentage of them promotes beneficial oxidation, by transporting oxygen to tissues and providing energy, for instance to kill bacterial invaders. These cells are responsible for all of the energy production in the body. However, if there is an excess of free-radicals, harmful oxidation and damage to the cell membranes and contents will occur. Think of it as a rusting of all the small organs inside the cell, like organelles, mitochondria and the nucleus, and the resultant great havoc in the functioning of the cell's inner sanctum.

Some forces that increase the production of free-radicals are *stress*, which feeds the anaerobic metabolism and causes free-radicals, *ozone* that produces superoxides, and *auto exhaust*, which contains carbon monoxide and hydrochloric acid instead of oxygen. The list also includes *cigarette smoke,* with similar but much greater effects than air pollution, inflammation, as *the body's immune* system creates free-radicals to fight germs, radiation, injuries that alter molecules by producing free-radicals and sunlight as a form of radiation. Impure water that has toxic material like chlorine creates free-radicals; foods that are processed with such chemicals and *preservatives* as sodium nitrites, toxic metals, and sulfites;

contamination of soil, water, air; lead, mercury, industrial chemicals and some drugs can also increase the production of free-radicals.

The body has a system of enzymes that neutralize free-radicals, providing they are not excessive. One instance is in the immune system that cannot handle excessive amounts of these free-radicals.

Free-radicals are oxidized and in order to neutralize them you can take antioxidants. See page 43.

Brain and Body Connection

Generations of people said "It is all in your head," implying that people with nonspecific symptoms are goofy or crazy or merely imagining these symptoms. Today doctors know that what happens inside our minds *very* strongly affects what happens to our bodies and vice versa. The doctor who says, "It's all in you head" usually is not knowledgeable enough to diagnose what your real problem is, so he/she blames you for this inadequacy.

The connections that occur between the body and the mind are so strong that the one regulates the other in an infinite number of ways. For instance: The function of the female hormone during menstrual cycles and the various effects it has on the performance and mood of this woman, both pre- and post-menstrual. Another is the attitude of young men with their maximum testosterone and growth hormones in the teenage years resulting in behavior that is often quite foolish and daring, because of this hormone's effect on the brain often destroys the judgment that leads to self-preservation. Another example is the variation in mood one has throughout the day, depending on the levels of insulin in the body mediated by excessive or deficient food intake, particularly carbohydrates. Perhaps you're a bear before lunch but a lamb afterwards.

Huge amounts of interactive functions occur between the brain and the body to create variations, and these mechanisms are wonderful and creative, but they also can be quite destructive.

One classic phenomena described by Dr. Hans Selie in his tome called *The Fright and Flight Reaction* is the immediate response of the brain to a perceived danger. He was working on this in Montreal while I was a pre-medical student helping him in the laboratories. Seeing or touching a fire, smelling smoke or seeing another individual's fear creates a very strong escape mode as an evasive maneuver. Dr. Selie recognized that the brain orders the secretion of adrenaline, noradrenalin and cortisol, which trigger an immediate escape reaction in the brain by stimulating the appropriate muscles to go into evasive action. This response increases heart rate and blood pressure, puts the whole body on red alert and gives the sense of intense fear that we all know.

The body also secretes various cortical hormones. One of them is called cortisol and, along with the two adrenalines (you may have heard of adrenalines under the name of epinephrine and non-epinephrine), will then affect the brain, particularly the *autonomic nervous* system of the brain. This system is a secondary nervous system usually referred to as a non-conscious system, encompassing functions that the nervous systems does automatically such as heart beating, breathing cadence, or bowel function. It protects the body against cold by constricting vessels in the skin so heat is not lost. It also protects the body against heat by dilating the vessels and then sweating so that evaporation will reduce some of the heat as evidenced during the second wind or warm up time in exercise. And many other such functions.

Stress is a very important part of this relationship. The adrenalines and cortisols are secreted during very tense moments. It either occurs at high levels for acute *off and on reactions* like in intense competitive moments or in very low sustained levels, as in chronic stress that is not dealt with to closure. People who suffer from the latter constantly secrete these hormones and are also constantly firing the autonomic nervous system. It has two components: *the parasympathetic* (PSNS) which is the slowdown mechanism of the organs, and the *sympathetic nervous* system (SNS) which is the step-up system as a counterbalance. Think of it as the Yin and the Yang relationship producing a balance. Because of the body's erratic control of these two systems when experiencing stress, the constantly irritated imbalance of these systems along with stress hormones totally deregulates and damages the function of some or all the organs. The heart may speed up and therefore create a racing heart and potentially atrial fibrillation. You can have high blood pressure because SNS is firing and constricting the vessels. The vessels become like stovepipes and the blood pressure rises and creates all kinds of damage in the body.

Another example is the inappropriate control of the intestinal tract being either too slow causing constipation or too fast causing diarrhea or the irritable bowel syndrome. This absolute imbalance will affect the immune system, the hormonal secretions of the body, sweat patterns, and even vision. All of these can create chronic disease, and these mechanisms have been ascribed to fibromyalgia, muscular abnormalities, rheumatoid arthritis, immunity abnormalities, and more. Dr. Leo Galand explores this very well in his book *The Four Pillars of Healing*.

Eliminating the original triggering mechanism, the stress— irritability, negative feelings, negative attitudes, or anger—*is very important*. In the long run, these stresses are extremely destructive to your body. A primary focus of this book is to try and prevent destruction to your body and this is definitely one of the ways it can happen.

A common thought used to be that stress could not be controlled voluntarily, but we now know it is entirely possible to do so. An elder Indian who has decided to die because he feels that he has been on this earth long enough and wills his heart to stop is an absolute real occurrence. This can occur by *biofeedback*, which literally uses the voluntary mind to will something that affects the autonomic nervous system to do what is demanded by the brain. The concentration has to be there. The repetitive use of biofeedback, which is just such concentration, has to be there for us to become better and better at it. Concentration, meditation and self-hypnosis are all forms of biofeedback. Each of them can be a form of controlling your mind to calm your body, or to speed up your body to do things that you want to do. Often a super athlete is just that because of the concentration, or meditation if you want to call it that, he or she uses in training to accentuate the stress reaction for peak performance and pre-thinking the exact motions necessary to win a competition.

While this system can be used to a desired effect, if under our control, if this stress or continued secretion of cortisol and adrenalins persists, then it becomes quite damaging. There must be closure. If the stress persists over a long period of time with mixed signals, these systems can become quite detrimental. Even sunshine burns, if you get too much!

Dr. H. Benson's book *Beyond Relaxation* is a good read about this. The book may help attain closure to stop chronic stress.

The immune system reacts fairly dramatically to these levels of stress and anger. Since bone marrow and the lymph nodes are controlled by the autonomic nervous system, the immune cells they produce are detrimentally controlled by anger, stress, anxiety, fear, or negative attitudes, dramatically reducing the formation of immune cells. The reverse—positive thinking, happiness, calm, loving attitudes—will greatly increase the production of immunity cells for protection.

Thus, fear and negative thinking often enhance disease, reducing the fighting capabilities in the body against any forms of diseases, including cancer and autoimmune diseases, as well as postoperative results or recuperation. A positive attitude can do the reverse. It helps the body fight and cure disease and increases the chances of beating cancer and many other diseases. I know from thirty-five years of surgery that a highly positive attitude leads to a significantly faster postoperative recuperation, with smoother and better results and far fewer complications. Blood pressure often can be controlled merely by alleviating stress. A positive attitude very often can reduce disease to a minimum or even cure it.

A person who has experienced chronic emotional distress caused by trauma as a youth may end up with a chronic disease. Statistics show a much higher level of disease in battered children, in post-traumatic syndrome cases, for those affected by the death of a child, mate or relative, and in cases of adult assault.

Closure is very important in these situations. One must forgive a situation or person before moving on. Forgive for your own peace of mind and move on. Not to forgive serves no purpose whatsoever and only causes an awful disruption to *your* mind and body.

There are many other mind-body connection mechanisms but stress is the most important one. I am sure that chronic stress was a major factor in my heart disease and elevated blood pressure. I had a difficult previous marriage that was constantly spurring tension. As I came out of it, all of a sudden I realized that life had become a coasting in wonderland. My blood pressure instantly reverted to normal, but the damage had been done.

One other mechanism that you will experience is the release of many hormones by the brain as you start exercising. This mechanism is triggered within the first ten to fifteen minutes of exercise, and is called the *second wind*. The brain secretes about thirty-six hormones that have multiple functions and cause readjustments to the body for the new need of severe muscle, heart and lung demand. An excessive amount of exercise can cause damage such as chronic stress would. Lowered immune system function is one deficient mechanism seen in some extreme athletes.

Everything that happens to your whole body is completely regulated by the brain. The brain sends mechanical nerve impulses consciously or automatically to control organs and muscles. It secretes hormones by way of the pituitary, the hypothalamus and the hypophysis to orchestrate all of the hormonal system throughout the body. It does a lot of thinking, which differentiates us from animals.

What to do about it.

You control your brain-body reaction by your mood. If you think it is cute or macho to be in a bad mood, think again. Besides being controlling, you are gradually killing yourself with the damage that this negative attitude causes you.

A bad mood perpetuates worst-case scenarios, whereas a good mood improves many body functions, from the immunity to the bowel. You will enjoy a more positive attitude after you get used to it, and so will those around you!

You must feed your brain the proper food, the right fats, the right proteins, and the right carbohydrates, to sustain a peak performance. See nutrition for this.

So:
Attain closure
Biofeedback
Meditation
Self-control
Exercise your brain constantly
Feed it well, not haphazardly.

You can do it!

Toxins

We are assaulted continuously by a multitude of toxins, some from within and some from outside.

Let us examine the hidden and not so hidden agents, toxins, that constantly assault our bodies. I am convinced they are the major causes of diseases. There are many questions surrounding health issues. Where does cancer come from? Why do people feel brain fog or lousy one day and not another? Do people ever feel that there is something in their body preventing them from feeling good? I am sure that there are many reasons for that. Toxic materials have to be a good portion of the problem.

There are a great many pesticides, preservatives, industrial chemicals, and various forms of radiation and heavy metals that should not penetrate the body, as they may cause severe diseases by gradual daily micro-accumulation. Some of these damages may be healed by the body, but there are many of these tiny undetected injuries that are permanent.

The biggest problem with this micro-accumulation is that we do not see it happening on a daily basis and denying it is very easy indeed. The older I get, the more I see destruction that finally surfaces years later as a disease. Radiation is such a flagrant example, ending up in cancers. Or, the various medications that have been fully tested by the FDA and turn out to have major flaws. But these flaws are found only much later. There is no way the FDA can foresee this in the "short periods" tested. Just look at pesticides or food preservatives. Of course they do not show damage when tested. It's only years later that the damage surfaces. First of all, because it took that long for the minute daily damage to accumulate and cause enough cell destruction. It is only then that symptoms appear. But the cumulative damage has been done by then.

Secondly, because there are so many agents constantly assaulting us that it is difficult to sort out which ones are responsible.

Today we know that many toxins previously believed to be harmless, usually by the industry producing them, are actually damaging to the body. The damage is imperceptible on a daily, even yearly, basis, but years later surfaces in the form of diseases. For example, cancer is often the result of many years of a specific irritation to a group of cells that eventually change and become cancerous.

Research has shown, for example, that cancer of the lung is caused by a long-standing irritation of the lung, such as smoking or radon. But it takes twenty to thirty years for that to happen. The same tar and nicotine from cigarettes can be associated with prostate cancer, cancer of the bladder, cancer of the ovary or breast. The micro-damages may result from a combination of one, two or three factors (called cofactors) working together to damage tissues. But just look how many decades it took for us to finally find that out and then lift our denial and go to action. We had to fight the industry at the cost of many lives.

Many others are suspect but have not been proven yet. Remember, it is very difficult to prove which particular agent is responsible for a disease or cancer. However we are making headway into this dilemma.

My suggestion is to stay away as much as feasible from anything suspected of being harmful. The old adage about an ounce of prevention being worth a pound of cure applies here.

However, do not become obsessed about all of this. It is impossible to avoid every single contact with these undesirable agents, as they are everywhere around us. But the less you are exposed the better. Although impossible to eliminate everything harmful, it is very much possible to substantially reduce harmful agents, at least.

I realized that mercury was a very toxic agent and although I had fillings for years, I had them removed. My reasoning was, eliminating the very tiny amounts that leach out into the body, added to the inevitable daily ingestion, would help. In this case it was easy enough to do something about it. Smoking is another obvious one. The campaign to stop people from smoking has reduced cancers of the lung by seventy-five percent.

You will be more prepared if you are aware of as many of factors as possible that could invade your body. The more you know about them, the less you will ingest and the cleaner your body will remain. If you understand the degree of damage foreign materials can produce, then you will try harder to avoid the specific ones.

I am extremely careful with pesticides, insecticides and even industrial wood finishing products, as I now seem to react a lot more to them as I grow older. For example, I used to love a wood finish made with turpentine, linseed oil and varnish. I got very dizzy and funky while using it in the last few years, even though I had used it for many years. So I learned to use different, less toxic products, and quite successfully.

Damage can be done in various forms. Free-radicals form or there can be various chemical reactions within the cell; absolute poisoning to the cell, such as can be caused by pesticides; destruction of electrolytes and their fine equilibrium; changes in the pH or acidity of the body; direct damage to tissues such as the sun creating a burn on the skin surfaces; immediate damage by certain foods that irritate the inner linings of the gastrointestinal tract; or lack of foods to feed certain cell groups, damage by infectious agents entering in various forms into the body and attacking it, especially if the body has no resistance to it, or a lack of oxygen. Ignoring other preventions can mean not wearing seatbelts or helmets that could protect from severe injuries, which to my way of thinking is just as toxic as brain toxins like pesticides.

Don't forget injuries. When younger, or even in middle-age, the injuries most often heal without undue consequences, or at least so we think. We thought we were indestructible. I know that a lot of arthritis or osteoporoses are due to improper usage of our joints or to earlier injuries. For example, if you sustain an injury to a knee while playing soccer as a youth, it may severely restrict movement later, and thus impede your exercise patterns, ultimately leading down the path of being in poor shape and finally atrophy.

I sustained a neck injury while being a macho football player as a young man. That neck has haunted me to this day. It has often stopped me from certain activities, such as swimming, since it always hurts when I do take part in those activities.

The lesson of all this is: Know the various damaging agents and you can do something about them.

From outside your body:

- Smoking
- Toxins in:
  - Air
  - Water
  - Environment
- Oxygen deprivation
- Bad, absent or excessive foods and electrolytes
- Heat-cold
- Radiation

From inside your body:

- The mind and stress
- Infections
- Inflammation
- Heredity

External Factors: those that come from outside our body

Smoking

Smoking has been present throughout the world for eons because it creates a pleasant feeling, as do most drugs. Gradually, smoking changes the inner environment of a body like the junction of nerve cells so that they start to require the smoking chemicals, and that is the state called an addiction. The body adapts by readjusting its chemical reactions, especially at nerve endings, to include nicotine. When a lack of nicotine occurs, the body has to readjust its chemical reactions. That process is called withdrawal, often referred to as kicking the habit, and much of the time it is very difficult.

I experienced this at age forty when I finally stopped smoking. It was difficult but I had to do it. And when I did, all of a sudden I could exercise better. The constant migraine headaches I had disappeared within a year but I gained weight. I still was not the winner in that race. I am sure the heart problems I had occurred at least seven or eight years later than they would have had I not stopped smoking.

If one stops smoking, a difficult chemical readjustment occurs in the body. But the readjustment of the psychological habit it created is just as difficult. Smoking is the greatest free-radical producer known, and it actually changes a lifespan, reducing it by about eight or nine years for men and about twelve to thirteen years for women. Smoking is a major cause of heart disease, even more so than cancer of the lung.

As a secondary effect, the embryo or the unborn child can have major abnormalities if a woman smokes during her pregnancy. There are many other irritating agents in cigarettes, but it would be difficult to cover them all so only the major ones will be reviewed. These can also cause cancer elsewhere in the body.

The mortality, according to Philip Morris, does not differ if a cigarette is filtered, non-filtered, low in tar, or smokeless. And people who sniff or chew tobacco absorb these compounds just as readily, although there is no carbon monoxide. Various cancers can still be caused like throat, mouth or larynx. Pipe smoking has the same effect. Pipes and cigars have intense smoke, so are not inhaled as deeply. Therefore, they may not cause as much lung cancer, but they are often associated with the dreaded squamous cell cancer in the mouth and throat where smoke gathers.

The fact of the matter is smoking causes many different diseases:

Heart disease

Heart vessels get damaged, usually by free-radicals often caused by cigarette tar. Once the arteriosclerosis is formed, it can actually reduce the size of a vessel. Let us say there is only twenty percent of blood flow left in a vessel that is feeding the heart. When someone inhales or absorbs smoke, the vessel size will reduce another eighty to ninety percent, therefore leaving very little blood to go to the heart.

Thus, heart disease or muscle damage will occur much earlier in life. You can survive on ten to twenty percent of blood flow, but not on one tenth of that.

Tar is a form of many chemicals, known as carcinogenic agents. Nicotine is a vasoconstrictor and, on its own, can cause major harm because the vasoconstriction causes a lack of adequate blood supply. A cigarette produces about one percent to five percent of carbon monoxide. Carbon monoxide actually captures hemoglobin two hundred times more easily than it does oxygen. Therefore, the hemoglobin transports much less oxygen, since a percentage has already been taken by the carbon monoxide. So, when oxygen and the volume of blood have been reduced in an already narrowed blood vessel by arteriosclerosis, the net effect is a much earlier death.

I find it interesting that although heart disease is not very common in young people, it is *twice* as common in young smokers as nonsmoking youths.

The smoker's heart rate increases substantially because of the effects of nicotine. The carbon monoxide has de-saturated the blood; therefore, it has to pump more blood in order to bring oxygen to the tissues.

Stroke

A stroke is caused by the same mechanism as heart disease. If vessels that nourish the brain vasoconstrict, and if vessels are already narrowed by arteriosclerosis and slightly damaged, then immediately part of the brain will lack the right amount of nutrients and oxygen. This could result in damage of the brain section fed by that particular vessel.

Aneurysms have a much higher occurrence rate in smokers. In an interesting study, the inside of the aorta in young people between ages seventeen and thirty-five who were killed by injuries showed that a large percentage, between fifteen and thirty-five percent, of these young people already had arteriosclerosis of the aorta. This occurred three times more commonly with smokers. If the aorta starts developing arteriosclerosis this early in life, aneurysms will occur later.

Elevated blood pressure, too, is associated with smoking because of the vasoconstriction effect of nicotine. Peripheral vascular diseases like arteriosclerosis of vessels in the legs, neck, and to the brain, Raynaud's phenomena (a blanching of the fingers with cold), Burger's disease, which is a vasoconstriction disease, and diabetes all have a very high incidence of occurrence in smokers. Ninety percent of smokers have these vascular diseases.

Cancer

There are many types of cancer caused by smoking. For example, eighty-five percent of lung cancer is caused by cigarettes. A true tragedy, this is a preventable disease just by eliminating the offending agent—the tar and nicotine of cigarettes.

The medical field considers that a twenty-year addiction of one pack a day is the trigger amount for cancers. Of course, the longer one smokes the higher the possibility of cancer. Another way to look at these statistics is that a one pack per day habitual smoker has ten times the chance to develop lung cancer than a non-smoker. And a two pack per day smoker has twenty-five times more chance of developing lung cancer than a non-smoker. Annual deaths from smoking have been reduced by fifty percent since the population has stopped or reduced smoking. Presently, twenty-six percent of the population continues to smoke.

Lung Diseases

Diseases in the lung such as emphysema, chronic bronchitis and asthma are directly related to cigarettes in many instances. As one grows older, the damage to the lungs caused by cigarettes will be amplified and have an inflammatory reaction in the lungs creating irritation and damage by depositing carbon and pollutants inside the lungs.

I remember when I was a surgical resident and performed many autopsies as part of my training. I was shocked to find the lungs of a smoker actually black. The newer smokers had some normal pink lung but these were also peppered by dots of black areas.

The longer the smoking history is, the darker the lung. An old emphysematous patient had lungs that looked like charcoal. Not being able to breathe easily is not a pleasant way to spend the last years of life.

Pregnancy Complications

There is a much higher perinatal mortality rate, a decrease in birth weight and an increase in birth defects as these children have been damaged during growth and development.

Teenagers

Teenagers who smoke can expect to be two to three inches shorter in their adult height. That is because the blood supply to the growth center of the body is substantially lower than normal.

Osteoporosis

Osteoporosis is significantly accentuated in people who smoke. This is due to the vasoconstriction and not feeding the high blood supply necessitated by the bones for proper transfers of nutrients and calcium.

Other Disadvantages of Smoking

- Increases peripheral vascular disease such as the blocking of leg arteries. Carotid arteries and all of the small vessels in the brain are also reduced by eighty to ninety percent
- Increases macular degeneration in smokers by two- and-a-half times.
- Triggers migraine headaches.
- Increases incidence of kidney problems.
- Increases incidence of peptic ulcers and heartburn.
- Reduces healing after injuries and surgeries substantially.
- Increases arteriosclerosis
- Reduces blood supply to flaps. I used to refuse to do certain reconstructive operations such as flaps or face lifts because there was only 10 percent of blood circulating in these flaps.
- Increases fibromyalgia.
- Increases wrinkles in the skin especially the face due to loss of elastic fibers in the dermis.
- causes yellow-brown teeth.
- Burns sofas, car seats, dresses and pants.
- Causes social rejection due to actual health threat to those around smokers, especially in confined spaces.
- Causes a constant guilty conscience.

I do not think that the temporary good feeling one derives from smoking is worth the consequences and the possibility of contracting most if not all of these diseases. Some smokers— like my cousin, for example—claim that doctors don't *know* that cancer of the lung is caused by smoking. They think a plastic surgeon like me knows nothing of the reasons for lung cancer.

I think that is a perfect denial, coming from smokers who are trying to justify their addiction. If you are a smoker, please do not deny this important information.

Many people in society today have reconsidered their opinion on smoking and have stopped the habit. There are many ways to do this but be aware of pitfalls like weight gain, and any drastic change in a health regime. Time is needed to substantiate itself. Physical exercise is one of the best components of a plan to stop smoking. Smoking is a powerful addiction and eradicating it from a lifestyle requires a sound battle plan. Research the most successful plans, talk to ex-smokers and create a smoke free environment around your most priceless property—yourself.

Marijuana is also smoke and has all of the same tars as tobacco. There are very similar chemical reactions, since it is a pseudo estrogen mimicker and destroys the body just as regular tobacco smoking does. It makes little sense to stop smoking tobacco and continue to harm the body with pot. Smoking is harmful, no matter what is smoked.

Air Pollution

You have to bring air from the environment into your lungs for proper body functions. Your lung's linings are a very avid absorbing mechanism. When air from the environment goes into your lungs, any pollution in the air is also included so contaminants have easy access to enter your body and irritate the lung lining.

Carbon Dioxide

The product of most combustion is carbon dioxide. If the levels of CO_2 are higher than normal, the amount of oxygen going into your blood is diluted by the increased percentage of carbon dioxide in the hemoglobin. The body also changes the pH of the blood, making it more acid and altering the whole chemical balance in the system. This is reversed in nature by the chlorophyll of plant leaves, which is the reason environmentalists are so alarmed. Your body requires a specific amount of carbon dioxide, as it is part of its combustion's by-products. The atmosphere around you must have a normally small amount to permit a proper breathing mixture for your lungs.

Carbon Monoxide

Carbon monoxide is the product of a fire or combustion that does not have enough oxygen to burn completely, a state called close combustion, like in car engines. Car exhaust is extremely damaging to the body because the hemoglobin, the normal transporter of oxygen, transports carbon monoxide two hundred times more readily than it does oxygen. Soon the whole oxygen-carrying capacity of hemoglobin could be totally destroyed. At high levels, it becomes lethal very quickly. Carbon monoxide poisoning is like having sudden severe anemia, as the capacity to transport oxygen from the lungs to the cells is totally lost. Symptoms are shortness of breath and typically the lips turn crimson red. Also, the lack of oxygen in various degrees makes the body very susceptible to heart attacks and strokes. Death is imminent if the red blood cell saturation is too high. Immediate hospitalization and hyperbaric oxygen therapy is necessary. By the way, *paint-stripper fluids* that contain methylene chloride become carbon monoxide in the blood, which is extremely dangerous and can even kill.

Sulfur Dioxide (SO2)

Sulfur dioxide is mostly an industrial byproduct and extremely damaging to the body. There are many products produced by industrial emissions, but sulfur dioxide is one of the most common and hazardous ones. If water is added to sulfur dioxide, it becomes sulfuric acid (H2SO4), which is acid rain similar to battery acid, a very dangerous acid that burns inexorably. This automatically causes a third degree burn if it contacts the skin. When sulfur dioxide does get into lungs and mixes with water in them it becomes a deadly situation.

I lived in a Quebec town called Noranda with abundant copper and gold mines in the area. The town had a smelter that extracted the copper and gold minerals embedded in stones. The stones had to be heated to melt the metals. The minerals contained a high tenure of sulfur, that would start heating the minerals to extract copper and gold. This created sulfur dioxide that was extruded through two huge chimneys that spewed it into the community, and the environment. The entire environment was damaged. The tree growth was quite stunted. The immediate area going into the Eastern pathway of the predominant winds was scarce in wildlife and fish and lakes were contaminated. The population had a very high level of chronic obstructive pulmonary disease.

The authorities at the mine finally did something about this heinous situation and stopped the emission of sulfur dioxide. That was done by a scrubbing technique that extracts the sulfur dioxide from the smoke and unites it with water to make sulfuric acid that they now sell. Now trainloads of sulfuric acid are transported and sold for use in various industrial applications. I shudder when I think of the unnecessary pollution this process previously created. Sulfur dioxide was responsible for major acid rain fallout. This very destructive gas actually destroys our lungs, wild life, fish and many crops. Concerned citizens and companies like Noranda Mine have set a fine example and contributed enormously to cleaning air quality. There is more pure air today and I, who have always been a nature explorer, notice a substantial resurgence of wild life such as ducks, geese, dear, fish, and even tweedy birds of all kinds. There is much less pulmonary disease in the area. Crops are more prolific and healthy to eat again. Noranda now has a lake in which people can swim and fish.

Oxygen Depletion

Another form of pollution that is quite harmful in certain circumstances is oxygen depletion. For example, if there is already a coronary artery obstruction and oxygen is reduced by twenty percent, this could be enough to cause a heart attack.

Airplanes usually fly at about thirty or thirty-five thousand feet, but the inside pressure of the airplane is pressurized at about six to seven thousand feet. Flyers probably breathe about fifteen to twenty percent less oxygen while in the air. It is not unusual to see people having mild heart symptoms in the air. This oxygen deprivation could also contribute to jet lag symptoms, the abnormal feeling you have after you have been flying.

I travel extensively and always thought that jet lag was due to time lag or time zone changes. But recently, I have traveled to Peru and there is no time lag with that country. However, I do get the dreaded time lag anyway. I have to deduce that it is altitude sickness instead of time differences. This may be one of nature's tranquilizers while you are up in the air!

In the airplane you will tend to dehydrate and swell up because you retain electrolytes and fluids as you do at altitudes and the cabin humidity is very dry (two or three percent). So wear loose clothing to allow for swelling. Bring bottles of water to keep up your fluid intake. Avoid alcohol and caffeine. Skip airline foods that have a lot of salt and preservatives.

Do isometric exercises and walk a lot while flying to prevent blood stagnation and clotting in your legs. Elastic stockings will prevent leg edema, swelling, also as a preventative.

If you get clammy skin, impaired vision and difficulty concentrating it may be a result of lack of oxygen causing hypoxia or low oxygen. Ask the attendant to turn an Air Pack on to increase the amount of oxygen in the plane. An air pack costs the airline about $80 /hrs so airlines tend to use the least possible. The pilots run the air supply at only seventy percent capacity until a passenger complains.

Take a good bath or swim on arrival to rehumifidy yourself through the skin and mucosa.

Scuba diving, climbing at high altitudes, or skiing can be oxygen reduction activities. If one stays in a low oxygen environment, then the body acclimatizes to capture more oxygen. Put your body in a situation so the lung and the body's cells, particularly the red blood cells, multiply and start capturing and exchanging greater amounts of oxygen with more competence. Although it's a gradual process, within three to four days the preliminary readjustment will occur. The harm, therefore, will only occur if you have not taken steps to make sure your body is not prepared.

Radon

Radon is a radioactive gas that is a degradation of uranium, often found in granite but not solely. This colorless, odorless gas is often found in home basements and in the water from wells dug in granite If not detected and removed, radon causes cancer of the lung on the long run. It is the most *prominent cause of that cancer, second only to smoking.* **Testing basements and every water supply for radon emissions is essential.** Obtain the test from your state's environmental protection agency or from private agencies. The test is simple and if the results are positive for radon, it can be eliminated by ventilation of the basement or filtration of well water. This is a very important issue and the aeration or elimination of radon should be handled by professionals.

Dust Particles

Smog is a product of multiple pollutants, usually from some form of combustion from cars, industrial or household heating and cooking. It also transports a positive ion on these particles along with occasional bacteria, although smog is usually produced by combustion so very little bacteria is present. However, there are many toxic gases around, such as sulfur dioxides, toluenes or benzenes, and being aware of where you are or what industries are emitting into your environment is essential.

Smog is carbon particles with many types of aliphatic contaminants that may be carcinogenic. In general, the quantity is small, but day by day it becomes cumulative. These can happen to nearly everyone in these countries. This situation is severe in countries that I have traveled to, so much so that the throats of many children I want to operate on are so irritated that surgeries must be postponed. If the children are affected to that extent, the long-term effects will be even more severe as they grow into adults.

Pollen is present during some seasons and is irritating to the allergic person's lungs causing several conditions like asthma or hay fever.

Home dust is generally a product of lint from drapes and rugs. Also, and perhaps surprisingly, a large amount of home dust has been analyzed and found to be the shedding remnants of skin, as keratin and hair that we shed constantly and naturally. Dust mites often feed on that shedding, as it is a protein. Therefore, dust occurring in homes is often a combination of lint, shed skin cells and dust mites. Dust mites are insects that die, but their carcasses can continue to be allergic irritants. Dust mites are one of the major causes of allergies inside the house.

Also dust particles pollen from outside will clog the lung and create many problems, increasing the inflammation in the lung alveoli, reducing the amount of air going in, and initiating the secretion of mucus, which then must be eliminated by coughing or by the action of cilia, small hairs that sweep it out. This is not a healthy lung. Varnishes, cleaning fluids and sprays, paint fumes, asbestos, and so many others, can all be factors with which to reconcile in our own houses.

Pesticides are meant to kill insects and many of them are neurotoxins that kill these little critters instantly. They very well can do the same to your own brain in smaller units but nevertheless cumulative. Now pesticides are still commonly neurotoxins to insects but nobody seems serious about it. They are not all bad. Do you remember DDT that was "so harmful" that it was withdrawn from the market?

I recently had a stunning conversation with an American physician in the Amazon, and she related to me that DDT had saved millions of people from mosquito-spread malaria. The countries that had been sprayed with DDT totally eradicated malaria. Only DDT ever helped this blight, and by removing access to the pesticide we thus permitted the death of literally millions of people by malaria.

Molds are another contaminant that is increasingly discussed. They grow in carpets and everywhere in houses or buildings, especially if in dampness.

It is extremely important to realize that molds are indeed quite harmful and should be taken very seriously. They cause much more harm than thought in the past. Many molds secrete various toxins, and some of these are neurotoxins that damage neurons, including the brain's. There is a syndrome called the *Old Building Syndrome* recently described by Dr. Shoemaker, who advocates that there is a variety of molds of specific species that produce a toxin that is very damaging to the brain and peripheral nerves and causes all kinds of diseases, including fibromyalgia and obesity.

This theory makes sense and is worth further research at <http://www.chronicneurotoxin.com>.

Dr. Shoemaker describes a comprehensive picture of these dangerous molds.

Asbestos, used for insulation, may still be found in some old homes. No longer used today as a building material, any existing asbestos is being detected and eliminated. The process of removal is costly and distributes dust into uninfected areas. One can prevent dust from old pipe insulators from spreading and it can be as easy as spraying them with a sealant. Much care should be taken with this mineral, as it is very dangerous. If asbestos is detected, make sure there are no dust particles in the air as the diseases of the lung like asbestosis or ultimately mesothelioma, a cancer, can develop and both are lethal. In general, the building industry has eliminated the problem, but be aware of the possibility for this danger.

Talc has been traditionally used for many reasons including facial and baby powders and is still used as a lubricant for rubber gloves. Fortunately, very little talc is used now but you still have to be very careful about this powder that is silicate of magnesium. Silicates theoretically can cause a lung disease known as silicoses. Many doctors and nurses develop severe allergies to talc and have to use powderless gloves instead. It is best to stay away from constant usage or large quantities of talc.

Bacteria and Viruses Of course, air is a strong transmitter of viruses as most colds and flu caused by viruses are transmitted via the air. Another way some bacteria and viruses spread is by depositing themselves on certain surfaces that hands are in contact with, like a counter top, and contamination not only occurs but also recurs. Bacteria have fewer propensities to be transported through the air but are still a real factor. Obviously, the worst environments for bacteria and virus transmissions are enclosed spaces like airplanes or rooms with no ventilation. Many times, I believe I caught a cold in a plane from coughing around me. These colds are usually relatively mild because I have developed immunity by repeated contacts. Please do not be overly concerned by these bacteria as they seldom create massive infections. Small quantities will just render you more immune, to the better.

Smell is actually protein and other chemicals that are transported by air and then penetrate into the nose and also the lung. One interesting fact I learned was that in order to produce perfume, the perfume industry uses five thousand different chemicals, in various quantities, for different perfume scents. This many chemicals simply cannot be good for our environment and do cause a certain amount of air pollution, albeit a nicely fragrant pollutant! I have not heard of serious problems except allergic reactions.

Industrial agents There are thousands of chemical agents used by industries and many of these have never been tested for toxicity. This creates very dangerous situations. Some examples of chemical agents include the following. Turpentine has been shown to cause lung damage, so eventually it was removed from paints and paint thinner. Carbon tetrachloride was used for years as a dry cleaning agent. Eventually it was found to be extremely toxic to lungs and particularly to the liver. For instance, If both turpentine and carbon tetrachloride were used simultaneously, as might happen if walls were being painted at the same time carpet was being dry cleaned, nearly automatic severe liver damage could occur to cause liver necrosis and death. Another example was lead in gasoline, now deleted because research showed it was extremely neurotoxic. Scientists discovered that DDT caused cancers and they have also banned MTBE in gasoline for the same reason. In the case of paint thinner, methylene chlorides are metabolized as carbon monoxide in the blood with dire consequences.

Solutions to these problems

Seek clean air as much as possible and do have the air tested in your house. Do not assume that your house is not contaminated. Many people have thought so, only later to find *Radon*. Air filters are very useful and ionic ones are probably the cat's meow today. There are all kinds of filters using that technology today.

I highly recommend you read an interesting little soft covered book called *The Ion Effect* that I first read more than thirty years ago. The book discussed the fact that there are many negative ion particles in the air. When it is sunny or calm, the environment is clean and people feel good, energized, optimistic, and enjoy a sense of well-being. The negative ions precipitate the pollution particles in the air to clean it up. Certain geographical sites such as Machu Picchu, Geneva, Olympia, or the top of a mountain, all have very high levels of these negative ions in the air.

Since water environments also have negative ions, you feel good around lakes or streams. Showers, baths, hot tubs and swimming pools are all places that provide relaxation and peace of mind. Amazingly, right after a storm everything seems cleansed and spirits can be lifted. People are more productive, have less brain fog and have a greater feeling of well being when the air is clean, with little or no pollution.

On the other hand, if the air is loaded with positive ions, usually associated with dust particles, you can feel tired, have brain fog, be apathetic or depressed, have low creativity, or just feel exhausted all the time. This is mostly seen inside closed buildings, inside cars that produce positive ions, or in a polluted environment such as large cities with smog or industrial pollution. All dust particles carry a positive ion. In a car, for example, the closed environment creates positive particles, and during long drives you can become dangerously sleepy.

There was a high school lab experiment called the Van de Graff belt that used a metal ball with a static electricity-producing belt. The outside of the metal ball had high levels of anions (negative ions) that created huge electric sparks similar to lightning. The inside of that ball had predominantly positive ions. A car is the real-life personification of this experiment.

Today most air cleaners are negative ion producers so they precipitate positive particles and thus destroy the particles contaminating air. This not only makes the air healthier and cleaner, but also provides a sense of well-being. In the long run, air cleaners are good for your health and attitude, and I highly recommend their use. They both clean the air of noxious gases and particles and add negative ions to the air, which make you feel terrific. There are negative ion producers sold for cars that can be plugged into the cigarette lighter, or in offices as efficient air cleaners that also will keep you alert and healthy.

Water Contamination

Water is the most critical component of life. Imperative in maintaining the best health, drinking the appropriate amount of water facilitates proper functioning of the body's mechanisms. Water is more important than food. You can live four to six weeks without food but just a few days without water.

Of course, air is the most vital component, but water is a very close second. Since you absorb water quite readily in your GI tract, all contaminants are absorbed along with it, so water becomes a transmitter of many pollutants and chemicals. Occasionally they may penetrate through the skin when you go swimming, but that is minor as the skin is more impervious than the GI tract.

These are some common contaminants:

Chlorine, used to disinfect water supplies, can react with organic matter such as decaying leaves to create trihalomethane, which is a carcinogen.

Fluorides have a good reputation, but there also is evidence that they could cause harm in the long term. There are two schools of thought on this. One thought advocates the benefits of reducing tooth decay which flouride indeed does, but there is ample evidence that it can cause cancers. Again, it is the problem of immediate damage that is very evident versus long-term damage that can be difficult to interpret since when statistics are analyzed they are often muddled with other factors and tend to be disregarded.

Algae, **bacteria** or **molds** that are normally found in lake and river waters are contaminated. Some are bad, most are not dangerous but it is best to rid the water of these contaminants.

Unicellular organisms like **Giardia Lamblia**, **Amoeba**, **Cryptosporidium** or **Parasites**, all of which may come from livestock or other animal contaminations of the water. For example, waters in which beavers reside usually have Giardia.

Livestock stool contamination may have bad **E.Coli**. Bad E.Coli are the ones that you are not immune to. There are many varieties of E. Coli and some can be very virulent, but that is more the exception than the rule. These can and will cause mild to severe diarrhea, and vomiting, or abdominal cramps. This is called "Montezuma's Revenge" or "La Tourista" when traveling to other countries, but you can get it in your own country as well, if you drink contaminated water. It is rare, however, as you are likely to be immune.

One recently-discovered phenomenon is that plastic water bottles, when frozen, leach out *dioxin,* a known carcinogen, into that water. Do not freeze water in plastic bottles.

Metal contaminants like lead and mercury are particularly damaging and will be discussed in more detail. There are many others that are less stringent. Iron is often present in well water but rarely in large quantities. Nevertheless it becomes a micro-accumulation of an oxidizer. See chapter five on Free-radicals. Manganese is not particularly a problem.

Volatile chemicals like **MTBE** that contaminate dumpsites with potentially dangerous chemicals are also noxious and have been found to be carcinogenic.

Arsenic will penetrate water through soil and bedrock with naturally occurring arsenic. Human intervention in apple orchards treatment with arsenic compounds which is now illegal.

Heavy metals are mostly absorbed via water, although sometimes can be borne by foods. Effects may come about as a result of either direct absorption or ingestion.

Lead

Lead has very high exposure as a contaminant because there are many sources. One classic exposure has been indoor paints. This was a huge contributor to damaging agents, as the paint used became a very large part of dust in the home. Drinking water used to be affected as old plumbing sometimes involved lead pipes. Even when copper was used instead of lead for pipes, lead sweating still leached into drinking water. Other sources included lead-glazed pottery and lead-soldered cans. Many industries or crafts were also using it—in stained glass creations, for example, or as a metal conduit or in the production of lead bullets. Gasoline contained lead stabilizers and when this gas was used, high levels of lead were in the air. Now that lead in gasoline has been eliminated, lead in the air is very low. Blood levels of lead in the United States have been reduced dramatically in recent years.

High levels of lead in children measured by a laboratory test were caused mostly from old indoor lead paints and dust from this source.

Levels over ten micrograms per liter are toxic levels for a child. Adults can absorb five to fifteen percent of ingested lead and retain only five percent of that amount. Children can also absorb five to fifteen percent of ingested lead, but will retain forty percent of that amount.

Lead levels in a mother's blood will cross the placenta and into her breast milk. Most of this lead is retained by the child with ninety percent in red blood cells and the rest in the liver, kidney and a few other areas.

Lead poisoning symptoms for adults include peripheral neuropathy, chronic neuropathy, nephropathies (kidneys), hypertension, GI problems and skeletal abnormalities. In children neurological problems mostly include encephalopathy, lethargy, decreased appetite, irritability, dizziness, ataxia (the loss of balance and muscle coordination), unconsciousness, epilepsy, mental retardation, optic nerve damage or even blindness.

Another important factor is that lead blocks the absorption of calcium in the membrane channels of cells, which changes the voltage and causes cardiac arrhythmias. Lead substitutes for calcium, and thus the calcium sodium pump in the mitochondria, making the process very inefficient. Lead poisoning causes anemia, immune deficiencies, serious bone defects, hearing deficits, IQ deficits and imperfect nerve conduction.

Treatment by source removal in the last fifty years has been very aggressive, since the discovery of the harmful effects of lead. The sources are lead paint, lead pipes and sweat in copper pipes. There was lead in gasoline. Chelation therapy is also a recommended treatment. This involves putting salts into the blood that will react with the lead to eliminate it via the kidney. You personally should assure yourself that no pipes with lead exist in your house. If you have an old house, check the paint to make sure it does not contain lead.

Mercury

Mercury is a natural product in many earth vegetations and the natural *de-gassing* of these vegetations causes the mercury to be released into the air as soluble salt called methyl mercury. It then proceeds into any body of water entering the aquatic chain where it is absorbed by plankton, then herbivorous fish, then carnivorous fish (which have one million times the percentage of mercury than the surrounding waters contain) and then absorption by humans.

Tooth filings called amalgams contain mercury and have been implicated in mercury poisoning because they release mercury as the mouth chews food. This occurs in very small releases but accumulative damage could be dangerous.

Toxicology of mercury: it is a major brain damage displaying itself in various forms of peripheral nerve neuropathies. The thyroid may enlarge and there may be a tachycardia (fast heart), muscle excitability, tremors or gingivitis.

Recently some studies indicate that mercury may be the cause of Alzheimer's and Autism since the classic damage to the nerves, the neurofibrils is typical in mercury poisoning. The *New England Journal of Medicine* reported that pregnant women should not eat fish, particularly the five species that have high levels of mercury like tuna, swordfish, king, mackerel and shark. They are the predator fishes that eat many small fishes and accumulate mercury. If you eat these fishes, do so sparingly.

For a normal diet the consumption of any fish that has levels of one part per million of mercury including shark and swordfish should be limited to about seven ounces (about one serving) per week. Canned tuna has about 0.3 part per million of mercury even though fresh tuna has .7 parts per million and therefore care should be taken not to eat large quantities of the fresh tuna.

In children, the problem is far more serious. As mercury is cumulative, it could cause more severe brain damage in a child's developing little brain. This damage is mostly permanent. It is possible to eliminate its water-soluble substance, methyl mercury, but only small amounts. For children the remaining amounts in the blood could cause extremely toxic problems. The damage varies anywhere from very subtle neurological changes to severe autism. A recent article suggests the possibility that mothers of autistic children have a hereditary defect that tends to retain mercury more than the average person and as it accumulates may be transmitted to the fetus. If the fetus has the same hereditary trait, then the levels will be even higher resulting in more severe brain damage.

I have only just heard about this, but it seems plausible, so the progress of this research should be watched closely.

The treatment for mercury poisoning is best accomplished by total avoidance, especially for pregnant women. In cases of acute mercury poisoning, hemodialysis is required.

Zinc

Several proteins, genetic activity, membrane stabilization of the cell, immune function, cytokines, the synthesis of vitamin A and many other functions require zinc. As a result zinc will improve wound healing and act as a cancer preventative as it boosts the immunity system.

In general, most people have adequate levels through a balanced diet. Zinc is used effectively by physicians to boost immunity and healing after severe injuries and other severe diseases.

Aluminum

Aluminum is the most abundant metal and element in the earth's crust. It is a fairly important component of acid rain and destroys fish by damaging their gills, which they use to breathe, and kills all aquatic plant species. It is not bio-accumulated.

For humans, it can be ingested by cooking in aluminum pots, drinking water and some pharmaceuticals. Found in Maalox, Gelusil, Amphojel, Mylanta, Rolaids, DiGel and many deodorants, it is also absorbed by the gastrointestinal tract through inhalation and exposure to air. Since not absorbed trans-dermal, deodorant is not a problem. Only one-tenth of one percent of aluminum in a diet will be absorbed by the body and it does accumulate, mostly in bones and a little in blood where it is excreted by the kidney.

Aluminum binds with phosphates in the GI tract and therefore can lead to phosphate depletion, which can then lead to *osteomalacia*. It also is a neurotoxin in the brains of cats and rabbits with over four micrograms per gram causing memory and learning deficits, poor motor functions with tremors, coordination difficulties, and severe muscle weakness. Actually, exactly the same symptoms have been experienced in human beings with levels slightly greater, 6 micrograms per gram. Some abnormalities at the end of nerve cells in the brain and the synapses, which are the junctions between the innervations, are either lost or very abnormal. Aluminum also prevents nerves from growing and developing and replacing the damaged neurons.

In Alzheimer's patients the same kind of lesions are found, however the present thought is that this accumulation of aluminum may be a consequence, not a cause, of the disease. Human dementia does accumulate aluminum and create damage to the brain. Dialysis is the only treatment in these cases. The best therapy for this is to avoid aluminum in all of its forms. Never cook in aluminum pots and pans and stay away from antacids containing aluminum. I understand that it is not absorbed by the skin therefore most likely deodorants are not a problem. It is found in water infrequently.

Solutions to heavy metals

If the quality of water is uncertain, the best way to protect yourself is to filter it before drinking. It behooves you to have your drinking water analyzed yearly to tell you precisely what you are drinking. Although it may be inconvenient and time-consuming to test your drinking water, it is one of the most important factors in your life and well worth the effort.

Contact your state authorities and they can direct you to laboratories that can analyze your water. Be critical, since you will be drinking water from that source for many years, and that means accumulation.

City water has been filtered, decontaminated, aerated, and disinfected by adding chlorine. This is all well and good; however, this clean water is brought to you through pipes that are less than clean. Pipes may have been polluted at one point, other contaminants like asbestos, lead from decayed leaves, animal contamination, even the material that the pipe is made of and so many other factors not known could have compromised the cleanliness of the pipes.

Cities do not provide pure water. The gazillion gallons that they have to furnish for such large populations simply prohibit city water from being pure.

If you analyze the water from your tap, then you can filter if deemed necessary. Most contaminants are acceptable to take baths, showers, and do laundry with but may be borderline for drinking. You absorb many more ingredients through the GI track, but very little through your skin. I still believe that some bacteria and viruses are good as they can challenge your immune system and improve it but you should get rid of all gross contaminants.

If you drink city water and dislike the awful taste, you can filter the water to improve the taste and quality. There are many simple filters you can use for purifying drinking water and most are easy to install. There are also many types of filters that can be used for water purification purposes. Some are sold in hardware stores and are very easy to install. Some have carbon filters and are a little more sophisticated but may remove more harmful elements. Some are very good like reverse osmosis filters. Very good water is attained by the combination of both the carbon filters and the reverse osmosis. Ask your dealer questions when you go to purchase a filter, but remember they are selling a product. Going online to research before you visit a dealer does render advanced knowledge.

Spring and well waters are often excellent sources for drinking water and many people have used these for centuries. By drinking well water these people have immunized themselves to some of the contaminants in these waters and that is good. Also, some of this water contains beneficial ingredients. However, please still have it analyzed. There could be radon or mercury or bacteria and you would not have a clue unless you tested the water.

My friend and neighbor, David, shares a family lineage that lives long healthy lives of more than one hundred years. His wonderful Dad whom we loved so much passed away just recently at one hundred years old. The entire family swears that it is the "Woodville road water" that keeps them all alive so long. I have been drinking that water ever since I heard that from David.

Bottled water satisfies thirst and is good to drink, however, it is very important to remember that bottled water does not provide beneficial zinc, copper and magnesium, very helpful to your body.

Bottled water is also not regulated and that may encourage inconsistent quality in the product. I also resent the great scamming of America, and for that matter the world, where a bottle of water that sells for $1.00 is more expensive than a bottle of soda requiring more ingredients. At $1.00 for an eight-ounce bottle, it costs approximately $16.00 a gallon, a huge markup, and the quality is often questionable as well.

You do not pay that much for gasoline, pop, milk or anything else for that matter. A good carbon, reverse osmosis filter will only cost as much as a six-month supply of bottled water, and will have better sustainable quality and after the six-month period will not cost you anything for many years.

Radiation

Sunrays

Sunrays are a fairly important part of radiation affecting you. Sunlight is ultraviolet rays A, B, and C, which can in the long run create free-radicals, doing damage causing skin cancers. Overexposure to these rays can lead to such conditions as basal cells, squamous cell lesions and melanomas. Squamous cells can be dangerous although not very much so if taken care of early. Melanomas, however, can be far more dangerous.

Typically it takes twenty or thirty years before they show up unless there is an acute and very intense burn and then they can develop very fast. Sunburns are most likely the cause of these cancers. They could have occurred twenty years before and caused the damage. Gradual tanning may not be as dangerous, but please remember that tanning comes from mini sunburns.

Beta radiation or cosmic rays from the sun definitely cause major problems. The ozone hole is a literal opening in the ozone layer of the stratosphere present mostly at both poles. As a result of this phenomenon we are being bombarded by a much higher intensity of sun and gamma radiation. The ozone layer was of the atmosphere was a good filter of theses rays. Therefore, there is far more radiation at both poles where the ozone holes are, as occurs in Australia, Canada, the upper

United States and Europe. We are seeing two hundred times more cancer of the skin including the dreaded melanomas.

One other interesting aspect of gamma radiation is that if you fly at thirty-five thousand feet you have more quantity of radiation from the gamma rays then you do on the ground because there is less air filtration. I have been told by a radiology friend that one hour of flight at that altitude is the equivalent of one mammogram's radiation. I admit this is not a large amount but is, again, cumulative.

Always wear sunscreen and do not bake in the sun. A sunburn is never a good thing and is a precursor for a future cancer of the skin.

Ionizing or x-radiation

These are all x-rays, cat-scans, radioisotopes studies and all the radiation treatments used for various afflictions *are all carcinogenic.* Any forms of such dangerous radiation are absolutely cumulative in our cells and eventually will surface given time as a cancer. Of course the higher the dosage of radiation given, the higher the possibility of cancer in the future. Patients who have developed certain cancers such as Hodgkin's lymphomas, cancer of the breast, colon, lung to name a few, will likely develop a "radiation" cancer twenty-five to thirty years later. In essence, they have been blessed with twenty-five to thirty years of extra life.

Try at all possible occasions to avoid any forms of radiation. Of course sometimes diagnostic radiation is imperative. Just look at mammography, it permits early cancer detection in the breast and is a must for all women. Admittedly there are very few units of radiation in that mammogram so the risk is little but the benefit of early diagnosis is so great that it is worthwhile.

Radon

Radon is a gas emitted from radioactive degradation of uranium in mostly granite and could accumulate in your house and particularly you basement. It behooves you to test your house air with test kits provided by states agencies and get rid of it. It is now a major cause of cancer of the lung and is actually easy to prevent. You just have to know about it with testing and get rid of it. See The Internet Sites for agencies to get kits. I have also discussed this in Air Pollution on Page 94.

Microwaves

Used extensively both commercially and for personal home use, many people still question the safety of microwave ovens and telephones. Are microwaves dangerous? Do they damage your skin and are they a dangerous part of your environment? My thoughts are that they probably aren't harmful, but they definitely can burn as they *do* cook meals and meats. However, major damaging process or association with cancers has not been proven.

My suggestion is to stay away from them as much as possible as many agents considered inoffensive initially have later been found to be quite dangerous. For example, x-radiation was used to examine feet for a proper shoe fit in shoe stores not too long ago. Today, people realize that this is not a safe practice and so is no longer done. The microwave may prove to be harmful eventually so meanwhile just try to limit your exposure as much as possible. Try not to be close to the microwave oven when in use and stay away from microwave towers that are more intense. There is no harm in minimizing your exposure. Do not use you cellular telephone excessively.

Light Depression

A very real dilemma, light depression can be a damaging situation occurring to people who live in varying climates, mostly in the upper part of the hemisphere like northern climates in our county or Canada, the Northwest territories and southern climates in Australia and Chile, etc. There are various psychological deficit disorders occurring in these darkened areas that are usually cured simply by natural sunlight. What happens in this situation is that melatonin production in the body is raised by darker climates and therefore the whole body can become sleepy or depressed.

114

Nighttime darkness is actually the reverse situation. If there is noise or light in your room at night then sleep will never be thorough, as the melatonin will not secrete appropriately with light or noise distractions. A very dark room is required to obtain a good night's sleep, as a dark room is helpful for better production of melatonin, and thus the whole hormonal system.

Food and Drink

Water

Drinking an appropriate amount of fluid every day is essential and of course water is probably the best fluid for this purpose. It is imperative not to drink more than four or five bottles a day, a quart or so, because it will dry you up. I know you don't believe this statement but the excess water will be drained by the kidney and in doing so needs electrolytes. The net result is a very poor balance of electrolytes in the overall circulation, which will be responsible for an offset of all systems in the body. You will feel tired all the time. I have discussed this subject in Chapter Six, hyperthermia and potassium.

Soft drinks

Soft drinks are acidic and have a fair amount of the addictive stimulant caffeine. These drinks also increase blood pressure and heart rates, and as they are an *acidic drink* they will offset the acidity of the stomach and change the Ph off the whole body fluids. This is probably the reason so many people have hyperacidity and heart burn. Along with creating an imbalance in the stomach, soft drinks also create havoc for the entire body's acid balance and can change the whole electrolyte balance of the blood.

They are a voluminous source of carbohydrates. Those that are not have sugar replacements that may be dangerous. There is also the history of saccharine that took many years to prove it a harmful carcinogenic.

Water is by far the best drink. Most juices, although they may contain helpful ingredients with some good chemicals,

115

have very high levels of basic carbohydrates and some as in citric juices are very acidic thus like soft drinks thus in general quite offsetting to the body fluid balance. Incidentally, excessive amounts of water can be as dangerous as not enough water since it can also deplete you of electrolytes by leaching them out in the urine with the excess water.

Foods

Damages from food can occur in various forms. Bacterial contamination can occur from meats and foods like mayonnaise that have developed major bacteria creating food poisoning. Typically, *meats* are a great culture medium for bacteria. Meats have contact with the normal intestinal flora of that particular animal like E.Coli for red meats and pseudomonas for fowls therefore they must be kept frozen or cooked to prevent the proliferation of these bacteria.

Once meat or fowl has been cooked or frozen essentially no damage can occur as all the bacteria have been killed or prevented from growing. Remember, a small amount of bacteria can probably be handled very well by the body. One caution is that *mayonnaise* in all forms has a *very* high proliferation rate of bacteria such as salmonella and this can create severe food poisonings. It is very important to always keep mayonnaise-like products refrigerated.

Prepared foods in general are not very good for a healthy diet. These all have a large amount of carbohydrates, hydrogenated fats and *preservatives* so try to stay away from these foods. Food is healthiest closest to its natural state.

For example, a freshly picked tomato is healthier than one that has been picked and sat on the kitchen counter for a week. Fruits and vegetables eaten in natural form, as opposed to being canned or frozen, are healthier. One friend from California recommended that grocery shopping be accomplished by purchasing only from the outer edge of a grocery store, where they keep refrigerated, generally fresher, food items. Anything that comes from shelves in the middle of a grocery store is generally processed food. Fresh food always contains more nutrition.

Vegetables in general are good but some do have phytochemicals that could be harmful. One example is soy, which contains an estrogen-like chemical that mimics the effects of that hormone when ingested.

If taken in a high quantity, men can offset their hormonal balance. Men can even develop breasts, gynecomastia. I suppose that women can do the same. Over-consumption can be dangerous as it can have deleterious effects like the question of cancer of the breasts. Some have replaced many regular foods by soy products and this offsets the balance. Again moderation is the key.

Cholesterol

Excessive cholesterol can be very dangerous; and there is no question about this. But the more I understand cholesterol and its mission in the body the more I realize that it is important not to have too low a level. I have mentioned that it is responsible for bile, hormones, myelin, cell membranes particularly in the brain and therefore it is not logical to lower it excessively. Another factor is the statin drugs, which by themselves can produce serious side effects as we are seeing more and more.

Excess can also become an important factor in arteriosclerosis so careful monitoring of cholesterol levels is advised. We must have moderation in order to attain balanced nutrition.

Food Allergies

Some people are allergic to lactose, gluten or have specific allergies to peanuts, crustaceans and certain drugs. Obviously the most effective treatment of these is to stay away from them. In many instances people who develop these allergies do not even know that they have them. The chronic allergic phenomena in their systems may become a major cause of disease. An example is the gluten allergies that are often

117

discovered after a patient is quite sick and the diagnosis is made by elimination.

Preservatives

Preservatives are an absolute necessity when providing huge amounts of food to feed large populations. There must be some form of it to prevent the deterioration and rotting of food and thus preservatives become very important. Damaging bacteria are killed by antiseptics like nitrites and sulfites.

Just think about this for a second: If nitrites, or any other preservatives for that matter, kill bacteria could they not kill some of our cells? Fresh foods are always best, but they can be hard to come by unless you have your own farm and make your own food, virtually impossible for the great majority of the population. In one form or another, foods must be preserved from deteriorating and becoming undesirable to eat.

Plant food must be protected from the invasion of natural predators like insects and molds. Pesticides are used for this and so by necessity the pesticides become a double-edged sword.

If food were not preserved, there would not be enough food simply because of the shear difficulty of the time lapse between processing food and eating that food. Also, much of the food would be contaminated with major microorganisms that could be very dangerous. This could be particularly true now that food is imported from other countries. You are not immune to the different bacteria in these foods and could become sick, just as if you encountered "La Tourista" problems when visiting other countries. Since the population increased, it now takes longer for food to reach your table.

On the other hand, however, the pesticides used are often neurotoxins and therefore dangerous for human consumption. It is essential to clean at least all of the vegetables and fruits on the exterior to rid most of these pesticides. There are probably five or six thousand forms of preservatives being used and they all have different side effects. There are only a few ways to preserve food from deteriorating by invading micro-organisms, including by freezing, by spicing the food (keep in mind that America was discovered because Europeans were looking for spices to preserve food) or by adding a form of antiseptic (preservatives) that will prevent the deterioration of the food.

Remember that all prepared foods and especially foods that stay on shelves for long periods of time, by necessity must contain some form of preservative. Cereal could have mold forming on it within a short period of time. Hotdogs, prepared meats, bacon, or for that matter any form of prepared salads, will always contain a consequential amount of preservatives, such as nitrites.

Nitrates and Nitrites

Nitrates are found in drugs, fertilizers, meat, food preservatives and perhaps all prepared foods. They are vasodilators that open vessels to provide a larger blood supply. Nitrates as drugs are used for coronary artery spasms, to dilate the arteries as for angina, like nitroglycerin.

Nitrites, often derived from nitrates such as vegetables that are fertilized, are mostly used in meats. This is also the functional mechanism of Viagra. Nitrites are used as a preservative usually in prepared meats like bacon, hot dogs and baloney. They have side effects like migraine headaches, creating a funny odd feeling after eating, weakness or dizziness. *Nitrites in foods can also cause low blood pressure, occasionally heart palpitation and even arrhythmias* if much is consumed. As you grow older you become more susceptible to chemicals and the symptoms are more accentuated. These same symptoms can also occur with nitroglycerin and similar drugs. Care must be taken not to over eat prepared meats when taking a nitroglycerine tab.

Nitrites do react with amines, some of the proteins, in other foods ingested in the low acid stomach, to form nitrosamines, which are *highly* carcinogenic both for the stomach and colon.

119

For years it was thought that a high consumption of meats caused cancer but researchers have since learned that nitrosamines are the culprits. The average American consumes 75 mg of nitrates a day, 0.8 mg of nitrites a day and produces 1 ug (one microgram) of nitrosamine a day. That is probably the "highest limit that is safe to consume" according to the FDA. Don't you think that it is too much especially if it is cumulative and it must be if it caused cancer?

Vitamin C, vitamin E and calcium will protect against the effect of nitrites and cancer. Fiber, especially in the colon, speeds up the movement of stool thus there is less exposed in the colon. Fiber also absorbs some of the nitrites.

Sulfites
Sulfites are natural preservatives in wines, more so in white than red wines. They may cause migraine headaches, particularly for allergic or hypersensitive people, as they also are vasodilators. No other major downfall has been found—yet.

Monosodium Glutamate (MSG)
Monosodium glutamate is an old product used mostly as a flavor enhancer. It used to be sold as *Accent* food spice mix although it has been removed by the FDA, I believe. Most though not solely Chinese restaurants add MSG to their food as it makes even an ordinary meal quite tasty.

Problems can arise from the side effects which include headaches, numbness in the neck radiating down the arms, tightness in the chest sometimes mimicking a heart attack; mild mood changes; heart palpitations; vivid dreams; swelling from water accumulation, and so on. The symptoms increase as you age. I like to think you become more astute as you get older and experienced so you can recognize the symptoms more easily but I found it is not always so. Older people are more sensitive to these substances, either because they are physically more reactive to them or because they no longer have the reserves to withstand these body challenges they had when younger.

Transfats

Transfats are essentially fats that have been altered either to make them produce a specific function or as a result of cooking. A hydrogen molecule added to oils hardens the oil so it can be used as butter like a spread or shortening. Transfats are used in most processed foods. They prevent rancidness and therefore are a form of preservative.

Also cooking actually changes the oils to either become hydrogenated fats or outright transfats. Unfortunately transfats *are* fats that act like free-radicals, and they scavenge ions and become harmful. Best prevention is abstinence from transfats. They are also discussed in Chapter Seven.

Burnt Meat

Barbecued meats that have been burnt or blackened contain benzopyrenes as well as other polycyclic hydrocarbons, all of which are well known to be carcinogenic agents.

In general, eating barbecued meat like fast food chains produce is acceptable as long as you do not intake a very high volume. The repetitive usage of barbecued foods can become carcinogenic and dangerous, mostly to the stomach. Did I ever mention moderation before?

Stimulants

Stimulants such as caffeine create a problem as they increase blood pressure, heart rate and stress levels. Other stimulants are cheeses, bananas and chocolate all of which have monoamine oxidase inhibitors that are actually stimulants in a similar fashion. They do alter the nerve conduction mechanism and thus are somewhat addictive I their effects.

Many people live on the stress edge and wonder why they stay in a constant state of being hyper, irritable and impatient. Yet they continue going to the coffee store for their regular fix. Incidentally, $2.50 for a cup of coffee at certain fancy coffee stores is $32.00 a gallon. If you compare that to the price of gas, then you have to wonder why we complain when we fill up at the pumps.

Don't forget that many carbonated soft drinks have caffeine, particularly Mountain Dew, which has up to five times the caffeine of one cup of coffee.

Stimulants have become a way of feeling good, a replacement for exercising and eating well. This is an artificial way to feel good, and carries a very high price of stress, hypertension and heart disease. And, if you remember, stress is cumulative.

Other Factors

Crowds

Crowds will increase stress as there is always jostling and the fear of injury, so it may be best to avoid huge crowds. The air contamination in crowds also is dangerous, as there are high levels of microorganisms and probably a lower amount of oxygen, along with increased CO_2. Claustrophobia is another fear factor, and injuries become a factor if the crowds are unruly. Airplanes are a good illustration of this unhealthy crowd environment, but they usually take you to such nice places. Today we may add fear of a terrorist attack,.

Automobiles

Automobile air has a very high level of pollution as re-circulated air is used if windows are closed. This air can be contaminated and also creates positive ions that make you apathetic and sleepy. See the Ion effect above under the sub-title *Solutions* in Air Pollution on page 101. With windows open, you can breathe outside "pure air," however, you could breathe fumes from other car's exhausts. In the countryside, you may breathe better air.

Seatbelts are very important protection devices along with airbags. Not using these devices has proved deadly or caused serious injury. Defensive driving is important, especially in today's society as calm and courteous driving will preserve your life much more than irritable and impatient driving. I live partly in Florida now and I see a lot of accidents as a result of impatience. Five to ten seconds gained could mean dire consequences.

Heat and Cold

Hyperthermia, as mentioned, is very dangerous as body temperature is elevated and serious chemical reactions and abnormalities occur greatly damaging the body. This is covered more thoroughly in Chapter Seven on *Physical Exercise*.

Hypothermia is the reverse and slows down many capabilities including immunity. Viral diseases tend to take a foothold during these periods of time. Severe hypothermia will cause serious injuries like frostbite and deep hypothermia can cause death.

Your body's defenses can adjust to both, if they are detected and recognized early but an appropriate time lag and acclimatization is required. Always seek a physician's advice on either of these situations.

Careful Travel

Travel is absolutely one of the most enjoyable activities in life. Stimulating your curiosity, satisfaction, learning, and understanding, therefore travel for leisure or business is greatly encouraged.

However, like everything, there are certain precautions necessary. Just as you wear a helmet for safety during biking, you need to take precautions during all stages of travel when you fly to other countries.

Prepare for your journey by researching the types of clothing best suited to your destination. Take proper clothing and gear, receive proper immunizations if required for travel to other countries, be cautious about foods and water you ingest and take great care of your passport, health insurance and money. They are your lifeline and are coveted by the local scam artists. Make plans well ahead of time and have a great experience. Third world travels is a little more difficult, but definitely worth the extra effort as many of the world's most vibrant sights and experiences are found in these countries, far away from the beaten path. You experience new cultures and learn how very wealthy and spoiled we are.

You should be especially careful about researching required immunizations for third world countries. For example, malaria may be a problem in a country and therefore you have to prevent this exposure from causing the illness by taking appropriate anti-malaria drugs before you travel. A physician who stays current on diseases and other health risks regarding travel is always helpful in these situations. He can give you advice about the appropriate vaccinations to help prevent typhoid, hepatitis, tetanus and polio. An ounce of prevention is invaluable in this situation because diseases that occur in third-world countries are not treated well there because they do not have the right medications or equipment, although they may have the knowledge. I strongly suggest a physician with exotic medicine training before, and after your trip, especially if any unusual symptoms occur.

If you are in third world countries it is very important to realize that the standard of medical care there is far below most U.S. hospitals. If there are hospital facilities, supplies may be limited and most likely you will find a low quality of medicine at least to our standards. This makes it even more important not to take risks that can cause injuries.

People are so nice when you respect them and they will bend over backwards to help you.

Besides you are an ambassador of our great country. It is a responsibility that you should not take lightly. Never think you are better than those in less fortunate countries. You are not better, you are only more fortunate. There are things they know that you don't. It is not a case of being better or worse, just different and that is the reason you went there in the first place.

Be as tolerant as you can of customs, views, opinions, ideologies and religions that are different from your own. Learn from them and grow.

Avoid stressful travel. Traveling with friends, making early and sound plans, and never drinking water in third-world countries unless it comes in a *sealed* bottle will all contribute to less stress on your trip. You will find it much easier to drink good water while traveling than it used to be as clean bottled water is sold nearly everywhere now.

Always request that hotels serve bottled water only, at meals, even if they claim their water in glasses is bottled water. Breaking the cap's seal yourself is the only way to truly know if clean water is used.

Do not eat foods that have not been washed and eat only cooked food. Remember also that salads may have been rinsed with contaminated water. Peeled and cooked are the best sources of food in foreign territory.

Also remember that foreign water is used for ice and is rarely made from clean bottled water. The glass or the icemaker could be contaminated and you would never know if your illness came from the water, glass or ice. Also, be sure that you drink all safe water, even while brushing your teeth or taking an aspirin or medication. One of your largest travel safety responsibilities is to ensure that your drinking water is safe. This may sound like extra work but a little care will avoid problems and the benefits are great.

Toxins Coming from Inside your Body

There are all kinds of damages that can come from within your body that you may not be aware of and these can be quite damaging. Just a few are listed here. One flagrant example is high blood pressure, a deadly silent killer. You must always be aware of this possibility and do something dramatic to improve the condition if this should occur.

Infections

Chronic bacterial invasion is extremely dangerous to the body as it creates numerous abnormalities that can cause free-radicals or *chronic inflammation* in the body that can be damaging, for example, to heart muscles. Colds and flu also cause infections.

Fungal infections such as Candida and Chlamydia in the sexual organs, mouth or fingers can create chronic bacterimia. Fungi like bacteria can create inflammatory mechanisms just like bacteria that can cause many types of damage to the body.

Gingivitis creates a constant flow of bacteria in your blood that deposits in the heart and elsewhere and could cause major problems. This can be a direct injury to the vessel lining or to the heart's inner lining or muscle. Gingivitis has often been blamed for heart disease as a major infective agent deteriorating vessels small increments at a time. It is mostly a cause for chronic inflammation.

Ulcers are usually the result of bacteria called H-pylori, which in the long run causes cancer of the stomach. Stomach ulcers that plagued people for so many years are now cured in a high percentage of cases by giving the proper antibiotics. Incidentally, heartburn patients sometime have those bacteria. Giardia, Lamblia and Chlamydia in the water can make you quite ill.

Boils on the skin will also make you sick in the same way. Warts, whether on sexual organs or elsewhere, can create problems. In particular, venereal warts (HPV) are especially harmful. Certain types or subspecies of these are also known to be carcinogenic but recently a vaccine has been discovered and all women should get vaccinated to prevent cancer of the cervix.

In general it is important to make sure that infections are completely cured. Make sure your physician shares that belief. Don't let any infections linger and take immediate action against any infection - gingivitis, vaginal infections, and chronic bladder infections and so on.

Inflammation

There are two categories: the acute inflammation and the chronic inflammation.

Acute inflammation is the protection and repair mechanism that does its job and disappears. It is brought about by injuries, infections that are quickly resolved and some allergies.

Chronic inflammation on the other hand is when the invader and the inflammatory processes are constantly battling. It becomes a major factor in the body and to the particular organ often referred to as fire in the heart, fire in the brain, as it causes a lot of damage and disease.

Causes:
- Chronic bacterial infections such as acne, gingivitis, vaginal fungal infections, hangnails, Lyme's disease, H.Pylori as in stomach ulcers, etc.
- Chronic viral diseases: rickettsial, AIDS, HPV, hepatitis, Herpes etc
- Immune reactions
- Insulin excess
- Free-radicals
- Stress
- Mechanical tear diseases: hypertension, arteriosclerosis, ligaments and tendon injuries, arthritis
- Radiation injuries
- Electrolytes imbalances

Treatment

- Keep up the immunity: vaccines, positive attitude, proper nutrition, electrolytes and supplements
- Find infectious agents (CRP test) and get rid of it
- Prevent or get rid of other chronic diseases
- Do closure on stress
- Avoid radiation
- Anti-inflammatories

Heredity

So much of what happens to the body can be attributed to heredity. Heredity is a silent inner toxin that many times can either kill you or make you ill during your lifetime. If you are fortunate, inheriting healthy genes works in your favor. But that is definitely the minority of us. The whole key to heredity is to find out if you have any of these defects that are remediable since you can correct them...if you know about them.

- Hyper cholesterol or hyperlipidemia are well known for causing heart disease and need to be detected and controlled. There is no question that too much cholesterol is damaging as the excess beyond what is needed is free-radicals and destructive.
- Homocysteine is a hereditary defect that is known to cause anywhere from five to fifteen percent of all heart disease and can be controlled with folic acid.
- Glutathione deficiency is hereditary and correctable.
- Gout causes all kinds of problems, mostly arthritic. It can also cause liver and kidney damage from kidney stones, and may even be instrumental in heart disease.
- Lactose intolerance can smother your whole body's system and prevent the absorption of food. This can be cured by avoiding lactose-containing products.
- Gluten intolerance is similar lactose except sometimes far more dangerous and involved. It can cause

anywhere from tiredness to serious problems like thyroiditis or schizophrenia.
- Specific food allergies such as to peanuts and crustaceans also must be avoided.

The task would be too great to list all the toxins that can come into your body, as there are literally thousands of them. The key is to try and understand as much as possible and read about toxins. Follow the basic prevention of not absorbing toxins, stay away from radiation, use sunscreen, wear your seatbelt and use common sense about reducing the amount of assaults that occur daily to your body. They are cumulative and the more you absorb them the more they collect in your blood.

Also remember that your body can naturally get rid of some of these assaults. It is impossible not to absorb some toxins, but you can reduce contact to the least possible. Your best interest is served if you understand which toxins are most dangerous and which ones you can safely live with. The more you know the better prepared you will be.

Do not be overly obsessed about this as it is impossible to avoid all the toxins. Often, some are absolutely necessary, as, for instance, are food preservatives. *Do not live the concept of paralysis of analysis*. Do not stop living because something *might* happen. Just be aware and careful, minimize the contacts, and everything will be fine. Be curious and learn as much as you can about potentially harmful agents, and then go on and live your life fully.

I am never afraid of what I know.
Anna Sewell   (1820-1878)

CHAPTER SIX

Physical Exercise

The objective of this chapter is not to provide specific exercises or information more easily obtained elsewhere, but rather to help you understand what goes on inside of you when you exercise versus when you *don't.*   I am hoping that once you understand the physiology any rationalizations you use not to exercise will be shattered and, even better, you will have new incentive to tackle a way of life that will revolutionize your golden years. Just watching yourself *grow* older rather than deteriorate is enormously satisfying. Growing older with good health and dignity is even better.

If you do not take care of yourself, *Numero Uno,* it doesn't really matter what else you do in life. You can have all the money or fame, be the most intelligent and imaginative person or simply being an ordinary Joe, you will deteriorate at the same pace as anyone else and it can be prevented. Culture, religion, sex, race, social status, riches and even heredity will not shield you from that deterioration.

Exercise is the most integral part of a healthy lifestyle. Just remember that heredity will not protect you from the gradual downward slope of atrophy. You *must* exercise to keep up your strength and many other functions in your body.

My good friend Gardner exercised until his last days at one hundred years old. Every day he exercised on his stationary bike and went for walks. Nobody is too busy. Find or create time for yourself, as nothing else is more important on the larger scale of life.

No other single component that I have mentioned in this book is more essential to an entire health regime than physical exercise.

As time goes on health professionals know this to be truer. The body simply atrophies, actually destroying or minimizing any parts not used so as not to have to service these parts. This is as true for muscles, ligaments, cartilage, and bone, as for the brain. I cannot stress how important it is not to deny the brain information to use.

I turned my life around completely after my open-heart surgery by committing to a fairly aggressive exercise regime. It has given me vigor, good mood, strength, gotten rid of a lot of my aches and pains and in general the satisfying feeling of doing some thing positive and creative for myself. It sure has reversed a lot of the vascular problems that were developing due to my arteriosclerosis.

I feel sluggish and gain weight fast if I do not exercise and this perturbs me to no end now. These third world trips I do are great but I don't get very good exercises nor good foods for that matter.

Unfortunately this atrophy is cumulative; the longer a sedentary period occurs, the more the body withers away. All you have to do is look at old people who do not exercise and you'll see what I mean. When you are young and have a good level of growth hormone, you have more leeway as the body will atrophy slower and faster re-growth can occur with diligent exercise. As you age and the hormonal curve dips downward, every system in your body slows down dramatically. What this means for each of us is that as we age, it is imperative to develop and maintain an aggressive, not wimpy, daily, or at least five days a week, exercise regimen to stay healthy.

If you have not been exercising, you may be reluctant to start but I assure you that you *can at any age* and you will be much happier and healthier once the habit of exercise is developed. You cannot be lazy and you will really need to focus to start a continual regime. You will have to stop being in denial if you are and change some of your life patterns. Remember that denial is a great killer in our society, and complete awareness is necessary to escape this.

It takes time to get back in shape. You will have to be patient. This process may be mentally painful initially, but that will quickly ease up and soon you will begin to look forward to exercise time. Remember that a long time lapsed before you got out of shape and you will need a fair amount of time to get back into it. If you start slowly then gradually increase your performance and then progress daily, you will also be building a good foundation for an exercise routine. For example, you might walk a quarter of a mile the first day. This isn't a huge distance but it is an honorable beginning. You can feel satisfied just because you *did* walk! You started the program. The next day or so you might increase your walk to a half mile and gradually increase your distances until suddenly you will not only be able to walk two or three miles a day but will *greatly miss* this wonderful physical and mental exercise on the occasional days when your schedule really does not allow your regime. *Do remember that exercise is for you only and your greatest priority.*

Do not make the mistake of thinking that you can begin an exercise regime with three miles if you're not used to it. Over-extending your muscles so swiftly could cause permanent damage. You could also become discouraged because the next day your body will hurt so much that you will be unlikely to continue with any regime at all.

My wife and I went horseback riding in Wyoming a few years ago and our guide, Doris, was a veterinarian who raced mules as a hobby. She always won these thirty-mile races and explained to me that she always starts training a mule slowly by riding short distances. She said that it took her six months to get the mules back in shape after the winter months. If a strong mule goes through this slow upgrading regimen, then logically you too must work your way very gradually into a regime. And *then* you must keep it up by never going through long periods of time again without exercising.

The less time that lapses between steady exercises, the easier it will be to rebuild muscles, and the easier for you to get mentally back in the groove. Lance Armstrong tries to have no lapses whatsoever between his regular exercise regime and his success is unparalleled.

When I reduce my exercise regime or do not exercise for a week or two, I start aching all over. As soon as I start my workout again, the aches surprisingly disappear. Sometimes I am angry and irritated at myself for having been so lazy until I remember to be grateful because I *did* get back on the regime and not quit altogether! It is difficult at first but then it becomes easier and eventually you will not want to be without it. There is a void that needs fulfilling. But what satisfaction when you do!

Advantages of exercises

Mental and emotional benefits
The first mental benefit you will experience from an exercise regime is pride. Once you begin, you will have broken the cycle of physical inertness. This all improves your body's appearance and you will enjoy a heightened sense of self worth not withstanding the physical benefits to the brain.

Due to the secretion of thirty-six hormones and enzymes during exercise, you actually feel better physically and mentally. One of these enzymes is a painkiller called endorphin that provides a sense of wellbeing. Some of these enzymes relieve the doldrums if not outright depression. These hormones are great for pain relief and elation. During individual exercise like walking or bike riding, the hormones and enzymes also promote thoughts such as planning your day, creativity or meditative thoughts that relieve stress.

When circulation is increased all of the brain functions are accentuated. More alertness, a better disposition, relaxation, memory and higher self worth will inevitably ensue. There is more on this in the second wind section later in this chapter.

The higher the blood supply, the more building materials get to an area and the better these cells will function and replicate. Cells divide and replace older less functional cells during aging. According to the National Stroke Association there is strong statistics showing that the stroke risk goes down when the amount of exercise goes up.

Reserve

When you are born every organ in our body has ten times the reserve power that it needs. As we age, these reserve powers of our youth are gradually lost in a slow but steady descending slope to a point where eventually there is no reserve left. Slowly, one may lose the capacity to climb stairs or may lose equilibrium and balance, start have aching joints, hearing loss, visual loss, cognitive loss, memory loss and so on.

The hormone endocrine system follows suite. For example the growth hormone secretion curve, as seen in the hormone chapter on page 47, is nearly identical to pattern of behavior that reserves have. They follow that curve closely down to eventually nothing. Exercise that changes many systems in the body for the better, can change that growth hormone and similar reserve curve positively although not greatly.

The decrease of reserve powers is caused mostly by disuse but can be slowly reversed by active usage of *all* of your faculties. You can be more independent and have less chance of injury because of better equilibrium, stronger muscles and joints, higher energy, faster healing, and overall a much improved self confidence and positive attitude. Also, because you are healthier, there is less chance of falling and injuring yourself because you have much better ambulation.

Circulation

The more you exercise, the more you need to increase the blood supply to feed every organ that has increased its function during the process. For example, when you run or bike, your calf muscle's (Gastrocnemius) blood supply demand can go from one percent at rest to one hundred and fifty to two hundred percent at full speed. There is an increased demand of oxygen, nutritional and energy supplies required by the cells at that high metabolism rate. This is aerobic exercise, which develops your heart and lungs very well. Your vessels have to readjust and become more resilient, elastic and dilated. This prevents or reduces clogging (arteriosclerosis) and more blood and nutrients are fed to the tissues it nourishes, and to the vessel walls themselves.

If the number or size of vessels are too small, exercise will stimulate the formation of collateral circulation, which in turn increases the amount of vessel network to fulfill new demands. So instead of the blood vessels gradually closing down for lack of exercise, they will start opening new channels to feed muscle demand. This improves the circulation in your brain, lungs, heart, bones, ligaments and cartilages and thus supplies the increased need for nutrients to replenish the depletion at the time of exercise and just afterwards.

The more circulation in a tissue the more easily that tissue heals if injured or depleted. Poorly vascularised muscles, or other tissues for that matter, will not develop well if not fed properly. A system *is* as weak as the weakest link. If muscles developed too fast, without the blood supply developing proportionately that is **anaerobically,** then the muscles will not be well fed. This will create lack of blood supply in times of need such as during exercise, for instance weakness and cramping.

Also trying to develop muscles too fast will also cause micro tears in them. There is also an increase in the production of undesirable amounts of lactic acid in unconditioned muscle. A conditioned muscle readily disposes of extra amounts.

Coordination
Think of a newborn baby who is awkward and has no specific

movement objective. As a baby grows, so will the purpose of movement and soon the capability of grasping a finger will develop. Next grasping a bottle, then playing with objects, then all hell breaks loose and you have to be on top of that little wonder as next you'll find them touching and playing with everything and soon crawling or walking everywhere.

We have the same capacity to develop coordination in aging. It may be slower but that changes as you use it more and more. This means you can readily learn new sports as you grow older. You may be awkward at first but your skills will develop as this brain interactive process is refined. The skill will not develop if your thoughts are negative and you think you cannot succeed.

The process of coordination is a huge series of muscles orchestrating together to create useful movements. The more they are used and focused, the more precise they become. Good tennis players, musicians, ballet dancers, painters or bikers each have refined movements governed by the process of coordination. Brain cells constantly fine tune interactions to produce more precise movements, which attain an objective or end product like creating an oil painting or playing a tennis match. The more you practice a craft or sport, the better you become.

This coordination process is not exclusive to youth and can definitely be developed later in life if the need arises. This may take a little longer during aged years than in youthful years, but the brain cells *will* connect and refine the coordination process. Do not despair. The connections will happen and you will attain the end result you are seeking.

Lungs

If you do not use your lungs, they will atrophy like any another tissue. Lungs need a good thoracic cage to expand and contract. This cage is composed of ribs (bone) and cartilages that lose elasticity and calcify if not used. The intercostal muscles and the diaphragm expand, contract the cage and subsequently the lungs also could atrophy so they too benefit from exercise.

The lungs themselves must be elastic with good circulation to exchange oxygen and carbon dioxide in and out as needed. When you improve your *aerobic capacity*, you improve the lung elasticity and its capacity to absorb oxygen (O_2) and rid carbon dioxide (CO_2). These attributes are greatly maintained and improved by exercise, and will also keep or improve important reserves.

Obviously, the better circulation, the better the oxygen exchange occurs in the body. Exercise is a win-win situation. Athletes who maintain constant exercise patterns, without periods of inactivity, lose very little aerobic capacity. Swimmers, bikers, and runners score highest in this capacity.

This dispels the myth that older people lose their capacity to exercise competitively. There is documentation that they can increase their aerobic capacity and strength by four to six times.

Better air circulation, which inevitably ensues, also will reduce the chances of lung diseases such as pneumonia and chronic obstructive pulmonary disease. In general people who do not smoke have very little chance of developing lung cancer. Smokers have found stopping easier while exercising.

Cardiovascular Benefits

Exercise will demand more blood therefore more function will occur from the heart and there will be a greater beat or stroke volume (the amount of blood sent by each stroke of the heart) to satisfy greater blood demand from the body. As a result, circulation will be stronger which will then increase the amount of blood pumped on each beat so the heart rate can slow down to attain the same circulation. A more powerful heart has more reserve and will be more beneficial to facilitate greater exercise output but also more reserve in case of a heart attack. A heart attack is much less likely if you exercise diligently.

By the way, congestive cardiac failure is an atrophic heart that no longer can pump adequate amounts of blood to the body. It may also not have enough CO-Enzyme Q-10 to sustain its mitochondria to pump adequately. I will explain Coenzyme Q-10 on page 310 in the chapter on Antioxidants.

Aerobic capacity affects the heart as much as the lung by improving the strength, the quality of blood vessels and the endurance of the heart muscle and the oxygen intake facility. The mitochondria are better nourished and more functional. This also increases the reserve power so if damage does occur, there is room to spare.

There are huge amounts of mitochondria in the heart muscle cell. Skeletal muscle cells contain about twenty mitochondria while heart muscle cells contain in the vicinity of seven hundred on average. If they are all fully charged, the heart will have a higher reserve and aerobic exercise builds up this reserve.

Through exercise, the coronary arteries, which are the blood vessels feeding the heart muscle will have a greater demand put on them and again will need to improve their performance. The likelihood is that exercise can reverse coronary arteriosclerosis, because the better blood circulation will heal damage to the arteries.

By the way, arteries also have smaller arteries feeding them. They are called vasa vasorum or arteries of arteries, and they have to be maintained just as regular arteries with aerobic exercise. Through exercise, the cholesterol and calcium deposits are reabsorbed, and there is repair to the damaged walls of the arteries. As mentioned above, the deficient arteries may also develop collateral circulation, which reverses the deficiencies created by arteriosclerosis. Of course, if you have no arteriosclerosis, which is unlikely, your heart will maintain a healthy status.

One important problem easily corrected is the lack of

potassium that can cause arrhythmias. The heart can go into fibrillation if the potassium levels are down. See further in this chapter— "potassium"

Muscles

Muscles are the powerhouse of our body. The skeletal muscles ambulate us, the heart muscles move the blood in our body, and muscles control other functions such as bowel, bladder, uterus etc.

Skeletal muscles are composed of large cells called muscle fibers. There are two types within a given muscle: *Fast twitch muscle fibers* concern speed, fast reactions, and lifting heavy weights upon demand. These muscles emit higher energy than the slow twitch ones. They are responsible for sprinting and the fright and flight reactions. You start losing these by age twenty and will continue losing them as you age. This is the reason sprinters generally retire at or soon after they turn thirty. It is easier to lose weight with them as they emit very energy to burn fat.

Slow twitch muscles are lower energy, slower of speed and decrease in strength but they can last longer. The older we get the less fast twitch fibers we have. They are the high-energy fibers and burn more calories. As a result it is easier to gain weight as we grow older. *But also we have much more endurance for long treks* as we age though we are somewhat slower.

You can increase muscle fiber size quite substantially by exercise. Even after menopause you can you can increase the size of your muscles if you are keeping the rest of your systems such as he hormonal system in great shape. Evans and Rosenberg in *BIOMARKERS,* which I recommend reading, have shown that you can double your strength *at any age* in three weeks by doing exercise at eighty percent of your single maximum capacity. That is the most weight that you can lift in one push. For example, if you can lift one hundred pounds, then eighty pounds is your repetitive lifting weight. This repeated lifting will procure the maximum muscle development potential and simultaneously your aerobic capacity.

Muscles have a high metabolic rate and thus create a higher caloric need, so will burn fat faster. Fat on the other hand has a very low caloric need so will lower the overall metabolism. The higher the fat to muscle ratio, the lower the metabolism, and the more difficult weight loss becomes.

- o   Muscles are responsible for vitality:
- o   They increase metabolic rate.
- o   They increase aerobic capacity for heart, lung and vessels by recharging their batteries.
- o   They use more glucose as fuel thus there is:
- o   Less fat deposition
- o   More fat re-absorption
- o   Higher HDL levels, the good cholesterol
- o   By reducing the levels of glucose in the blood, muscles also reduce insulin levels that reduce cell resistance, and thus there is less likelihood for diabetes.
- o   Remember the daunting fact that just one week of inactivity will cause muscles to atrophy and three to six weeks will be needed to bring them back to normal. During the atrophy period the body will accumulate fat. This atrophy is often seen after surgery.

Muscle fibers do not as a rule multiply; instead they hypertrophy, or enlarge. They do not form more cells to rise to a need but basically just enlarge existing cells. So if muscles are very large like a weight lifter, you have the same amount of cells, muscle fibers, as if you did not lift weight.

The older we get the more the atrophy of the muscle but it is not inevitable as exercise will reverse the atrophy or prevent it altogether. Thus you should not wait until atrophy is advanced before you start exercising. Your will power also weakens proportionately to the muscle atrophy and becomes more and more difficult to reactivate yourself the longer you wait.

If a muscle loses its inner functional mechanism, it becomes shorter. It is called contracture of the muscle. The end result is that you are weaker, stiffer, less agile, have less equilibrium, and will be much more insecure in your movements, thus increasing the chance of injuries. Does that not describe older people well? The flip side - the side where you exercise adequately - means you are stronger, more secure, have less chance of injury, better circulation to muscles and improvement to your whole being. You will feel great about yourself as you become stronger and may also look better!

Incidentally, strong muscles support joints much better and protect ligaments, tendons, and cartilages from injuries. The stronger the support muscles, the fewer injuries in sports. Consider football players for example. They would sustain extreme injuries if they were not in absolute perfect condition. Well the same protection will happen to you if you shore up your muscles regardless of age.

Think of a joint as being like a microwave tower that must be supported on all sides by guy wires; otherwise it will buckle disastrously at the slightest wind. Your muscles are these guy wires, or reinforcing struts, that can stabilize the joints and ligaments from injuries. If you build these guy wires stronger than necessary, the likelihood of damage to these joints is less. You can see how fragile our joints can be if they are not protected by this support mechanism especially as we age.

Understanding this concept clearly will prevent many injuries in daily life and sports alike.

- o Think of a motor (muscle) that has a pulley (joint) and a rope (tendon) that can lift eighty pounds. No harm will come to it as long as you stick to that weight limit.
- o Using your muscles is the same: active sports and work actions like lifting require spikes of power such

as sprints, lunges or weight lifting beyond that weight. If the motor system can lift only eighty pounds then one hundred pound spikes will damage the system, tear or rupture muscles, tendons or ligaments. Besides the joint cartilage might be crushed as they are more friable. That is why it is a good idea to do both aerobic training and weight training, to cross train, so the muscles are prepared for both spike power needs and long distance needs.

o Again when the muscle is not in good shape it will produce lactic acid and micro tears in the muscles that could bring about an inflammatory reaction. This is the pain and stiffness experienced for the next day or two. If you exercise more gently the next day, instead of nursing your wounds, you will increase the circulation in the muscle and reabsorb the inflammation and lactic acid and thus heal the tears and reabsorb lactic acid much faster. Graduated exercise will minimize this.

o You tire easily due to lack of proper muscle endurance.

o You have a greater chance of injury as stated above.

o You will not enjoy exercise as much as when you are in better shape.

o There will be less pain, a better balance and equilibrium, more coordination and no fear of injuries.

Only you can determine the right amount of exercise for yourself.

Remember that the right percentage to lift is eighty percent of your maximum lifting capacity. So, eighty percent of your full capacity when running, biking and so on is also a goal. This provides a solid workout that you can do safely without injuring muscles yet simultaneously increasing your strength. Constantly readjust this upwards as your strength increases. Avoid situations that will cause damage like running that constantly pounds on the knees. This may be very small damage, imperceptible at first but again the cumulative damage to the cartilage is what becomes lethal to it.

Giving your muscles the proper food is necessary to help build them. Carbohydrates are acceptable in small amounts to provide energy just before you exercise, as that is exactly what they are good for. But carbohydrates do not help build new muscles or repair damaged ones. It is proteins and fats that do so. Electrolytes are necessary to replenish the immediate deficiencies that are experienced during exercises. Remember, carbohydrates in excess of what you use for energy will only build fat storage. A good schedule is to eat about two or three hours before you exercise. You could take a small amount of carbohydrates just before exercising, but only if going on a long stint of biking or other activity.

Stretching also helps by keeping muscles longer and elastic, rather than allowing them to become short, stiff and inflexible and more easily ruptured. Yoga and Pilates are perfect sources for stretching to increase strength and equilibrium. I used to think that it was a wimpy thing to do, but boy have I changed my opinion on this! These practices also enhance the brain-body relationship. Combined with aerobic exercises this wonderful combination creates a good overall program.

You *must always warm up* before aggressive exercise to loosen the muscle and to increase circulation. Muscles are tight before use and more prone to injury so you must use caution. Warm up first for ten to fifteen minutes then stretch every muscle and tendon and ligament. A torn or pulled muscle is slow to mend so plan your exercise regime with care and allow time to build your endurance. The warm up period is most important for preventing injuries. You should reach your second wind before reaching your full capacity.

Tendons

Tendons will also atrophy, stiffen, shorten and lose the lubrication of the synovial fluid, which is the 'grease' that makes them glide well, with lack of use. This is what makes you stiff and awkward in demeanor when you do not maintain a healthy exercise regime.

When this happens, you are quite prone to injuries like tendonitis, carpal tunnel, sprains or outright ruptures. Tendonitis is an inflammation of a tendon caused by a lack of lubrication. This lack of lubrication (synovial fluid) is due to inflammation and aging disuse and the resultant stiffness. The tendon becomes frayed just like a rope would if rubbed inside a tube without lubrication, or it could be caused by tendons being too weak and that partially or totally rupture. Chronic tendonitis is seen mostly in muscle-tendon systems that are too weak and the repetitive motions are above their capacity, resulting in the inevitable chronic injuries.

Weak ligaments or tendons will not sustain the greater stress of sports or exercise and eventually as they get weaker and weaker, they will not even support normal daily living. As soon as you put a slight demand on them, they partially tear, then heal, then tear again, creating the chronic cycle of tendonitis, like carpal tunnel, tennis elbow, or plantar fasciitis of the soles. Of course, the prevention or treatment is to strengthen the system by a good graduated exercise regimen.

Most tendonitis and carpal tunnels happen to people who push the envelope just a little beyond the capacity of the strength of their tendons and ligaments. If they had exercised well and built themselves up, this would not happen. Stretching often and painlessly is also important. The trick is to exercise regularly *before* this happens. This naturally will happen more and more as we age.

Stretching

Stretching is particularly important as we age as our tendon-muscle complex are stiffer and it prevents tearing injuries. Stretch often and work every muscle that you will use. Also remember to put tension slowly on the muscle up to the point of tension, but not to the point of pain as it indicates you are microscopically tearing the muscles. You would only aggravate the damage if you continue after hurting begins. Sometimes if you have a knot or a spasm of the muscle, stretching will hurt so you would be better off massaging the knot away first. You could massage that hard lump in the muscle to gradually soften. When your muscles rest they naturally shorten to their resting length, thus the importance of stretching before you begin to exercise.

Yoga is an excellent way to stretch and offers balance, equilibrium, isometric exercise and a great way to unwind and reduce tension. Pilates is similar but offers more strength training. Incidentally, stretching in the morning as soon as you get up is the body's way to automatically do a morning tune up. This re-lengthens the muscles that have shortened all night. This often is the cause of backaches. Also do a small session of isometric exercises to keep muscles from atrophying. Do not be afraid to do this often through the day when you have the opportunity. If you sit or are otherwise inactive, get up occasionally and stretch. This feels good and is good for you.

Joints and Bones
Bones atrophy just like every other structure in the body if not used. It is called osteoporosis and is eighty percent the result of disuse. Hormonal changes, particularly in women but also in men are another factor although less so.

Osteoporosis
If the body is in disuse, it gradually reabsorbs calcium, which is normally deposited on a framework of protein mesh. Just think of reinforced cement structures that are made of steel bars, rebars, around which cement is poured. This reinforced cement structure is ten to twenty times stronger than cement without the rebar. The same concept occurs in bones. Calcium is the cement and the protein network acts like the rebar. As calcium gets reabsorbed by disuse, the strength of the bone diminishes as the protein mesh weakens. The structure is now too weak to support the body and bones crack easily or are broken.

That mobilized calcium circulates through the body and will

deposit anywhere, in vessel walls, tendons, muscles, or excreted though the kidney where kidney stones are formed. You should recognize this very serious danger by annual bone densitometry x-rays to find out if this is happening. If so, immediately replenish the calcium and magnesium. Make sure you have adequate vitamin D either by one-half hour of sunshine a day or by taking supplements. But of course you must also get rid of the main causes, the lack of exercise and hormonal replacement.

Let me tell you a little story of my experience as a plastic surgeon. I treated paraplegics for years taking care of mostly their pressure sores that are such a problem for them. What was very eyes opening for me was that the lower part of their bodies that was paralyzed had absolute osteoporosis. Mind you they had normal upper bodies with normal hormone production, normal nutrition and electrolytes and vitamin D.

The only difference between the upper body with normal bones and the lower body with severe osteoporosis was paralysis or absolute disuse atrophy. That sure tells me that *osteoporosis is not a disease of aging but one of not using the body*. Another example is the older person who plays tennis with the right arm holding the tennis racquet being normal while the left arm gets osteoporosis.

Take this as a lesson and go and exercise.

Cartilages

The cartilages are like plates of polyethylene over the bone ends preventing them from crunching onto each other. The more the blood supply feeds nutrients to the cartilages, the healthier they remain. The increased blood supply due to exercise will preserve them. And that increase feeds more nutrients, which permit the cartilages to stay thicker, more elastic and secrete more synovial fluid. User-friendly exercises are beneficial.

For example, running naturally pounds excessively on the knees and the cartilages eventually and inevitably crumble. If you bike instead, the motion at the knee is very smooth and gliding, not pounding and crushing. I play tennis and I shouldn't because my knees swell. If I go biking for ten to fifteen miles, then afterwards the swelling and the pain go away. I deduced that I increased blood supply to the joint and reabsorbed and healed faster. Beside that I am cross training.

Active joints stay much better lubricated than inactive ones. They also a have much better blood supply to sustain and heal if the joint is damaged. The less damage there is the less inflammation and deterioration. Arthritis and the products of its inflammation are damaging and can create a vicious cycle. Osteoporosis by itself also causes damage to the cartilage and thus promotes osteoarthritis. By the way, they both cause chronic inflammation.

A great tragedy occurs when a person has a joint damaged by osteoarthritis and does not have it operated on, usually because of the fear of surgery. Inevitably, it puts one in a no-exercise mode with the inevitable weight gain, loss of muscles, equilibrium, stiffness, pain, and thus a downhill mode. The whole body follows suit and this unavoidably leads to disease and ultimate demise but only after very unhealthy and unpleasant last years of life. And it is totally avoidable. To do maintenance is crucial to keep you in good repair and function. You would do exactly that to your car wouldn't you?

Also remember that if, after consideration, you decide you will have surgery, the longer you wait the more the support muscles to that joint will atrophy and the more likely an operation will be less successful, or at least will require a much longer recuperation and therapy. Always remember that it takes longer to rebuild muscle than to lose it.

The various surgeries are getting so sophisticated today that results are excellent and will permit you to go back to exercise fairly soon. This may set you back a few weeks but not having surgery could remove years from your life and severely mar the quality of your remaining years. Take the bull

147

by the horns and do whatever it takes, even surgery, to repair bones and joints.

Keep your body like a car--running! Replace worn out bearings and continue driving that wonderful old body you have! You cannot buy a new one; it's the only one that you will ever own, so do the best you can!

Hormones

Exercising in later years will increase growth hormone levels by two or three percent, which is not a great deal, but it is much better than zero percent. It is surprising how much good this small percentage does to your body and particularly to your muscles. It is the only reason why you can enlarge the muscle bulk after menopause, male and female.

Muscles and Insulin

Two premises: One is that muscle needs fuel or energy to function, and that is glucose—sugar. Two is that you need a facilitator to absorb the glucose in your muscle cell, and that is the insulin.

Glucose is only absorbed into the cell during heavy exercise or when insulin permits glucose absorption in the muscle cell. Insulin in general renders the membrane permeable to glucose at rest. Under the influence of insulin, the storage hormone, when you ingest sugar, the muscle and nerve membranes open pores and permit glucose to enter and be used to fuel activity. During exercise, the glycogen, which is glucose in storage form, is mobilized and transformed by insulin into glucose to be used as muscle fuel. When the glucose and subsequently the glycogen are totally used from burning too much energy in exercise, only then are fat and triglycerides allowed to be mobilized to use as energy. This is a difficult process for the body.

This can be noticed during long exercises when there is a period of physical depression, tiredness when the body's metabolism mobilizes fat since carbohydrates are no longer readily available.

Weight Metabolism and Exercise

Surround yourself with supportive people. Weight goals can be attained and maintained simply by replacing an attempt to control weight with an attempt to create a healthier lifestyle.

Exercise increases the combustion rate in your body. In doing so, it burns a much higher amount of calories than when the body is at rest. Exercise burns the excess calories of carbohydrates and other excessive, unused nutrients in your body. It actuates the *Fat Mobilizing Factor*, which permits the re-absorption of fat in the fat cells, mostly triglycerides.

The fat mobilizing factor does not go into play unless you have very low levels of insulin. Without this process, no fat ever leaves these storage cells. You are seldom or ever hungry while you exercise, or afterwards. The period without hunger lasts longer the longer you exercise. You produce little or no insulin during this period. Exercise dramatically reduces diabetes. Current figures show that sixty-four percent of the American population is obese and thirty-six percent of them develop secondary or late onset diabetes. Keeping weight down is likely to prevent late-onset diabetes. Very few normal or overweight people ever get diabetes type II if they exercise.

Other advantages of regular exercise

- o Builds muscle mass.
- o Reduces fat by actuation of the 'fat reabsorbing hormone'
- o Improves ability to repair tissue.
- o Improves strength and confidence.
- o Reduces pain by the secretion of endorphins, which is your body's own morphine.
- o Improves vision.
- o Helps smokers quit.
- o Improves sleep; however does not exercise before bedtime as the secretion of the brain's enzymes may

keep you awake.
- o Reduces cancer by reducing free-radicals and improving the immune system.
- o Increases the numbers of t.lymphocytes in blood, which protect against cancer.
- o Improves physical appearance and body image.
- o Improves balance and coordination with more security and less falling.
- o Improves relaxation and relieves stress.
- o Reduces bad cholesterol and increases good cholesterol.
- o Reduces the risk of stroke by thirty percent or more.
- o Prevents or reduces high blood pressure.
- o Reduces Type 2 diabetes by thirty percent.
- o Prevents osteoporosis and bone fractures.
- o Dramatically reduces the risk of dying prematurely.
- o Makes a healthy lifestyle more attainable.
- o Creates more independence, since you will be in good physical condition to take care of yourself as you grow older.
- o Improves your health so you live longer but you also will be much healthier, happier and satisfied during your golden years.
- o The risk of heart disease is reduced by 40 percent with only three hours of brisk walking a week. Exercise is a pretty powerful tool. The more you do, the more you lower the risk of heart disease (Harvard study JAMA October 2002). The more brisk the exercise, which improves both the quality of your muscles and your aerobic capacity, the better these statistics, will be. Moderate exercise does not seem to provide these same high results, but obviously anything is better than nothing.
- o Years ago studies showed that farmers, who regularly work hard physically, have an average of eight more years of life. The same is true of exercising people.

Let me reiterate that *the easiest thing to do in life is not to exercise*—yet that is the worst thing you can do.

The more I read and experience life, the more I surmise that exercise is the most important factor in preventing the destructive mechanisms of the aging disease.

Second Wind (Warming up)

There is only one thing to say about warming up before exercising--just do it. Always warm up before you start any active exercise. This will prevent many injuries and your body will readjust to the new stronger demands much smoother and faster. You will be less likely to experience aches and pains afterwards or injuries and cramps.

This is when the brain secretes thirty-six hormones that change the whole pattern of the body to accommodate itself to the new regimen called exercise. You have started slowly and attained your second wind

Your body will secrete vasodilators that open vessels to satisfy this greater demand of blood. Your heart will speed up. Your lungs will adjust to accept more oxygen. Muscles and ligaments will loosen to make them more elastic and less susceptible to injuries. Endorphins are secreted, which are your body's morphine, thus reducing pain during and after exercise. You might notice if you hurt yourself during exercising that you hardly noticed the pain while it was happening but the pain became more intense when you cooled down because the endorphins had left and inflammation occurred.

The second wind process takes about ten to fifteen minutes to occur after you start exercising and it should be recognized because when you start exercising, it is not pleasant and there is a natural tendency to quit doing something if the results are not pleasant. You must start slowly since your body can be stiff and muscles and ligaments are not as elastic as they will become once warmed up. Starting too fast may injure muscles, tendons joints even though these injuries are very minute to a point you may not recognize it. Always do five to fifteen minutes of slow aerobic exercises until you start sweating slightly, and then stretch for five minutes. After this, your body is ready and you can proceed exercising whole-heartedly. The least amount of exercise you should do is to start slowly until you detect the changes of the second wind. You will recognize the arrival of the second wind by the diminishing pain, the start of sweating, heart rate increase, less shortness of breath and an overall well being.

The longer you stay in that second wind, the longer the pleasant effect will stay with you during the day. The endorphins will linger during the day to reduce aches and pains and improve mental attitude. I believe this feeling of second wind is what perpetuates the avid runner's addiction. If you exercise without attaining the second wind, you will not achieve the good feeling that lingers throughout the day since you have not secreted the endorphins.

Many quit before this phenomena occurs because it is not really pleasant to exercise up to this point but if they waited just a few more minutes, the satisfaction of the exercise would demonstrate itself. Knowing about the second wind gives hope that once you get into a regular regime, you will start feeling good and improve rapidly! The older you become, the more important the warm up is as older people usually become stiffer and are more prone to injury.

Essential Exercise
The most important factor in feeling good and staying healthy in aging is exercise. It *is* essential. I know I repeat this but perhaps repetition will sink this concept deep in your mind and give you reason to incorporate an exercise regime ***now!***

How to Start a Regime and Maintain It

- Consult with your doctor first and be safe.
- Do not push exercise if you have unusual symptoms
- Do not think that problems will not exist if you go

without exercise.
- o Establish a starting date, now is best, not much later.
- o Sign a contract with yourself, a la Bob Green's "Get with the Program"
- o Start slowly and easily and do fun exercises.
- o Record your activities and times. List times for exercises on your calendar and stick to your plan. You must alter your life pattern to accomplish this important challenge. It is the primordial golf ball.
- o Invite a friend to join you so that you can encourage and stimulate each other.
- o See an exercise physiologist or a trainer in a health facility like the local Y.M.C.A.
- o Do not compare yourself to others. You are only competing with yourself and you are the only one who can improve your exercise regime.
- o Do not despair if you stop your exercise regime; just begin again. Beginning this time will be even easier than your initial start-up.
- o Do exercises you enjoy so when you return after a break in your regime, you'll feel like you're returning to a fun activity.
- o

Exercise is not taking a walk in the park; it is a dedication to your health. Do not rob yourself and think that a slow walk or a slow bike ride will accomplish your goal. Continually improve your endurance until you can get to, or close to, your eighty percent maximum capacity. You must use an honest effort to reap high benefits. A slow walk or bike ride is better than no exercise at all, but will not substantially reverse a poor physical condition to a healthy vigor. It will not provide the aerobic capacity that is so essential. This sedentary exercise may maintain the shape you are in now but will not offer any improvement. Limited exercise is better than nothing, but once you experience the great benefits of aerobic endeavors and the second wind, you'll understand why this elevated exercise is so important.

Remember that other people have had your same concerns

and justifications and have overcome them. A majority of the population hesitates to start an effective exercise regime. You will be in much better company once you actually begin and maintain your exercise regime.

Types of Exercises

Aerobic Exercises

Aerobic exercises involve any activities requiring an increase is oxygen absorption and thus an increase in heart rate. This covers most active sports. When muscles become more active, the required nutrients and oxygen are met and the demand must be met by the providers, the heart and lung. In previous references about exercise, I emphasize the importance of exercise for the development of a good heart-lung-oxygen system. Aerobic exercises should be a primary goal in an exercise regime.

Isometric Exercises

Isometric exercises are a convenient way to preserve muscle strength or even develop it between exercises. The whole premise of Charles Atlas's program was based on isometric exercises. The downfall, however, are those isometric exercises do not develop the cardiopulmonary system proportionally to the development of the muscle, and this eventually can create severe problems. Therefore isometric and aerobic exercises must be combined.

Isometrics are exercises by which you tighten your muscles without moving the extremity. The resistive force is the opposing muscle. This is a great additive way to keep your muscles developed in between exercises. But think of it only as an additive used between sessions, because in the long run these exercises do not produce a balanced workout as your blood vessels, heart and lungs do not follow suit. The morning stretch is such an exercise. Both Yoga and Pilates are excellent isometric exercises.

When you are younger and participate in group or team

sports, they can be challenging, active and competitive. That is excellent. But it is also very important to learn sports that you can do by yourself, as these will be with you the rest of your life especially after fifty. You will be very glad you did, as learning later is more difficult. Examples are tennis, golf, skiing and swimming which all require skill and if learned early in life can benefit you for the rest of your life.

Team sports tend to be played less later in life. There are exceptions such as softball, volleyball, tennis and such.

Familiarity with a sport makes it easier to start. Do not despair if you want to participate in a sport you have no experience with as learning a new sport can be fun and beneficial. This is also a new brain growth that you will be very proud to accomplish. It may take a little longer to learn but you can learn it.

Indoor Sports

Indoor sports have the advantages of being unrestricted by weather or temperature and are usually available year round. The equipment sports are predictable. The weight training ones are excellent for selected muscle training. Upper body strength is important and weight training can provide this very well. Aerobic exercises on machines are also good but unfortunately can get so boring unless you use this precious time to think and meditate which may also relieve stress. Ideas seem to churn out in your mind as miles on a bike slip past. This can also be a good time for reflection, an opportunity to catch up on news via television or light reading. There are always creative ways to spend time while doing a worthwhile exercise.

Less time is consumed when exercising indoors and you can hit and run, like do a mile in the morning and a mile in the afternoon. Sometimes people let other schedules become more important than their own health and splitting exercise time is certainly best if that is the *only* way it can be accomplished. The most effective method, however is to do complete exercise sessions. Try to ensure that you choose an exercise that you do not find boring and definitely do more than one type for variety and cross training. Notoriously, some people buy machinery to exercise, use it for a short period of time and then stop altogether for lack of stimulus. This is where the correct choice of exercise and the dedication to a regular regime coincide. You have to do both. If particular exercises become boring, do another type or try another activity so the novelty will peak your interest again. Participate in water polo, a water competition, Yoga, Pilates, Dancing, Judo or Tae Bo. You are only limited by your imagination! There is nothing wrong with doing all of these, alternately, and they will become cross training, which is a great benefit.

Outdoor Sports

Outdoor sports are more varied and entertaining, but the weather is less predictable although most of the time it will not be an impediment. Sometimes you can get a little wet or cold but that can provide character and resilience. More time may be required to get going, but the payback is very high. You are far more entertained in the great outdoors so the exercise is more interesting and consequently you are more likely to last longer and participate with more gusto and enthusiasm.

Here are a few examples of sports for different interests:
There are as many different sports as there are people to undertake them. Just to name a few, think about adding to your own exercise regime such things as: walking; skating; tennis; line dancing; hiking; trekking; biking; ballroom dancing; waterskiing; Rollerblading; kayaking; canoeing; yoga; Pilates; softball; volleyball; badminton; judo; karate; racquetball; squash; bowling; water exercises; taebo; flossing your teeth. Water exercise

(Well, flossing may not burn very many calories, but it *is* beneficial.)

I am cautious about recommending running, as I believe the constant pounding on knee cartilages in the long run destroys them. Tennis and hiking may do the same damage, but to a lesser degree depending on how they are done. I have seen very few old runners as most end up with severe knee problems and have to stop running or have knee replacements.

An orthopedist friend who performs many knee replacement surgeries told me that ninety percent of his cases are from runners. He does not recommend that they run after knee replacement. A good friend who shares my opinion of the damage running may do to the body, once said that he had never seen a runner smile while running! If you are a runner please consider this advice and shift to other sports early so as not to damage your cartilages.

Exercise Mission Statement

The goal to aging well is to have a vital functioning system with a strong heart and lungs and good supporting bones and muscles.

Very interesting studies have shown that even at eighty years of age, you can reverse your physical shape from body deterioration. So don't ever use the age card to get out of changing at any point in your life.

It really *is* all in your mind. *Those who think they can't, don't. Those who think they can, do.* It's a choice. You reap only what you sow so make sure your exercise regime is adequate to keep your body in the best condition possible.

The worst thing you can think as you grow older is to say, "you are too old to accomplish an active exercise regime". This creates immediate defeat so keep your thoughts positive in this matter. The more extensive the exercise program, the better your health and well-being will be. You must strive to do both aerobic and body strengthening exercises. Walking "ten miles" at work does not count, although some physical jobs will count, such as farming or construction.

Aerobic exercise is very important in attaining over-all fitness. To strengthen muscles, weight training or resistive exercises should be done. Also important is enhancing balance and equilibrium as this prevents falls and provides better stature and security. Even a sit-down bike is better than nothing, but riding a regular Lance Armstrong upright type of bike is best of course.

User-friendly Exercises

Especially as you grow older, do exercises that will not harm you. Do smooth exercises. Bicycling is a good example of a user-friendly exercise. Ride a two-wheel bike when you can as the exercise workout is very effective and equilibrium and balance can be regained.

Joint-gliding exercises will be easier on your joints. Swimming, skiing, cross-country skiing, biking, and walking with only mild pounding are a few examples. Do different sports, as often one will supplement the other. Beside, it is less boring and more fun to do different activities.

For example, play tennis but also do a good amount of biking. This reinforces your joints by surrounding them with much stronger muscles preventing injuries and deterioration. Upper body strengthening prevents tennis elbows, tendonitis and osteoporosis.

Since constant effort is required to exercise, the rewards are great. Please remember the great importance of exercising in keeping your good health especially in aging. Nothing is more important. Make exercise a priority and you will have no regrets. Even the President of the United States makes time in his busy schedule to participate in a regular exercise regime. Your friends and family will respect any new dedication to your health and you may inspire them to also exercise.

Hyperthermia, Dehydration and Electrolyte Imbalances

It is very important to know the following factors about heat, electrolytes and water as they can be disastrous. The dangers, however, are easily prevented if you know about them. All this becomes an important part of your life if you exercise. Staying well-hydrated is essential for good health and especially so when exercising in hot weather. Water is good but in general should be laced with electrolytes...read on. During exercise you not only lose fluid via sweat, but also via heavy breathing. Muscle activity byproducts are released into the blood and need to be contended with through adequate hydration. The more fluid available, the easier the clean up, the transportation and the elimination of byproducts through the kidneys or sweat. This dilutes byproducts and permits the kidneys to eliminate what is not necessary. Too much fluid or elimination can also be a problem.

Just to give you an idea of the large volumes of water we can lose daily—normally and with heavy exercise. (in milliliters; 1000 ml is a liter, about a quart)

	Normal Temp	Hot Weather	Prolonged Exercises
Lung	350	350	350
Skin	350	350	350
Sweat	100	1400	5000
Urine	1400	1200	500
Feces	100	100	100
Total	2300	3300	6600

From Guyton Textbook of Physiology

Proper hydration will also help prevent hyperthermia, which can be very dangerous and very destructive to your body. This will improve your body's performance by facilitating circulation and transporting oxygen and nutrients into the cells. There are over two-and-a-half million sweat glands that constantly are secreting sweat. Sweat is ninety-nine percent water but it also contains sodium and chloride, salt, and a low concentration of potassium, except during exercise when the muscle releases potassium in the blood and surrounding fluids, increasing the concentration of potassium. The resultant sweat has an increased percentage of potassium, so more is lost in the sweat, thus depleting the muscle of it.

Sweat, which is an important cooling mechanism of your body, obviously needs water. Sweat's evaporation mechanism requires heat, which it draws from the body, thus cooling you down.

One of the major signs of severe dehydration, or hyperthermia as they are often together, is lack of sweat, and not long afterwards urination will stop. In mild dehydration, you may lose four to five percent of body weight, in moderate, six to nine percent, in severe, ten percent or more.

Hot climates are obviously more dangerous. Your body temperature rises proportionally from 98° F to 105° F. Also be cautious of saunas and hot tubs before or after exercising, which could exacerbate the problem multifold.

Athletes who train consistently do not lose excess hydration. Their bodies readjust to control kidney dilution or concentration level, sweat volume and composition and body temperature control. This is one transformation occurring in a body's physiology with constant training. These athletes experience less water and electrolytes loss and have less fat to insulate thus permitting heat loss during exercises. Drink one or two glasses of water before, during, and after serious exercises and, of course, more in lengthy cases.

Potassium
You need salt and potassium (K+) and magnesium (Mg+) in the water you drink to replace sweat.

This is important information for avid athletes. You must understand it. The older we get the more sensitive to these factors we are. Not that we will exercise that strenuously, but in a good tennis match in the sun, we are there!

Very few people seem to know this as evidenced by the fact that many times super tennis stars and marathon runners have cramps during competitions and could even die from potassium loss in sweat. Simple potassium replacement could have averted that severe handicap.

The inside of a muscle cell is high in potassium and magnesium, while the outside of the cell is high in sodium and calcium. Exercise that causes sweating tends to reverse that ratio temporarily. The muscle cell must leach out some potassium outside of its cell into the fluid around the cell, interstitial fluid, and into the blood stream in order to contract. Once the cell relaxes the potassium goes back inside the muscle cell for a further contraction.

If sweating is profuse due to heated environment or to excessive heat in the body from the exercise, it will derive its water and the excess electrolytes from the blood. Thus the sweat become high in sodium but there is huge quantities in the body and is relatively less consequential. It also becomes high in potassium, which depletes the small volume in the blood resulting in very low blood potassium. When the muscle cell needs its potassium for a subsequent contracture, it no longer is available so the muscle has weak contractures and cramps.

The cardiac muscle does the same but individual muscle fibers cramp which cause fibrillation or irregular heart beat, arrhythmias. This is very dangerous, as during fibrillation the amount of oxygen circulating in a body can be reduced by twenty percent. This may also cause a turbulent flow of blood in the coronary arteries, which potentially can result in clotting and causing a heart attack. That is why potassium must be replaced immediately or better still, should never be allowed to progress to this stage. It is speculated that is why young runner dies of heart disease on the trail.

You need 200 to 400 mg or more of potassium replacement. I like Emer'gen-C by Alacer that has sachets containing 200 mg of potassium along with vitamin C, which diluted in water is a good replacement. It also has 60 mg of magnesium. I have no relationship with Alacer other than I use the product as it has a good formula and have had good results. I wonder if the vitamin C in it does not help in a situation of the some inflammation and resultant free-radicals formed in the muscles during exercise.

A can of V8 has about 800 to 900 mg of potassium with some salt, but I find it difficult to drink while exercising. Other sources of potassium are far too weak to replace all that is lost. For example, a banana or sport drink normally has less than 30 mg of potassium. In very warm and humid climates, you may want to substitute table salt with a salt substitute, which is potassium chloride. There are newer sport drinks but I have not analyzed them yet.

After a period of good exercise you may notice that you feel tired, sluggish and start slowing down. Try replenishing potassium and see how quickly your energy will return. I used to think that I was missing carbohydrates when this happened, but now realize that it was potassium, water and some sodium that I needed most. Once I replenished these, my previous high energy level returned. Only on long duration exercises will glycogen deplete and sugar replacements become necessary.

You can take too much potassium so take care not to do this. It is not appropriate to take potassium as a daily supplement, instead it should only be used when there is cause like after exercise, cramping, sweating, or in high heat regions. If you have fluid retention like swollen legs, or if you have kidney problems, be very careful not to take too much or any. Don't go over 1000mg of potassium. Swollen legs may also be a sign that you have taken too much water and/ or potassium already. Excess potassium can also be a problem but is not seen in the normal athlete.

If you take ACE inhibitors such as Captopril, Primivil, Vasotec or Zestril, be careful not to take potassium as this may create accumulation and become dangerous.

If you have kidney problems do not take an excess of potassium.

Sodium

If you lose sodium, hyponatremia, low sodium, may occur. This can mimic hyperthermia or occur with it. It is early heat exhaustion and can be very dangerous. This is most likely caused by drinking *too much* water as the sodium is leached out through the sweat and the urine as the body tries to get rid of the excess water. Urine and sweat always carry electrolytes with the water so the more you sweat the more electrolytes leach out.

So replace the sodium with salty foods or drinks containing sodium. Many of these contain magnesium as a bonus.

Excess sodium (salt) intake will cause swelling because of the fluid retention this initiates. This is one of the causes of high blood pressure. Sodium loss, although important, is probably less important in exercise than potassium loss as it has less impact on the intrinsic skeletal and cardiac muscle function. You can also take too much sodium.

Magnesium

Magnesium is covered in great detail in Chapter Ten and it would be beneficial to review that information.

Hyperthermia (Heat Stroke)

Heat stroke is a fairly common occurrence especially in warm climates or in large heated rooms, such as gyms. The body temperature rises and a chemical revolution occurs in the body when this happens. In high school chemistry lab, when you wanted a chemical reaction to occur, you heated the experiment to greatly accelerate the reaction. Chemical reactions in the body are exactly the same and for this reason the body must maintain a steady temperature with very little variations. The normal temperature is 98.6 F or 37.0 C. The body has a very good regulatory system, a thermostat that always keeps the temperature at this level. There is a thermostat in the brain controlling the system, which will adjust to your environment.

If you live in the desert, you will handle heat better than a Northerner. Arctic Eskimos are much more resilient to cold than Southerners and so on. As you grow older, you have less body temperature control than when you were young, most likely because you do not use it.

We become wimps as we grow older but shouldn't. You can alter that situation by constantly exposing yourself to changing temperatures and readjusting. You lose temperature control just like you lose equilibrium. I believe that it is purely a lack of usage weakening that thermostat. People may have avoided cold and thus lost the capability of adjusting to it.

If over-heated, your body can become seriously damaged. Cells function appropriately at a given temperature and damage occurs to all cells if the temperature rises too high. This is like a mild, medium or severe burn to all cells, damaging them and depending on the level and length of time the overheating occurs, can even cause death.

If you have an infection, the body goes into overdrive and inflammation occurs. To rid the invader, heat is produced by the intense immune mobilizing mechanism.

That overheating is called a fever and if this goes over 106° F can be lethal.

The body usually overheats from too much exposure as in very hot climates, in the mid-day hot sun, from exertion, hot tubs, too much clothing or if too much fat is acting as insulation. High muscle activity produces overheating along with concomitant factors like ambient heat and humidity that increase the metabolism in the body. That in turn affects all chemical reactions, which become quite detrimental to the whole system. Alcohol consumption aggravates the situation in a multitude of ways.

Your cooling down or refrigeration system necessary for you to lose heat is mostly by sweating. Sweat requires heat to evaporate so it draws it from the body thus cooling the body's core temperature. If the environment is too humid, sweat will not evaporate well and thus less or no heat is lost. If you are not well hydrated there will be reduced, or no sweat production and no heat loss.

If the sun hits your skin and heats it, then your body's cooling efforts will not be as efficient. Wear a light clothing or even sunscreen that filters UV rays, a practice that makes a positive difference. If you over-exert, your muscles produce a huge amount of heat so the sweating will not be able to keep up with cooling demands. Sunrays will just aggravate the injury by adding radiant heat with added sunburns. Sun blocking lotions like SPF 25 to 40 will avoid this problem. The body will gradually readjust to this with training.

Don't forget that sweat contains electrolytes like potassium and sodium. We have a large supply of sodium but little of potassium so they must be replaced particularly the potassium as I have mentioned above.

There are three levels of hyperthermia:

Mild Heat Exertion
Body temperature is slightly higher and you feel tired with no energy and are red faced or flushed. There is a three to four percent loss of your body weight. *Treatment*: Hydrate, replace potassium and sodium, stop exercising, take a cold bath or a dip in the pool.

Heat Exhaustion
Extensive fluid loss, gradual loss of ability to sweat, nausea, vomiting, syncope (loss of consciousness), fainting, pale grey clammy skin, weak slow pulse, low blood pressure, faintness

with up to five to eight percent of body weight loss. *Treatment*: Put your head down, replace fluid and electrolytes. Take salt and potassium and take a cold bath or dip in the pool and stay out of the sun of course.

Heatstroke

The body has a failure of heat loss as described above. Body temperature soars up to 104 - 106 F (40 C). Headaches, nausea and vomiting, weakness, dizziness, and even loss of consciousness are the classic beginning symptoms with hot, red dry skin, little or *no sweating*, rapid pulse, high temperature and over ten percent body weight loss. *This is a life-threatening situation* so do not be in denial. *Treatment*: Immediate cooling in cold water or ice and hospitalization to re-hydrate and receive the proper electrolytes. Even life support maneuvers may be required.

A good friend related to me that one day during tennis in the sun and dry heat became nauseated, tired, weak and gradually stopped sweating during a hard tennis match but continued playing despite some nausea. He felt sick for a whole week afterwards.

I think he was lucky not to have more damage and that he skirted tragedy unbeknownst to him. Had he been aware of the danger he was in, he would not have skirted possible tragedy but rather cooled himself in a pool, drank lots of water and replaced potassium.

Prevention of hyperthermia

Drink adequate *fluids with electrolytes*. Carbohydrates will not contribute to this. Use *sunscreen* generously or wear light clothing as this cuts the sun's heat absorption substantially. The Bedouins move about the desert with heavy cover-up clothing and even though this may seem hotter than less clothing it actually acts as protection from the relentless sun. *Do not expose too much skin to the sun.* Instead, cover up as much as possible. Increase your resistance by graduated increases in exposure. The function of a suntan is protective if it has been acquired very gradually without ever getting sunburns.

Do *not overexercise* in a hot environment, especially if you have not yet acclimatized to the warmer temperatures. Sweating will dehydrate you much faster than you think. Learn your limits and be aware of what your body is telling you.

Maintain a high awareness about hyperthermia and dehydration in any form. Do not ignore the severity of this dangerous occurrence.

Go and sit in a car or building with air conditioning for a period of time.

Lactic Acid

Lactic acid is a by-product of the chemical reactions that permit the muscle fiber to contract. The more contractions there are, as with heavy exercises, the more lactic acid is produced and excreted both on the inside and outside of the muscle fiber. This raises the acidity level in and out of the cell proportional to the severity and length of exercise. The increased level of acidity in the muscle and in the fluid around it weakens its chemical and electrical reactions causing contractions. This makes you feel weak and tired and can cause a burning sensation in the muscles. Ultimately the blood becomes acidic, resulting in a feeling of extreme fatigue.

Lactic acid is produced when oxygen levels are low as in lengthy or sprinting exercises or in low aerobic capacity. Lactic acid forms when the maximal capacity of the muscle has been reached. If your muscle is weak it easily reaches that level. The raised acidity of the cell environment will bring some inflammatory reaction which is the pain experienced after working out the first few times. Gradually your body adjusts with better aerobic capacity (more oxygen) and less formation of lactic acid. Some of the pain experienced the day after exercise is caused by lactic acid around the muscle cell. If you exercise the following day despite the achy-breaky feeling, you will increase the blood supply and reabsorb the lactic acid much faster. Then you can continue the exercise routine and suffer less.

The pain you experience after exercise, especially at the beginning of your training or if you use different muscles in different sport, can also be caused by micro tears to muscles and to a lesser degree to tendons and ligaments. This is an excessive use of muscles and tendons that are weaker than the demand imposed on them. The stronger the muscles become, the less this occurs.

In other words, the more gradual the exercise capacity, the fewer injuries and lactic acid and the less chronic pain will occur. Ruptured muscles and tendons occur when a structure is weaker than the sudden increased demand imposed. If you impose a one thousand pound weight to a five hundred pound. capacity cable, it will never hold the weight. The same is true of tendons and muscles. It is an important part of the mechanism of injury in tendonitis, in tennis elbow and with carpal tunnels plantar fasciitis, and Achilles tendonitis.

Cramps

Cramps are a muscle spasm or painful contraction usually caused by some form of irritation inside the muscle fiber due to inappropriate levels of electrolytes, blood supply, oxygen, nutrition, inflammation or drugs (sometimes statins as an example). They hurt and are often in the legs or in the back muscles. They feel like painful knots in the muscles.

Probably the most common cause of cramps is a *potassium deficiency* in the muscle fiber. If you awaken at night with cramps after fairly good exercise or after a hot day, you are probably low on potassium for the reasons described above and need to replace the potassium. This always works for me and for many friends who follow this advice. You will need 400 to 500mg and it will take thirty minutes to absorb in your system to relieve the cramp. Again I suggest Emer'gen-C as each sachet has 200 mg of potassium and you can get them in natural food stores. Sport drinks have only 30 mg, which is too little potassium. 8 oz of V-8 has 800 mg.

Cramps can also be the result of weak muscles or inflammation around the muscle caused by micro tears, inadequate blood supply or excessive use causing lactic acid to irritate the muscle fiber. That is the reason bodybuilding for Charles Atlas had so many problems with cramping as his big muscles were not supported by a proportional growth of blood supply.

Again, if you demand too much of a weak muscle, the muscle will go on strike ...that's a cramp.

Blood supply deficiency, one reason for cramps, can be caused either by vasoconstriction due to cold, smoking, cocaine use or outright vessel obstruction problems such as arteriosclerosis, diabetes or a vascular supply not adequately developed due to lack of aerobic training.

For example, if your legs are cold at night in bed, the vessels are constricted by the cold and your blood supply in the legs does not have the benefit of gravity, so you get cramps. If you swim after a meal, the majority of your body's blood supply is busy digesting and the muscles are starved of blood supply and thus can complain with a cramp. The same is true if you exercise just after a meal and experience how inefficient the body muscles have become. If that occurs please see a physician, as this can be serious.

Cramps are caused during a heat stroke. They are very often associated with over-heating or mild to moderate hyperthermia. That is a potassium deficiency. Muscle fibers will only function well in a very narrow range of body temperature, and too low or too high a temperature will cause malfunctions.

Irritated nerves can also fire too many impulses to the muscle. An example would be back muscles from a nerve irritated by a herniated disk, or carpal tunnel with muscle cramps in the hand. Even here potassium can be helpful.

Statin drugs such as Mevacor, Lipitor, Prevacol, and to a lesser degree Zocor, may in some, albeit rare, instances cause myolysis, which is a breakdown of muscles. In essence, if a patient on a statin drug starts getting serious muscle cramps for no apparent reason and has tried to supplement potassium and magnesium with no result, that person should stop taking cholesterol-lowering medication.

These medications can cause muscle aching, cramps and outright breakdown of the muscles with bleeding, which will show as ecchymoses or black and blue marks. You must stop the medication and see your physician, who will likely change the statin drug to another one.

If your cholesterol is high, it *is* imperative to lower it, but if such complications occur you will have to find alternatives to statins. In the bodybuilding world, the rumor is that you cannot develop well if you are on statin drugs as they alter the muscle function. I have not seen any medical articles on this, but the complication does occur.

If cramps occur often despite potassium and magnesium supplements, see a physician. Quinine is often prescribed but not with great success. There are also muscle relaxants that can be used. After these steps, an investigation of the blood supply may be required to find the cause.

Conclusion
Your own personal exercise regime can only be determined and followed by you. There may be friends who join you in some of the pursuits but only you are ultimately responsible for the initiation and endurance of your exercise program. Make it a good one! You will love the shape you can be in!

It will improve your quality of life by allowing you to meet many nice people. I live in a community that has such congenial people that I would play tennis *just* to be with them.

The exercise tennis provides is another reward for being with these friends who have added a total new dimension to my life.

My life is far richer as a result of meeting all these delightful, goofy and supportive exercising people. It satisfies curiosity. Exploring your environment and satisfying your curiosity by climbing, kayaking biking and is always pleasurable.

Those who abandon their dreams of staying healthy will often try to discourage yours.

Old Chinese proverb from author of *Almond Cookie*

Personal comfort is not the only thing worth seeking.

Lance Armstrong

CHAPTER SEVEN

Essential Nutrition

Please understand the following concept: you will eat an average of a thousand meals a year all your life.

The function of food is crucial to feed your cells for proper functioning and health in all circumstances such as growth, stress, high demand of work and exercise. It is by far the most important thing that you will do for yourself if you understand it and if you feed the proper ingredients to you body. Yet if you feed junk don't expect good results. So why not spend precious time knowing what the most influential factor to proper aging is along with exercise?. Why would you ever do something three times a day all your life and know very little about it?

Why would you trust anybody who has a product to sell or a splash to make in a magazine, journal, on the radio or television—most often pseudo-experts who read one or two articles, become "experts," and feel they can teach you the A-B-Cs of feeding your body to stay healthy?

Sure, I fall in this category you will say! But I have read books and articles avidly for ten years to understand what to feed my body. The flabbergasting revelations shocked me into reality. Really, all I had to do is read and learn and understand. Why don't you do that? You are the most precious person you know. This should be but a starter that will change you life, I promise.

Food was particularly the major factor in the production of this book since it was always a prominent problem in my life as it is in the lives of many of us. I played a lot of sports as a youth and ate to satisfy my ravenous appetite and high energy needs during that period but in the process developed bad habits that made me eat anything, anytime I wanted. Of course I kept the habit of eating too much and gained weight. I figured I could diet it off anytime I wanted...Ah! It did not turn out to be so.

I had high cholesterol, maybe familial. Then Dr. Dean Ornish published the "fat-free diet" that was going to save my life and reduce this high cholesterol. To accentuate all of this, I stopped smoking on my birthday at forty, as a birthday present to myself.

From that moment on I was totally and continually hungry. I was a busy surgeon and ate anything and everything I could put my hands on since I was so ravenous. This meant I was eating mostly carbohydrates as junk foods full of carbs as available and handy foods. I gained weight and did not understand why carbs more than fats did that to me. After all they did have fewer calories per grams than fats. (Carbs four, Proteins four, Fats nine).

Well after my heart operation I knew there was something wrong with that premise. I immediately started to research foods. Obviously I had been doing the wrong thing and my body was diseased from it. That is when it dawn on me that I ate one thousand meals a year and I knew very little about this most important factor in my life.

It was Dr. Atkins who opened my eyes and mind with his explanation of the high spikes of insulin caused by the absorption of simple sugars and starches. Then I learned that insulin was a storage hormone: Bingo!

That meant that all the excess carbs that we have eaten so much of are stored in fat cells (as triglycerides). So fat was not the culprit, carbs were. Then I studied what happens to food when absorbed in our system. I reviewed what our cells are made of and consequently what they needed to survive in health.

I hope this chapter will help you, like it did me.

Fat Free vs. Atkins diets

Let's look at these two diets and compare them with an open mind. They are the key diets that shaped the last thirty to thirty-five years of foods. The fat free diet definitely did lower the cholesterol levels but it ended up being a major problem with obesity and its consequences. Though many people oppose Dr. Robert Atkins I have found many concepts in his book that suddenly made me realize that sugar and the insulin rise associated with it was a major harm to our body and the culprit of most of our woes! The concept he emitted was very logical and helped me both in my professional and personal life.

The Fat Free Diet;

About three decades ago Dr. Dean Ornish started promoting fat free diets in an attempt to reduce cholesterol and heart diseases. His intentions were excellent and he did attain his objective of reducing cholesterol and heart disease. I know he could not have anticipated the serious consequences that it would bring about: the obesity and diabetes epidemic. This diet advocated eating no or very little fat and very little meat since red meat contained saturated fats. It advocated eating low fat meats like chicken and fish and otherwise mostly carbs as vegetables but mostly in the forms of sugars and starches.

Interestingly enough, the fat-free diet became popular and along with it a resurgence of some infectious disease, various degenerative diseases, obesity, and diabetes. This diet, while promoting a low fat intake, inadvertently promoted a low meat diet, since mostly red meats contained a lot of fat.

It thus re-established the whole cycle of a predominantly high carbohydrate diet like that found at the beginning of the century, before meat became generally affordable through proper husbandry, *but much worse.*

174

The industry added their easily accessible prepared foods, mostly made of very high sugar, starches and preservatives, and then shamelessly promoted them as healthy fat free food with massive, invasive advertising techniques. That easily got us *addicted to carbs* and they had us hooked: the carbohydrates addiction with its constant cycle of hunger that is insatiable. It also created a very high diabetic epidemic that I will explain later.

At present the American diet consists of about eighty to eighty-five percent carbohydrates. It is not what Dr Ornish wanted, but because of the pathway of least resistance, encouraged by the food industry and the media, it ended up that way. This is very close to being a vegetarian diet, but worse as it emphasizes high glycemic carbohydrates, which are the sugars and starches of pastas and breads that cause such *high levels of insulin* when absorbed. I will explain this further in this chapter as *it is one of the most important concepts for you to learn* in the food consumption knowledge. This realization is what suddenly made me understand what I was doing wrong and how to correct it.

The Atkins Diet;
Dr. Robert Atkins brought us back on the right track to the path of a balanced diet particularly including meats and fish. Of course he had to emphasized meat and fish since he had to shock us out of the fat free craze. If you read his first book carefully and totally you'll see that he advocated vegetable and grains along with the meat and fat and fish. The fact is that a good balanced diet is still the most epidemiologically ideal diet to maintain. Dr. Atkins advocated a weight loss diet that included intense proteins and fats; the first stage is two to four weeks.

The maintenance diet in the second stage involves more of balanced diet with very little high glycemic index, sugars and starches. The first concept he explained was indeed that relationship between carbohydrates and insulin. I will explain this further beginning on page 189.

The most important message I believe Dr. Atkins advocated was the fact that a diet high in carbohydrates was very damaging to the body, creating havoc by totally skyrocketing insulin levels and loading the body with excess, unused carbohydrates that are, after all, only a fuel not a building block.

That created the constant hunger cycle, a total loading of our fat cells with sugars (triglycerides) and eventually a resistance of the cells to constantly high levels of insulin (causing diabetes). A more balanced diet toned down the high levels of insulin. The startup Atkins diet is excellent to shock you out of that dreaded predominantly carbohydrate fat free diet. A steady diet of balanced nutrition is ultimately best...in moderation of course.

Balanced Diet

So then why am I advocating a balanced diet? Because it will furnish all the very varied ingredients the body needs to nourish itself totally.

The trend is fortunately changing back to the more balanced diets. There are many diets now that fundamentally tried to balance food intake In *The Zone* Dr B. Spears illustrated the importance of fats, particularly good fats Other good books to read on this subject include *Carbohydrate Addicts*, *The Perricone Prescription*, *The South Beach Diet* and *Get with the Program*.

They all emphasize certain nutrients in a more or less balanced diet. But all of them seem to ignore certain food products and I believe that is a failure. All of them are weight loss diets. And most sell a product.

A balanced diet must be maintained for proper body growth or maintenance as we get older. The body needs *all* the proper nutrients to develop or repair all its components. Sudden elimination of foods with crash diets and then, gorging on those same foods after the crash diet is confusing to the body and further alters the inner manufacturing processes of cells. To maintain good health, you must maintain a constant lifestyle of nutrition and exercise, not a lifestyle of ups and down of weight depending on your mood. You have to take the bull by the horns and will power yourself out of these very damaging cycles. If you eat a little bit too much everyday, will it not accumulate and ultimately you discover you are fat...and can't get rid of it.

What is food?

Let's go back to the basic premises: Food is predominantly two things: a *building material* and secondly a *fuel* for the body. If you do not eat the appropriate foods, the building materials, your body will not grow normally, will not maintain top performance, will not ward off noxious invaders and will not be capable to reconstruct or protect itself during injury, disease or natural aging deterioration. If you do not give it appropriate fuel it will stop dead in its tracks. You will not feel it for years to come, as these are cumulative damages.

If you want to operate your car to run dependably you have to do constant maintenance You need to do preventative maintenance with new oil and grease and water in the cooling system. When parts break down due to wear and tear or accidents, you have to replace them, not with fuel but rather with metal parts, rubber, paint, glass, plastic, and so on. You need fuel only as an energy source.

A gasoline-engine needs gasoline to function properly and it will not operate adequately with diesel, alcohol, or a cord of wood. In this same manner, it is impossible to feed your body edibles like junk food and expect to maintain the body's proper function of feeling good and energetic, fighting disease and aging more slowly.

You must have a clear understanding of this important concept that individual food categories do not do everything. Some are meant to build cells when they grow, reproduce or are damaged. That is predominantly proteins and fats. Yet we need fuel in order to energize the cells, and that is mostly carbohydrates. There is some crossover on these functions, but the greater percentage is as stated. And then there is a need for all kinds of other additives like phytochemicals and vitamins. If you eat of everything as in a balanced diet, you will be more likely to provide all these ingredients available to use.

Various components of food

Proteins

When nutrients enter the gut they break down proteins into their smallest components, which are amino acids. The gut will not absorb proteins any other way. These are the basic bricks and mortar that you need. Many vegetables contain some proteins but the percentage is minimal. Large quantities are needed to build or rebuild the body. The quality is not provided in vegetables as all the essential amino acids necessary are not present.

Occasionally in abnormal situations the gut's lining is defective and will absorb longer chains of amino acids and create havoc in the body in the form of an immune reaction such as for instance rheumatoid arthritis and celiac disease.

To build healthy brain cells, muscles, ligaments, cartilage, blood cells, immune cells, immune proteins, bones matrix and any other cells in the body, you need various amounts and different qualities of proteins as building blocks. The major component of the cell is proteins as I have mentioned. Proteins cannot be replaced by, or totally manufactured from other components.

By the way if one takes growth hormone by mouth, as an example, none of that growth hormone will be absorbed, only its amino acids, once broken down by the gut lining. This is the reason that one cannot take that hormone and many others like it by mouth.

Since proteins are the major element of our bodies, besides water and calcium, they are a very important factor in nutrition since you must provide the proper nutrients to build or replace them. Your manufacturing processes will occasionally take other materials such as carbohydrates and change them into proteins but it is an incompetent system used only in necessity when other, proper nutrients are not available. That system does not produce all the amino acids necessary and very few essential ones.

These are the basic bricks and mortar that cells need. Many vegetables contain some proteins but the percentage is minimal considering large quantities needed to build with, and the quality is not providing all the essential amino acids necessary. Another interesting fact is that Eskimo meat eaters did not get scurvy. The animal meat provided enough vitamin C to prevent scurvy.

I cannot understand people not replacing the most important ingredient for the reconstruction of the body. It defies my reasoning that this simple fact is totally ignored. Unless it is because people do not understand why and how proteins are of utmost importance in a diet to construct or reconstruct the body.

There are essential amino acids and non-essential ones. If a diet lacks essential amino acids, there will inevitably be a failure of a system, and sooner or later life will not be sustained.

The body cannot fabricate the essential amino acids. They must be ingested as food. Without them the basic fundamentals for cell creation replacement and repair are missing, *essentially the basis of life itself.* One-half of the dry weight of a body is protein so it is essential to provide that crucial component adequately.

These are the twenty amino acids. Nine of them are essential. I name them only to make you aware that they are the most important nutrients and very few references are made of them. You do not see them listed on food packages, but you must recognize the necessity for them.

Essential	Non-essential
Leucine	Aspartic acid
Isoleucine	Asparagine
Valine	Glutamic Acid
Phenylalanine	Glutamine
Tryptophan	Glycine
Hystidine	Alanine
Threonine	Serine
Methionine	Cysteine
Lysine	Proline
	Arginine
	Tyrosine

All these amino acids are necessary. The body cannot build some of them efficiently, or at all. They must be provided in the diet. It is almost a miracle that some Americans survive or are not bombarded with life-threatening diseases when one considers the diets most maintain. Many good minds, such as Drs. Atkins, Sinatra, Klatz, and Goldman, Sears and Eades, to name a few, strongly believe that many ills are caused by a deficient diet. It is easy to understand their beliefs when the basics of nutrition are analyzed.

Considering all this, you must supply your diet with these fundamental necessities, and when the need presents itself, must also supplement with specific nutrients. For example, during exercise food is needed for over-used muscles and is depleted of components like glutamine, carnitine, potassium and glucose. *These must be replaced.* Much of this has been known for years but has not penetrated public knowledge, and for that matter, much of the medical profession. Certain enthusiasts of other ideology may have also distracted from these basics.

Fats
I want to explain fats to you since they have such a bad rap from all the years of bad publicity that is not deserved. If you

180

get to know them you will have more respect of them and eat them appropriately. They are absolutely necessary in the right quality and quantity.

Fats are a second food category consisting mostly of *essential fatty acids* (the smallest building blocks of all fats and *eiconasoids).*

They are a very important building block for the body. Their functions are not as involved with energy supply, if at all.

The American public has developed a phobic aversion to this food category because of years of brainwashing with the fat free culture. That aversion is very unhealthy.

Fats (Lipids) are very important for proper nutrition. *The Pericone Prescription* and *The Zone* are two good sources for information on this.

What is the function of fat in the body?

- The *cell membrane* is made of proteins and lipids (lipoprotein) and both are required to build a specialized membrane actively transporting nutrients into the cytoplasm, the inner sanctum of the cell.

- Inside cells, fat are the building block for all the important *eicosanoids*, discussed below which are the inner cell's hormones.

- Fats are also necessary to transport fat-soluble vitamins like A, D, and E.

- These building blocks of fat molecules are also necessary for the creation of brain cells and important for their insulation. Many nerve cells are surrounded by an insulating fat layer called the *myelin sheath*, which is essential in the transport and regulation of electricity as nerve impulses in the brain and all nerve cells going to the body. The important ones here are mostly Omega-3 and Omega -6 which eventually become good eicosanoids. By the way *the Brain is eighty percent fat by weight.*

- Fat is necessary for the production of all hormones like sex hormones, paracrine hormones, the ecosanoids. *Hormones necessitate cholesterol for their syntheses and cholesterol is fat of course.*

- The body can synthesize 'fat' from carbohydrates, but not in exactly the quantity and quality necessary. The 'fats' derived from carbohydrates are mostly triglycerides and are eighty-five percent of the 'fats' stored in the fat cells. They are not used for the production of hormones, ecosanoids, bile, immune cells etc. They may, according to research, even damage the inner lining of the vessels.

- Bile is derived from cholesterol that the liver transforms into cholic acid, one of the important digestive fluids whose function is to absorb fat. Eighty percent of cholesterol becomes cholic acid or bile.

- The mammary gland needs the proper fat to create milk needed during breast-feeding. This is to feed the growing baby thus has to be the most sophisticated food in the world.

- The sebaceous glands constantly secrete oil to lubricate skin otherwise it would become leather.

- Fat is also a source of energy and is stored for use in time of need like during long exercises or hunger spells and hibernation. So as such are not used very often. I question this fact since bears eat very little fat, but mostly berry before they hibernate. So it would be triglycerides that are used for energy.

- In the right amounts subcutaneous fat is an insulator and a shock absorber and so can be around organs for this reason. Obviously too much fat in this area can become a real handicap.

- Fat also adds taste to food and has satiety value, giving hunger satisfaction when eaten, and not promoting hunger between meals thus reducing total calorie intake. Diets without fat cannot be successful for that very reason.

- Butterfat is directly absorbed into the blood and then used as building blocks. The other fats are absorbed in another system, the lymphatic system, to be transformed into specialized fats.

To quote Dr. Barry Sears in *The Zone*, "Nowhere in the world is fat phobia more extreme than in the United States and nowhere else are people fatter. While Americans think of carbohydrates as the savior of mankind, fat is considered the messenger of doom. Dietary fat does not make you fat; you have to eat fat to lose weight."

What are the types of fat?

Ecosanoids

Eicosanoids are very important factors as inner cell hormone. They are called paracrine hormones and are present in all living matter. They regulate all cell functions and coordinate all, or nearly all, cell interactions in the body. Since they are produced inside the cells and do not circulate in the blood stream, they cannot be measured by standard means. Special equipment called micro-bioassays had to be developed to find and analyze them. Dr Barry Sears has done a fair amount of this research on eicosanoids and calls them the most powerful biological agents known to man. So we can't just ignore them just because they are not well known to us.

They play a very important role in inflammation and the immune system. It is essential that you know they exist and have such an important role in your well-being.

Just know that there are two types, and one is good and the other not.

Type One *are beneficial*. They lower high blood pressure, prevent clotting in the vessels improve immune response, act as an anti-inflammatory, and so on. They are also produced when the alpha-omega 3-6- fatty acids are absorbed and when there is a *low ingestion of carbohydrates (thus a low level of insulin)* and a high percentage of fats and proteins in a diet. They come mostly from fatty fish like salmon mackerel, bluefish etc.

By the way, new studies show that if we feed fatty fish that contain alpha omega-3 fatty acids, the producers of good ecosanoids, to depressed people we are very successful in pulling patients out of their depression.

Type Two, *the "bad" eicosanoids*, are, in essence, the reverse of type one,. or the yin and the yang.

They are produced by the absorption of alpha linoleic acids. A high level of carbohydrates will necessitate a high level of insulin, and will tend to cause them. Transfats or partially hydrogenated fat will also produce the linoleic acids and are the worst offenders.

Saturated and Hydrogenated Fats

Saturated fats hold all the hydrogen they can carry. In general they are animal fats They hold up well at high temperatures and are used in frying. They produce cholesterol when absorbed so should *not be taken excessively*. Although we need cholesterol, very high quantities can be dangerous as they become oxidized and act like free-radicals. Fats in this group are *butterfat, animal fats, palm and coconut oil and all hydrogenated vegetable oils as present in most prepared foods.*

Probably all fat that gets heated such as during frying becomes hydrogenated and become trans-fats that will produce free-radicals and bad eiconasoids thus harmful. Fats that are hydrogenated by the manufacturers as this process hardens fat so it can be used in margarines shortening and all processed foods. Ordinary fats, non saturated are destroyed by heat, becoming hydrogenated or aliphatic, trans-fats. Of course, excess fat intake will create high levels of cholesterol but please understand that only excessive amounts are damaging. A balanced amount is necessary. So eating meat, whether red or white, is necessary to a balanced diet to furnish the appropriate amounts of proteins.

I know that meat of any kind, especially red meat, gets a bad rap since it contains "all kinds of bad fats." But these bad fats are necessary, although not in *excess.* Just avoid indulging in excessively fatty meats. Rather, eat lean red meats in moderate quantities. Saturated fats tend to revert as good eicosanoids. They are the sole providers for the construction of endocrine hormones. For that reason, they should not be shunned, but intake monitored.

Partially Hydrogenated Fats
Partially hydrogenated fats are not totally satisfied with hydrogen. They are less likely to form cholesterol unless they are totally hydrogenated, which stabilizes and hardens them. They are present in *safflower, sunflower, corn and soy oil.* They are also found in many processed foods. They tend to form bad eicosanoids.

Monosaturated Fats
Because they are susceptible to oxygenation, Monosaturated fats tend to become rancid faster and are more liquid. They are thus less used in processed foods as they deteriorate faster and are not solid. They produce less total cholesterol and more of the better cholesterol fraction, HDL. They are found in *olive, peanut, cottonseed oil, canola oil and avocados.*

Transfats
Transfats are primarily the hydrogenated oils. We use hydrogenated oils to harden them and to prevent them from

becoming rancid. Most margarine and processed foods contain them. They tend to create free-radicals, are very harmful to chemical reactions in the cells, and are cumulative in the long run, and should be avoided. They revert as bad eicosanoids in the body, so they should be shunned completely. Because they produce free-radicals, they are far more dangerous as a cause of heart disease through vessel damage. For that reason you are better off eating real butter in reasonable quantities than hydrogenated oils or fats in margarine. All fried foods have transfats since most oils revert to transfats when cooked with a few exceptions such as olive oil, sesame oil and grape seed oil.

An interesting fact is that they were developed to prevent heart disease by replacing animal saturated fats in butter, but today we know that they are far more likely to cause heart problems than act as preventative. Thus fats in processed foods increase LDLs, reduce HDLs and produce detrimental free-radicals. Transfats have to be one of the major damaging substances humans ingest, especially since they consume such large quantities. Combination products such as Smart Balance have no transfats.

Cholesterol

When some fats are absorbed, mostly the saturated fats, they are immediately brought to the liver, which produces cholesterol and then transforms eighty percent of it as cholic acid, which in essence is bile. This bile is necessary to digest fats in the small bowel. The rest of the cholesterol is used for cell membrane construction, hormone production, and the brain, which requires a huge amount. Remember that the brain is seventy-five to eighty percent fat and absolutely needs it to function well. There are proportionately far more cell membrane in a brain cell than in a regular cell.

Why is cholesterol bad? First of all, cholesterol is not bad. The HDL is beneficial and does not harm vessels. Secondly, LDL, the bad cholesterol has two factions: on is oxidized thus can act as a free radical in the body, particularly in the vessels. This is where its bad reputation comes from. It actually reacts in cooperation with other chemicals in the blood. Only the remaining excess is in circulation and can be deposited in vessels and protrude in the vessel to obstruct its lumen. Thus very high LDL should be shunned.

Parallel to this knowledge is the new belief now that arteriosclerosis is not caused entirely by high cholesterol blood levels. There has to be damage done to the arterial walls by other factors. Research has shown that certain deficiencies in foods like proteins, fats or minerals plus low levels of potassium, high levels of insulin, toxins, nitrites, low potassium and radiation and so on *are the cause of this* damage to the arteries. It then becomes *inflamed and only then it loads up with cholesterol and calcium*. Only then does cholesterol and eventually calcium deposit themselves in the walls of the arteries and become an obstructive factor to the circulation.

Thus the primary factor for arteriosclerosis is not high cholesterol but rather the damage to the arterial walls creating a nidus for this deposition of cholesterol. The lack of appropriate nutrition that should deprive all the building blocks of proteins, fats, minerals and vitamins, to the arteries is the factors causing the blood vessel damage, and cholesterol is but an opportunist invader

There is no doubt that an excessively high cholesterol level by itself is damaging but it is not the primary factor as cholesterol does not by itself damage the vessels and if it does it is only one of the factors responsible for the damage.

Dr. Steve Sinatra reminds us that fifty percent of people having heart attacks have normal or low cholesterol blood levels.

Carbohydrates

They are fast-absorbing, high glycemic index carbohydrates and slow-absorbing low glycemic index carbohydrates such as green vegetables. Carbohydrates are not only sugars and starches, but also vegetables and fruits.

Sugars are simple carbohydrates and consist of one or two molecules like sucrose and fructose in white sugar. They are easily absorbed by the gut. They are table sugars of all sorts, honey corn syrup, fruits, molasses, etc. Some fruits have some fiber content but all are high in sugars and please don't kid yourselves about this.

Starches are made of thousands of these simple molecules and are also easily absorbed. They include pastas, breads, corns and cereals.

White vegetables are mostly starches such as potatoes, corn and rice. Green vegetables are more complex since they contain cellulose fibers which make them more difficult, and thus much slower, to absorb. You will see this in flatter the insulin curve later in this chapter. The fibers have hundreds of thousands of these molecules. Humans cannot process this cellulose fiber in their small bowel thus fiber becomes bulk in the large gut that facilitates the elimination of our stools. This is believed to lessen cancer of the colon by speeding the elimination out of the gut. Cows need two stomachs and re-chewing 'their cud' to be able to absorb these cellulose fibers. Some vegetables do have proteins like all sorts of beans and nuts, but they do not have all the proteins necessary for the body.

It is easier to understand carbohydrates if you think of them as links in a chain.

- *Monosaccharide:* One link is simple sugars such as glucose. Honey, fructose, corn syrup, lactose in milk.
- *Disaccharides:* are refined sugars with two links as in table sugar, sucrose.
- *Polysaccharides:* 10 to 20,000 links of these make up glycogen inside the blood for storage, starches like pasta and breads, and white vegetables like potatoes, corn and rice.

- *Cellulose* whose many and complex links are in the hundreds of thousands. We refer to them as 'fiber' in food and is very difficult for the body to absorb. Most other vegetables called *green or cruciate* are in this category.

Glycemic Index

The High Glycemic index is the capability of a carbohydrate to be easily absorbed by the gut into the blood and usually is a simple sugar. Put in another manner, this determines whether the sugar is promptly absorbed to immediately produce a high blood sugar, which promotes immediately high insulin levels. They are not building materials. They are fuel for the cells. They are the sugars, pastas and white vegetable. *All* prepared foods whether they are hotdogs or doughnuts have them.

The *low glycemic index* is the *complex carbohydrates.* They are slowly absorbed by our gut.

Green and other vegetables are essentially low glycemic index as they are absorbed much slower and incompletely mostly because of the high amount of indigestible fiber and the low proportion of absorbable carbohydrates. Conversely a much lower and slower glucose blood levels occurs and concurrently insulin. See the charts on pages 192 and 193.

All carbohydrates must be broken down into one link to be absorbed. Once in the blood stream, they all are transformed to predominantly glucose, the standard sugar to be distributed by insulin to the various cells in the mitochondria for energy. Once they are filled, they are stored as glycogen for future use. The excess is then deposited as triglycerides in fat cells by insulin.

Starches are pure sugar in longer chains and relatively easy to absorb and greatly elevate the blood glucose levels.

Vegetables are mostly composed of cellulose fiber and starches, which are far more difficult for the gut to break down, and thus are absorbed slowly. Some of the fibers are not broken down at all and create bulk in the bowel for proper elimination as I have mentioned. Vegetables also provide a myriad of beneficial phytochemicals, the good hormones of vegetables.

Remember, carbohydrates are not building blocks but rather are only fuel for the energy furnaces, the mitochondria in all cells.

On a side note, the mild consumption of alcohol, which is a pure simple carbohydrate, at three to five drinks per week seems to reduce diabetic incidence. Only five percent of obese people who drink moderately get diabetes. This connection has not yet been explained but the statistics show this to be true. Of course, if you drink too much it will greatly increase calories, increase free-radicals and cause severe liver damage.

What are we feeding ourselves?
If you do not eat the appropriate foods, your body will not grow normally, will not maintain top performance, will not ward off noxious invaders and will not be capable to reconstruct or protect itself during injury, disease or natural aging deterioration.

If you operate your car to run dependably, you need fuel as an energy source and oil to permit the parts to work smoothly and not prematurely wear out. A gasoline-engine needs gasoline to function properly and it will not operate adequately with diesel, alcohol, or a chord of wood. But if you have defective parts due to wear and tear you need new fenders, pistons, axles, not gas to rebuild it.

In this same manner, it is impossible to feed your body edibles like junk food which are mostly carbohydrates and transfats *and expect to maintain the body's proper function of feeling good and energetic, fighting disease and aging more slowly.* Remember that cells are made of seventy to eighty-five percent water, twenty percent proteins, two to four percent fat and very little carbohydrates, about one or two percent or less.

190

With very few exceptions, carbohydrates are used primarily as fuel and not as building materials. There is no question that carbohydrates are crucial as energy suppliers but that does not mean that humans need huge quantities. The brain needs this glucose as witnessed by the mental sluggishness before a meal when you are hypoglycemic.

Human metabolism requires multiple building blocks to construct cells, the foundation of the whole living organism. These come from all three categories of foods--fats, carbohydrates and proteins of all kinds plus water, electrolytes and supplements. Human bodies, unlike herbivorous animals, do not have the manufacturing capability to produce all necessary proteins, fats and carbohydrates and supplements so the entire range of foods are necessary to provide nutrients to produce all essential fatty acids, essential amino acids, some carbohydrate molecules and all vitamins, supplements and enzymes.

Proteins and fats cannot be obtained solely from vegetables; they also come from animal meats. Remember that animals manufacture all the necessary ingredients for their good health and that is also available in their meat that humans eat. There are at least two amino acids, *lysine and methionine,* provided by a diet especially of red meat that are crucial to heart and skeletal muscle function and also to the immune system. These are not available in other foods and are found in carnitines. It would not surprise me if more amino acids are missing beside these two.

Being omnivorous means that human cells need *all* the nutrients as building blocks, not just a few of them. A good balanced diet is the best approach as this does include most of the right ingredients. However, some vitamins and antioxidants need to be supplemented and this is discussed in Chapter Ten with more depth. Remember, an aging body requires more proper building blocks to constantly renew itself has little or no reserve to rely on as do youthful bodies

What happens when the food is absorbed?

Insulin and Carbohydrates

When food enters the G.I. tract, components get broken down into the smallest parts of the molecules. For example, if a protein is ingested the gut will break it down into amino acids which are then absorbed into the blood vessels and sent to the processing plant., the liver. It then distributes it to the various parts of the body. It also manufactures specialized proteins as necessary.

Fats get broken down to fatty acids and carbohydrates into the simple sugar glucose. At this point, insulin, a facilitating and storage hormone, is secreted by the pancreas to process the nutrients entering the blood stream. Fats and proteins require much less insulin secretion than sugars.

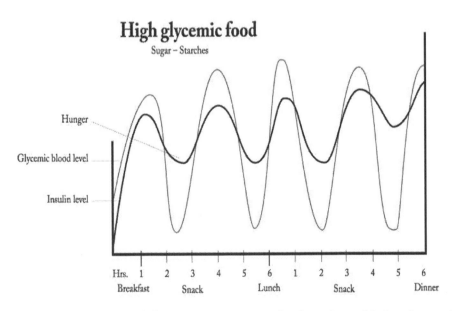

Insulin is secreted far more aggressively when high glycemic index carbohydrates, sugars and starches are ingested. The insulin level rises to high levels proportional to the amount of sugar levels. The sugar gives a temporary spurt of energy. As

the insulin has done its work, the glucose and insulin levels both recede. At this point we are hypoglycemic i.e. low glucose levels, and become very hungry, ravenous and even irritable so we eat more carbs and continue the cycle. The insulin levels then rise again and again and again always in the same approximate two-hour cycles.

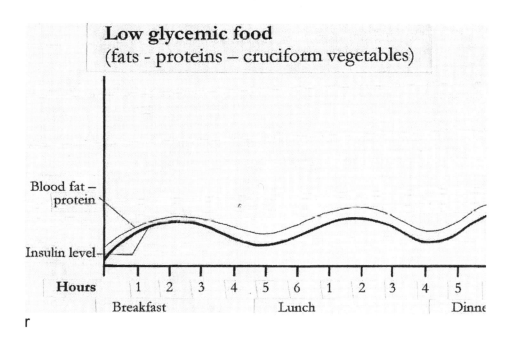

However, if fats, proteins and low glycemic carbohydrates (mostly green vegetables and whole grains with high cellulose or fiber contents) are eaten, the levels of responding insulin will be much lower. Since cruciate carbohydrates take much longer for the intestine to break down and absorb in the blood, the commiserate secretion of insulin will be much lower. Since the need is lower the absorption of the molecules is much slower. As a result fats, proteins and these cruciate vegetables are less likely to promote the hunger cycle inappropriately. Thus it is easier to go from one meal to another without constantly being ravenous and irritable. The period without hunger is therefore much longer.

Current thoughts indicate that *insulin at high levels* damages tissues such as the blood vessel lining, the heart and skeletal muscles, and in the long run is most likely very damaging to many cells. The outsides of cell membranes have receptors, the docking stations for insulin, to absorb nutrients; eventually they become resistant to this overproduction of insulin. This is what causes type 2 diabetes. The process of storage occurs so fast that insulin does not have a chance of being metabolized. Therefore, it causes excessively low-level of sugars in the blood, a condition called hypoglycemia that may be very dangerous.

If there is too much insulin in the bloodstream, the body will be in a state of hypoglycemia, or low blood sugar. This causes the brain to have too little carbohydrate. The brain requires constant carbohydrates to function and uses the circulating glucose as well as the stored glucose in its own cells.

When the brain does not receive glucose, as during hypoglycemia, such as before a meal, the brain function becomes very abnormal causing symptoms like irritability, anger, tiredness, poor performance, mood changes and even in extreme cases unconsciousness. So if insulin is very high and the blood sugar goes below average, these symptoms will occur.

There must always be a balance between these two to sustain a proper level of glucose to feed the brain. This hypoglycemia is not seen except in high carbohydrate diets or in diabetics taking too much insulin.

Summary of the function of insulin:

- Insulin is a *storage* hormone.
- Insulin permits cells to absorb carbohydrates until they are saturated
- Insulin permits cells to store glycogen.

- o Insulin takes excess carbohydrates, makes triglycerides with them, and deposits them into the fat cells.
- o Insulin, because a storage hormone, blocks the release of fat from fat cells.
- o It is also known to be an oxidizer (thus creating free-radicals when there is an excess of insulin).
- o Insulin influences the cell membrane to absorb carbohydrates and some amino acids.

Excessive insulin secretion (as in high carbohydrate diets) has these effects:

- o Blood vessel damage
- o Excess fat deposits
- o Increased production of cholesterol, especially LDL, the "bad" cholesterol
- o *Cell resistance* to insulin itself. That is diabetes
- o type II.

The high levels of insulin-glucose created by high glycemic diets are *very addictive* as they change the whole body physiology.

So it is impossible to lose weight as long as insulin is secreted. Insulin not only stores fat when carbohydrates are eaten, but keeps you fat as long as you eat carbohydrates.

The total portion of glucose deposited in *all* muscles is about 200 to 400 grams, about the equivalent of one cup of pasta or three candy bars or a single doughnut. This glucose is not accessible to use except by muscles during exercise and then only the muscle can utilize it. The other portion is deposited in the liver, about 100 to 200 grams as glycogen. Here the glucose is usable for other energy needs.

Over and beyond this, all excess carbs will become triglycerides and will be deposited in fat cells. The speculation is that triglycerides are highly important in the development of arteriosclerosis, as is insulin.

Glucagon, another hormone, is secreted by the pancreas and acts somewhat as a counterbalance to insulin. Its function is to keep the blood glucose at a minimum level. It is the yin and the yang.

Hunger

First of all, hunger is a very complex mechanism that we do not totally understand. There are two types of hunger—the ravenous stomach wrenching hunger, and the tired, weak, slowing-down feeling of hunger that indicates you need food. The latter is the ideal, as it does not incite you to eat constantly. The former is the bane of some lives, as it creates a continual *need* to eat. That was me in my hunger years. I had never understood until recently why I was always hungry, and of course always needing food to satisfy that hunger.

Hunger is usually a brain's signal that demands you eat for nourishment. Ideally, hunger occurs only when a body needs nutrients and the storage of these nutrients has been depleted. However, three systems cause hunger.

Insulin levels and their effect on the glucose level in the blood cancel the hunger factor, as *leptin* is secreted by the stomach lining when filled with food. Then the leptins go to the brain neurons and tell them not to be hungry anymore.

Low blood glucose, hypoglycemia causes the brain to perceive it is starved and to cry hunger. It actually needs that source of energy.

Stomach size is another interesting phenomenon in that the more food eaten, the greater the stomach size becomes. Eventually, large volumes must be eaten to satisfy this larger stomach Otherwise, it constantly screams that it is hungry until it is filled again.

Low Fat Diets

Food consumption has changed drastically. In the early 1900's, the average American consumed thirty-five pounds of refined sugar per year. In 1990 the average American consumed on average one hundred and thirty-seven pounds of refined sugar annually.

That's possibly hard to believe, but all the processed foods eaten on a daily basis contain sugar. And then, of course, there are those doughnuts and bagels.

This is one of the factors that I believe is creating the obesity epidemic in our country. The concept of a low fat diet leaves only high protein or high carbohydrates to replace the fats. Since meat contains some level of fat, it has nearly been banned from low fat diets, thus removing important saturated fats, fish fats and red meat from the menu. I agree that meat and fish eaten in too great quantities are dangerous, much like any excess.

But, if you refrain from eating fats or proteins in appropriate proportions, most of your food will be carbohydrates. And sugars and pastas are then ideal foods; besides they are good and readily available. The body's metabolism will use a small amount for necessary energy. *Since there is no other way to get rid of excess carbohydrates, they are transformed into triglycerides.*

The triglycerides are then stored in the specialized cells called fat cells.

To demonstrate that body chemistry can do this, look at cattle that eat only carbohydrates like hay and corn as fodder. They are easily fattened by this diet. Remember that cells are filled with eighty-five percent triglycerides coming from carbohydrates. Cows' metabolic processes can be maintained on an herbivorous diet only because they manufacture their necessary building blocks from that type of diet.

But the *quality* of the cattle is better if we add animal meats to their fodder. They can actually be healthier, since they develop more muscles and meat, having been fed more of the necessary amino acids for that purpose. The human body's metabolic processes cannot fabricate all proteins from carbohydrates, but they can store the excess carbohydrates very easily in fat cells.

The low fat diet addiction actually was caused by high carbohydrates and caused major damage to our bodies, although we thought we were doing the right thing for our health. At present, the American diet consists of about eighty to eighty-five percent carbohydrates. This is very close to being a vegetarian diet, but worse as it emphasizes high glycemic carbohydrates, such as the sugars and starches of pastas and breads. Also please remember that low fat diets will result in the loss of fat from the fat cells, but they will also lead to the loss of fat from the brain. The brain is eighty percent fat. Is it logical to do that?

Crash Diets

Crash diets are essentially a reduction of the quality and quantity of the food ingested. The body needs all the categories of foods to be healthy. Crash diets, however, are mini anorexia nervosas in that they damage the body by not feeding it properly and result in accumulated damage that is eventually is very harmful. These diets get rid of all tissues, not selectively fat cells. But even if they got rid of fat alone, you have to ask the question: Is it a good idea to get rid of the fat that is so much a part of the brain? Please go and read more on this in Obesity, page 209. I urge you to do so, as this understanding is an intrinsic part of your food knowledge.

Food and immunity

Let me digress for a second to explain this: in the mid-nineteenth century people ate mostly vegetarian foods, due the difficulty in providing animal meat. Tuberculosis was prevalent at the turn of the twentieth century. There were no antibiotics or vaccinations that could stop the disease and a high percentage of those who came down with the disease died. Yet its incidence gradually decreased in a steadily descending pattern from 1900 to the mid-fifties.

By 1955, tuberculosis had become very rare. About forty-five percent of people in that era were tuberculin positive, in other words had contacted the disease, but they had quelled it with their strong immunity.

Tellingly, epidemiologists found that the only curve that was inversely proportional to the descent of tuberculosis was animal husbandry. As animals were raised as a food source, meat became cheaper and more prominent in the diet. Consequently, the general population developed sound immunity and were able to eradicate tuberculosis. We were treating TB in sanatoriums "with fresh air," but in reality these patients were eating three square meals a day of meat and vegetables.

Another parallel story to note in that era: I was a surgical resident in the early sixties when I read a paper that impressed me so much. A large study from the 1930s to the 1940s was conducted with breast cancer patients.

These people had never been treated with radiation or chemotherapy, as these treatments did not exist in those days, and surgery was rarely done.

Yet despite the fact they had never received any treatment for cancer, this group had a twenty-five percent survival rate. It is presumed that the patients' own immune systems were strong enough to eradicate the cancer and save their lives. And that was the era when meat was readily available.

Today, with the frenzy of sterility—i.e. using all kinds of antibacterial soaps and solutions to clean everything—we are going to need ever so much of our immunity, and it is not on a fat free diet that we will succeed.

Vegetarian diets

I totally understand love for animals and the people who do not want to kill them for food. But I also love humans, and they are far more of a priority to me than animals. In order for humans to be healthy and vital, they must eat meat and fish. God created us the way we are within the food chain hierarchy. Even if you don't believe in God, but do believe in the Darwinian theory of humans achieving the sophisticated level of development through evolution, then you know that humans are omnivorous. There are many carnivorous animals and humans were that originally.

So accept what you are instead of bucking the logic of nature and damaging your body in the process. Proteins and fats cannot be obtained solely from vegetables; they also come from animal meats. Remember that animals manufacture all the necessary ingredients for their good health, and that is also available in their meat, which humans eat. There are at least two essential amino acids, *lysine and methionine,* provided by a diet especially of red meat that are crucial to heart and skeletal muscle function and also to the immune system. These are not available in other foods and are found in carnitines. It would not surprise me if more amino acids are missing beside these two.

Being omnivorous means that human cells need *all* the nutrients as building blocks, not just a few of them. A good balanced diet is the best approach, as this does include most of the right ingredients.

However, some vitamins and antioxidants need to be supplemented and this is discussed in more depth in Chapter Ten.

Remember an aging body requiring building blocks to constantly renew itself does not have the resiliency of youthful bodies. In youth, bodies are either growing or performing at peek, trying not to lose reserves as they age. The minimum amount and quality of appropriate ingredients ingested is absolutely crucial.

Some older people who tend to eat small and mostly carbohydrate meals, like the proverbial tea and toast, promote systems that are degrading alarmingly and who eventually die due to lack of proper nutrition. The body cannot survive, especially at this later stage, with such a lack of building materials. On the other hand, too much food can accumulate and become a burden on the body's ambulation, functions, healing and reconstructive performances. So a moderate, balanced diet remains the only way to maintain a healthy body.

If a body is predominantly provided with just one main nutrient such as carbohydrates, it will lack essential ingredients to rebuild important organs such as the heart, liver, immune system and cells. Excess carbohydrates are then turned into triglycerides that the body stores in fat cells. Some of the carbohydrates will be processed into some essential amino acids and essential fatty acids, but by far not all of them and in a much smaller quantity that the body requires.

As a result the body becomes deficient in appropriate reconstructive materials with disastrous results. Do you really want to decide for your body what amount of building materials it needs? Or would you let your physiology decide what is best for it?

There is no way to rid the body of triglycerides unless exercise burns calories so first intake fewer carbohydrates and secondly burn off the excess with exercise. Triglycerides are the excess of glucose that gets deposited in the fat cells.

Generally one hour of aggressive exercise will burn about three hundred to four hundred calories. A slice of bread is about one hundred to two hundred calories and a doughnut between two hundred and fifty and three hundred and fifty calories.

Toxins in Food

Preservatives

There are five thousand FDA approved food preservatives. It is impossible that these all be totally non-toxic. We would have to follow each one individually for years to prove them inoffensive. But that is nearly impossible as we would not know which one causes harm and which one does not.

Of course, if toxic additives are introduced into the system, the body needs to rid them or it will become damaged, either acutely initially or in the long term by small, cumulative increments. Because of this the best choice is to avoid these toxic additives. Unavoidable toxins need to be neutralized or detoxified and this is done mostly by the liver. The liver gets rid of the garbage via bile, or through the blood via the kidney. Toxins are like viruses and worms that affect computers. You do not know until your system has been infected and it is too late. More on this subject beginning on page 84.

Processed foods

Processed foods contain high levels of carbohydrates, along with hydrogenated fats, additives and preservatives. When absorbed the liver must process them and becomes overtaxed, resulting in a diseased liver called "fatty liver," a precursor of cirrhosis. It is seen mostly in overweight people since they tend to eat this kind of foods.

It is impossible that these all be totally non-toxic. We would have to follow each one individually for years to prove them inoffensive. But that is nearly impossible as we would not know which one causes harm and which one does not. There is no way we could keep these foods on the shelves without the preservative. Even cereals would rot after a while. Could you imagine if you opened a box of cereal and it was rotten?

Adverse reactions to certain foods

There are a few foods that for acquired or hereditary reasons become partially toxic or outright destructive to our systems;

peanut allergies, gluten allergies also called celiac disease or Sprew, lactose intolerance, allergies to shellfish and others that can be difficult to detect. You must be aware of this possibility and correct it.

Diet Recommendations

I say we should never be on a "diet" which implies weight loss from specific food category restriction and quantity restriction. The logic is to mostly have a stable diet eating moderately without highs like binges or lows like starving periods. If we need to lose weight just adjust the food intake along with the exercise to gradually lower your weight over a longer period. No harm comes to your body that way. And the likelihood is you will continue to follow the regimen.

It is essential to understand why a diversified diet is so important and why a low fat diet is so detrimental. Some foods are detrimental like excess fat or excess carbohydrates, so staying away from them is in your best interest. Just balance your diet with the three food categories: proteins, fats and carbohydrates, with very little sugar and pasta and no excessive saturated fat.

If the body is not fed well, it will eventually fail. Don't expect that you will see the result or failure immediately since it is a micro-accumulation like the grains of sand .It may take years to discover it.

Chronic fatigue, damage to organs, inability to exercise well and eventually major diseases are results of not providing the proper building blocks for the cells of the body. It becomes an outward demonstration of the body deteriorating and crumbling, also called aging. It is not a tea and toast diet that will keep elderly people alive and vigorous.

The diversity of the body's cells and their functions and products obviously requires a diversity of building materials. These are found only in an adequate diet with a variety of foods that provide appropriate amounts of amino acids, essential fatty acids, carbohydrates, antioxidants, minerals and phytochemicals all from different sources of foods. Any diet that eliminates specific food categories such as a low fat diet does will unbalance the nutrients by replacing fat with carbohydrates. On a low fat diet, meat quantities are reduced or eliminated because they contain fat, mostly saturated fat.

What is left are mostly carbohydrates so this diet has a great lack of essential building blocks. The original purpose of this diet is to lower cholesterol. But we now know first of all that tissue damage is the predominant agent in heart disease, not solely cholesterol. There is also much evidence indicating that a low fat, high carbohydrate (and thus high insulin levels) diet may damage blood vessels and the rest of the cells to boot.

Balanced Diet

So the *emphasis should be on a balanced diet* of proper nutrition and not focusing on only one factor. Cholesterol is only part of the equation. You can have the lowest cholesterol in the world and if the rest of your tissues are failing, including your arteries, this low cholesterol is irrelevant. Remember that fifty percent of people who die of heart disease have normal cholesterol levels. So please don't focus only on that cholesterol obsession.

I believe the low fat diet craze, along with my coined feed-on-demand characterization, is among the leading causes of the obesity and secondary diabetes epidemic in our country. Many factors cause this damage. Many aging citizens gradually gain weight if they do not stay physically and mentally active. This becomes nefarious, especially as they grow older and the body should be getting thinner instead of larger to facilitate ambulation.

If a balanced diet in moderate quantities is eaten, and an appropriate physical exercise regime is followed, aging people would be much more comfortable and healthy. The most productive diet I have found, and the one I follow myself, is a diet that consists of forty percent protein, thirty percent fat, and thirty percent carbohydrates, mostly in the form of vegetables—primarily colored, with few white ones. These percentages are approximates and used here only to give you a very rough guideline.

Don't forget milk products, as they have good fats and a lot of calcium. It is believed today that osteoporosis starts when people are very young, and in low or milk free kids. They like fruit juices. They also do not exercise. If you are so worried about too much of these saturated fats, then just get one or two percent fat milk.

The proteins have to be of a great variety and must include meats and fish of all sorts and some red meat but choose lean meats. Tend to stay away from prepared meats such as bologna, hot dogs and various meat loaves, all of which contain fillers of carbohydrates and other parts of the animals and require *mucho* preservatives.

The diet should include at least weekly, or better bi-weekly, fish that are mostly oily. This group includes, for instance, salmon, bluefish, mackerel and haddock, foods that contain omega-3s. Eggs are good and I choose a variety called Eggland's best simply because they have 100mg of omega-3 fatty acids each. I think that is significant.

Do not overindulge on excessive saturated fats, but you do need them. Thus vegetable oils like olive, canola and grape seed should be the staple cooking and salad fats. It is acceptable to enjoy milk and butter but, again, in reasonable amounts. Stay away from transfats such as fried foods and margarine. Use spread blends like Smart Balance. I have no relationship with that company except that I personally use their Smart Balance instead of butter and I like its composition. It has no transfats and very little cholesterol or cholesterol producing fat once in your body.

As for carbohydrates, vegetables are slowly absorbed and contain much fiber so are a good source for carbohydrates;

they have a lot of excellent phytochemicals those rare important supplements for us. Sugars should be mostly eliminated and some starches like breads, pastas, potatoes or rice should be consumed *sparingly.*

It is acceptable to consume some of these foods but caution should be exercised as it is easy to fall into a carbohydrate addiction pattern. Just be careful and don't give in to that weakness. Many people are addicted to carbohydrates and it will be very difficult to go without these carbs at first. Soon it becomes easier to get rid of this problem especially when the benefits show up—more positive moods, more energy, less constant hunger, gradual weight loss and more vigor to exercise.

Dr. Barry Sears also makes a good point that this balance of nutrients stimulates the secretion of a balanced ratio of insulin-glucagon (the yin and the yang), keeping the right levels of glucose in the blood and properly feeding the brain.

Eating moderate quantities is important. If you absolutely have to eat carbohydrates like doughnuts or other sugary foods, it is best to indulge in a *"reasonable"* binge once in a while, rather than consume them every day. Think about this for a minute; eating carbs daily will continually stimulate the insulin-glucose system while once in a while it will have must less of such an effect. Fruit juices naturally contain much sugar and, more often than not, have added sugars to boot so stay way from them. Whole fruits however are better than sugars as they are mostly fructose and have 50 percent slower absorption, more fiber and thus a somewhat slower insulin response. If you must eat them, do so only occasionally and in moderation.

Organic foods are best because they generally do not contain chemicals like insecticides, fertilizers, preservatives and God knows what else. In other words, cook your own meals and rely as little as possible on processed foods, as they contain too many non-natural additives and nearly all of then contain tons of sugar and transfats.

I suggest that you grow foods in your own garden in the summers in northern climates, or year-round in the south. Gardening however, may be a problem for some, especially if your residence is on East 94th Street in New York, or a similar locale!

Some things ingested, like certain spices, excess alcohol,, and many anti-inflammatory drugs like ibuprofen and aspirin can damage the gastrointestinal lining, so go slow on these. Also, be sure you are not lactose our gluten intolerant. If you are having symptoms you cannot identify, go to one of the websites I gave you and research your symptoms. Then talk to your doctor about them.

Alcohol, though a sugar, has been shown to have beneficial advantages like anti-oxidant properties, the ability to lower the incidence of diabetes in obesity and seems to lower cholesterol and heart disease. The medical field does not yet know why but this will be figured out eventually. This is true only in moderation, like three to five drinks a week. Beyond this level of consumption, it becomes toxic, forming free-radicals and damaging tissue cells particularly the liver cells that it put on detoxification overdrive.

Conclusion

Nutrition is an essential factor in keeping your body healthy. I encourage you to read as much as possible about nutrition as it affects your diet to gain a thorough understanding of the fuel your body needs. Do not read junk flyers, infomercials and super diet recommendations but find good books that explain what proper nutrition is and what to include in your diet. Make sure you read the whole book. So many people have made comments on some of the diets, for instance Atkins and did not see his more balanced approach at the end of the book. This information is your life blood. Couple this logical approach with great curiosity, common sense, good humor and exercise and you will feel proud of yourself being healthier and live longer.

If you must absolutely follow a diet to lose weight, please go to Weight Watchers, as they essentially do and have done for years exactly what I have recommended and they will give great support. By the way I have no relationship with them so this comment is based only on my analysis. There could be other organizations like it but I do not know them. Weight Watchers does not financially gouge you, while they give you knowledge support, boost your courage and keep you healthy and encourage you to exercise properly.

Please remember that moderation and balance are always the best choice. Invariably, too little or too much of anything is a bad deal. That is true in nearly every aspect of life. The attitude, exercise, food, money, work, play, sex and everything else in life is best if balanced in the right proportions. Since my wife understands the science and sense of the information in this book she feeds us a proper balance diet with moderation in all ingredients of food choice, care in preparation and abundant love. From firsthand experience, I can say it works *very* well for us! Please enjoy your food and don't be afraid of it. It is going to keep you going for years and years. Those who are obsessed with or hate their foods will never attain bliss since they are always afraid to do the wrong thing, and their whole life suffers the consequences.

Please read the next chapter on obesity, even if you are not affected by that condition. Regardless of your weight, it will give you more concepts of food psychology and cultural behavior.

You are what you eat.
Author unknown
(but it makes sense)

CHAPTER EIGHT

Overweight and Obesity

I originally intended to include obesity in the Nutrition chapter, but because this has become such a serious epidemic in America, I concluded that the topic warranted a chapter of its own.

Even if you are in good physical condition you should read this chapter. If you understand the physiology of obesity you can more easily prevent its occurrence, since it can creep in, especially as we grow older. Our systems are no longer as efficient. Part of the reason for this is that depletion plays a major role not only in our aging, but also in fat accumulation (particularly around our torsos, hence the term middle age spread!).

For clarification, obesity and being overweight are both an unhealthy increase in body weight caused by fat accumulation in specialized storage cells called fat cells. These fat cells are situated all over the body but most particularly under the skin. They also deposit around the abdomen and heart organs. Obesity is a large amount of weight gain while over weight is only a moderate amount. The more weight you gain the more damage ensues to your body.

Obesity alters many of the body's chemical reactions dangerously. Diabetes is a flagrant example with its high levels of insulin and the cells' ultimate resistance to these exaggerated high levels of insulin. It is important to realize that by gaining weight the whole inner functioning of the body is substantially changed detrimentally. Being super sized is not just an added physical weight problem or a vanity issue. Obesity is a deadly *disease* that affects all body systems including the brain, the liver, the heart, blood vessels, blood, cell membranes, the hormonal system, the immune system, cholesterol, body image, and overall mental health in more or less the proportion of the weight gained, although not necessarily so.

Fat cells seem to be the only ones that do not atrophy with disuse. As a matter of a fact, the more you do not use your body the more they multiply and "grow." You must accept that *obesity is a disease*, or an abnormal state of the body leading to severe morbidity and at the very least shortens life. This may sound very harsh but is a reality that must be faced.

Every tiny bit of weight gain multiplies the number of fat cells and these new cells will always want to stay filled with fat.

The very real effects of micro-cumulative damage are particularly damaging—and particularly true—with weight gain. Adding a minute amount of fat every day will indeed end up with a ton of fat eventually.

In general, someone is considered overweight if there is a slight to moderate increase in weight compared to their norm. Obesity on the other hand is an excessive weight gain. The difference between the two diseases is only a question of degree.

For simplicity, I will refer to both degrees as obesity in this chapter.

Obesity accumulates fat very fast and makes you miserable. But you are miserable for a long time before you die. It is easy to gain the weight, but very difficult or nearly impossible to get rid of. And, the older we get the more important it is not to gain unnecessary weight.

Obesity is an irreversible problem that you will have to fight the rest of your life.

THINK SERIOUSLY ABOUT THIS!

Statistics

In America today, sixty-four percent of the population is obese, and thirty-six percent of these obese people are or will become diabetic. Besides diabetes, a high incidence of disease is associated with obesity. This condition carries a huge risk of heart disease, fat emboli, cancer of the breast, osteoporosis and arthritis, which all have a high level of disease complication, morbidity, and mortality rate. Either directly or indirectly, three hundred thousand deaths occur annually from being overweight. Over one hundred billion dollars in health care costs annually occur as a result of obesity.

One number that is impossible to calculate and can only be imagined is how many individuals are discouraged, depressed and in very serious health quandaries because the dreaded disease of obesity crept up on them.

Often times, on the way to being obese, people think that it will be easy to resolve an obesity problem "later, I'll just go on a diet" but soon find out that the problem becomes permanent.

Causes and Concepts

What fashioned our minds often is responsible for what care we take of our bodies. What we were taught about nutrition as children has gotten us in some trouble.

But now *we* must deal with it and not expect someone else will. We can do something and it does not have to be one hundred percent correction but at least we can give it some improvement.

What frustrates me so much is to be subjected and bombarded by the constant brain washing of media onslaught that gives so much bad information for the sake of selling and only for that, despite the harm they do.

Let's look and learn all the factors and once you know them try to alter them to improve your aging years to make them as healthy and pleasant as possible.

Heredity

Genetics may increase the chance of obesity, but this only makes a person susceptible to it with no guarantee that they will actually develop obesity. Other factors must also be present and contribute to the problem.

The pure genetic component on its own is not known to be a very common cause. But other factors like force of character to deal with the environment battering you constantly and being down in the dumps will certainly be contributory. Certain metabolic changes in the body may also facilitate obesity.

Rare cases are fully genetic and these are generally demonstrated very early in life by extreme morbid obesity. An essential point here is that it is very easy to blame heredity for weight gain problems. But just because your parents are obese does not mean you have a bad gene that will also make you obese.

Sometimes the words *in my genes* are an excuse, a way not to take responsibility for a weight problem. We must face reality and be totally honest with *ourselves* about our entire lifestyle – exercise and eating habits. If indeed a weight problem is hereditary, you *can* beat the system and overcome the odds, albeit more difficult.

So a genetic background can be contributive to a weight problem but this is more about the combination of genes affecting metabolism of sugar processing, stress mediators and hormones that together may lead to this type of obesity.

Family and peer pressure

This is a problem of pure copycat and/or role model issue. There is a natural tendency to copy the parents as examples of behavior. "If my parents or brothers and sister can do it must be okay" Children often mimic what parental figures *do*, and not necessarily what they *say*. If adults in a child's life are obese then the youth often will assume this is an appropriate state of health. This creates a circle of family that soon becomes supportive, even accepting of overeating behavior and an overweight lifestyle. The immediate influence of your family is quite intense in the developmental years.

Your immediate family is the most powerful and profound influence you have. The familial aspect is important as children get their primary education from families and this has the most lasting effects on the brain of little kids. This early training and these impressions last a lifetime and are difficult to erase. The environment children are raised in fashions their minds, knowledge and particularly their personal habits and behavior. They actually become part of the character of these future adults.

Mom suggests that children *put meat on their bones* because they "look sick or frail"; she is negatively influencing those children on several fronts. While family members may have the best of intentions, they are actually encouraging children to develop bad excessive-eating habits. A thin child is not unhealthy. This is a false concept in society. It would be much easier to prevent than to encourage and later to reverse a bad pattern

I recall, as many of you might, my Mother encouraging *me to finish my plate* because she told me to think of the little children starving in China. To this day it is very difficult for me not to clean my plate, even though I might be full and satisfied and *I know* I shouldn't eat any more than what I need. I often wished, however, that there were a way to send some of that food to those children in the world who were starving.

Feed on demand

Feed-on-demand is the term I use for the lack of discipline developed in children because parents allowed them to eat as they chose, so they do not have to listen to them even though this is not in their best interest. This causes irreversible psychological and physical damage haunting children for the rest of their lives. Establishing a feed-on-demand routine in youth causes an *intense psychological need to inappropriately satisfy every need on all levels at all times* instead of imposing discipline, which is a much more difficult and time consuming disciplinary strategy, but infinitely more important for the child. That discipline, or lack thereof, stays with us the rest of our lives.

Although not intended as abuse, allowing a child to develop unhealthy habits that harm and lead to severe complications and potentially a difficult life is indeed abuse.

This stop-gap method of satisfying a child's demands unfortunately permeates many other demands from the child who will soon take advantage of this reaction from the parent in all other areas of development. *Some parents even cook special meals, different from what the rest of the family is eating, to satisfy a child's bad food habits*.

Look at the problem of milk and osteoporosis developing in children. Once the child has had a taste of juices he/she of course will not want to drink drab milk. That immediate gratification becomes a habit. If the habit of immediate gratification and need for sugars stays with children as they grow into adulthood, they can become isolated as they push people away from relationships when nobody wants to become their servants.

There is a high possibility of obesity in these adults. If they become obese, they will expect the problem to be resolved immediately by someone else. They will gravitate towards the crash diet-of-the-day or a magic pill without exercising. These people support the diet industry. Or is it the diet industry that takes advantage of these targets?

These unhealthy lifestyle choices *alter the character* of children, and subsequently the adults they become, for the rest of their lives.

Lifestyle choices are learned; even those you have learned to do differently. Bad lifestyle choices are a direct cause for most obesity. I have the sense that most people in society do not even recognize this as a problem, much less how gigantic this problem has become.

Daily micro-accumulation

"A grain of sand a day will end up as a ton later." So every day you must be conscious of eating too much, as even a tiny bit will accumulate mercilessly. Is it not the worst accumulation of harm you can do besides disuse?

Need I say more?

Educating the Child

The child we educate will become old very soon and *all the false concepts that child will have will stick in his mind the rest of his life.* Amazingly, one of the most important aspects of good physical and mental health knowledge—proper food consumption—*is not being taught profoundly in educational institutes at any level.*

Institutions like schools traditionally use less expensive and less nutritious foods in their menus. They of course have to satisfy stupid political budgets at the cost of the health of the future adults they are 'educating'. Schools tend to listen to parents dictating diets to please their children. They become weather vanes changing direction at any small winds. I question the fact that a parent be allowed to change school policies that may have been decided by "nutrition experts". Can you imagine hot dogs being part of a school's diet? It has to be the worst food on the planet.

A balanced, nutritious diet is necessary especially at this stage for proper growth of a child. Prepared foods and carbohydrates are not appropriate building blocks. A sound body supports a healthy mind. Just look at the low quantities of milk issue. We know today that too little calcium renders the child borderline osteoporotic very early on, called *brittle bone syndrome,* and that it will be a pattern until they die. Why are we even providing soft drinks, still present in many schools, to them? Why are parents giving children soft drinks and sweet fruit drinks that will spoil the taste of young children for life? Of course, they will choose these instead of milk, which is not as good tasting.

A child must be well-fed and the body should receive nourishment on a regular schedule to eliminate going through hunger pains or low sugar. Only a balanced diet with all the ingredients, with very little or no sugars will do this. If the body and mind are taught early to eat this way, it will become engrained in the mind and followed easily as a natural pattern or habit of life behavior. Why teach bad habits when good habit with a little discipline is nearly as easy.

Denial
Obesity is a major disease in our present time and yet there is enormous denial surrounding it. *There will never be a pill to cure it. You won't do it through a crash diet* or *walking a half-mile once a week.* If someone is obese, it most likely happened in a gradual process and took some time to develop into a huge health risk. Because it took some time to happen, it will take some time to correct, but you *can* correct an obesity problem – remember that.

A problem cannot be corrected until acknowledged by the individual. Do not put your head in the sand. If you are obese, invest the depth of commitment and length of time needed to bring your weight back to a balanced, healthy one for you. It may seem easier to play the denial game. You may think that you will not have to work hard if you do not acknowledge a weight problem, but believe me; you will end up working much harder in the long term. And the work in *that* game involves keeping not just your lifestyle, but possibly your life. Obesity is a burden for the rest of your life.

Above all, obesity involves a great amount of *denial about the consequences* that unquestionably will result from it.

216

Denials are active with thoughts like "I'm just a little fat," "I'll lose the weight later," "One more doughnut will not make a big difference," " I love beer and I'll just have one more," "I'll exercise tomorrow," " I've always eaten pasta, why should I stop now?" "Why should I forgo sugar with my coffee in the morning?" or "I know that I shouldn't eat doughnuts but I love them!" Unless arrested, these thoughts grow into larger denials, inside of a much larger person as excessive food is consumed to mask other problems.

Young people think that they can eat anytime, any volume of food, in any form. These young people expect their bodies to develop healthily even though they are, in fact, abusing their bodies. They may think they can get away with these poor nutrition habits at their age but do not realize they are harming themselves for the rest of their lives. One little grain of sand at a time. They are ultimately preventing the proper construction or development of their bodies and guess what? They will awaken at fifty or sixty and realize the harm they have done to themselves. It is more and more difficult to get rid of fat as we grow older.

I wish I had known this when I was the macho, indestructible youth that I thought I was in my teen years. *It is so very easy to think that this will not happen to you – while it is happening.* This is especially true if a young person exercises extensively and remains slim although eating anything and everything. They seem to get away with it but as soon as they no longer exercise aggressively; the eating habits created become drastically detrimental to their health, and very quickly. That's why so many athletes gain weight after their careers end and they no longer follow a regular exercise program.

The quality of food

The quality of foods is very important in this whole dilemma. Americans previously lived on a mostly balanced diet with all the food nutrients required and more likely relatively fresh foods. But commercialism changed that by promoting low fat foods, expedient foods, and good tasting foods easily accessible, and promoted through inaccurate infomercials to make them enticing. These are all the potato chips, packaged pastries, doughnuts chocolate bars and candies and the list goes on. They are all addictive and hard to resist. Food companies flooded the advertisement market, bombarding the public with false information while presenting mouth-watering Pavlovian reflexes that you might not, but should, resist.

They have totally skewed the knowledge of foods quite detrimentally but to whose benefit? The food industry certainly does not manufacture food to make the public healthy. I wonder if money as anything to do with this? I wonder if greed has anything to do with this?

Please learn foods well. It will dramatically change your whole life and particularly the aging process. It will make your aging years so much more pleasant and vigorous. We are living longer so this is particularly important.

I figure I have eaten seventy thousand meals in my life so far. I can just imagine how much healthier I would be today if I had known what good foods were and what harm bad foods were. The calories that go in must go out.

Even though all fats have 9 kcal/gram (compared to 4 kcal/gram for all carbohydrates and 4kcal/gram for proteins), the fat quells hunger faster and ultimately yields a gain in the total caloric consumption. We are less likely to binge eat, since we are not hungry. A good balance of moderate amounts of good fat in our diets is best.

Obesity is mostly the result of a *high carbohydrate diet*, and this type of diet creates a constant hunger that is very difficult to resist at all, much less forever.

Triglycerides are the product of excessive carbohydrates that are transformed to be stored in the fat storage cells. Diets where fat is balanced will quell hunger thus there will be much less weight gain. Again, it is impossible to permanently lose weight on a low fat diet.

The *carbohydrate addiction* is a process that slowly alters the entire metabolism system to crave carbohydrates, through higher insulin and non-effective leptins that delete the hunger signal to the brain. Unaware, those who followed the promotion of fat free dieting for lowering cholesterol unknowingly did so at the very high expense to the rest of their bodies. Following the penny-wise, pound-foolish theory while cholesterol levels are good, diabetes and many more serious problems occurred as a direct result of it.

Indoctrination

Society is totally confused and ill informed on many crucial medical concepts regarding obesity. The advertising media have accomplished a massive brainwash with the onslaught of persuasive infomercials. These not only mislead the public but also entice them to practice fast-loss diets, low fat diets, or low carbohydrate food diets that advertisers claim are healthy. From advertising people actually well trained in persuasive techniques, the average citizen finds it hard not to believe or resist these ads, especially if they have no solid medical knowledge. Heck! Now they are even selling low carbohydrate beers!

Just remember that advertisements are created by shrewd experts who want to sell the most products and they target many who are gullible and fall for this garbage.

Also the relentless mental battering that the media and industries send out to the public from all directions is difficult to ignore and pervades all aspects of communications. It is like a well-orchestrated virus by geeks infesting computers. Knowledge is your Norton anti-virus software.

As you gain knowledge, you will see and understand the fallacies that are presented and how they put information in people's heads with innuendos. The more you know the more you will ignore them.

Believe me, your brain computer will work a lot more efficiently and will be able to adequately sort out a lot of information. *The alternative is to remain in denial about this detrimental media blitz of modern times.*

What I find most regrettable is most people have based their knowledge on having read one article or heard one or two comments and listened to a person not qualified to give this info and the they establish a whole life style on it. Better still they start preaching these false concepts to justify themselves.

There are some excellent health reporters who pass on accurate, helpful information, but they are nearly lost in the onslaught of media garbage so that the average Joe simply cannot discern what can be trusted or believed. Logically it would be virtually impossible for reporters in any media - TV, radio, magazines or newspapers - to have comprehensive knowledge on every subject they report. Some books or articles are written with an intended inaccurate slant, or maybe it is their over-enthusiasm, but they sell a product. Not mine of course!

My intention is to provide an unbiased view and that is specifically why I do not sell any products. I am sure that false information in advertising is the worst factor in the epidemic of obesity. Making money should not be done at the expense of the public's health and well-being.

If other people are hurt in any way while some are making money, the concepts our society is based on have failed. Society is ripe for the picking to all the forms of media that exist in advertising. In a society hungry for nutritious food, selling food especially if labeled healthy, is easy, whether true or not. It is no surprise that the public is constantly brain washed by all forms of the media in order to sell products.

Since meat, fish, fat products or green vegetables cannot be inexpensively or conveniently packaged as fast foods, the food industry reverted to easy, convenient and prepared foods.

They can charge more for these and most consumers do not realize they are paying more.

Constant barrages of advertisements with claims of healthy contents further entice people. When advertisers *then* claim these are also healthy for the consumer – snap – done deal. By the way, statistics in 2004 indicated that ninety-two percent of potatoes eaten in America are potato chips or French fries.

Most Americans have faith in their government and do not even *consider* that false food advertisements *can* occur. They believe that if something is on TV or in the news, it must be true and safe. The government promotes big business above all, as it pays taxes and contributions. I hope you are beginning to know different.

The whole advertising technology is extraordinary, invasive, scheming, resilient and, indeed, quite successful. For example, Dr. Atkins reversed the fat free craze. So advertising moguls jumped on the Atkins bandwagon to continue their ploys. Now we are flooded with the concept of low carbohydrate foods. There are even grocery stores and restaurants chains that sell low fat and low carbohydrate sandwiches. If you carefully at these carefully they are not what is advertised, but you bought it anyway.

A balanced diet does not make money for the big food industry. This is evidenced clearly by the fact that it actually costs more to buy organic foods or free range chickens. Many supposedly miraculous crash diets come and go easily. When one diet does not work they quickly move on to another supposedly miraculous, crash diet without losing a heart beat.

Preparing food at home is 'too hard' for many busy families because they are so tired after very long days. And some people think that preparing food at home is opening a frozen pre-cooked lasagna or pizza. Some even recognize the difference and still make conscious choices to serve half prepared and half home cooked meals.

Preparing food contributes to a healthy lifestyle in many ways, not just the obvious one of simply ingesting food that does not harm but rather helps the body grow, develop and stay in good shape. Food prepared at home contains fewer preservatives and trans-fats. The process of preparing a meal also bonds family members. There is an intimacy in cooking, a sense of fun also and it is a time together as a family to educate to communicate to appreciate. This does not occur with fast dinners and fast foods, the get it out of the way approach.

Exercise

A dangerous cycle of indoctrination is clearly seen with people who turn into couch potatoes. Besides not exercising, they continue to get more brainwashed by watching TV full of advertisement garbage about diets and beer.

I know I have belabored the exercise issue many times in this book. I think it is that important. I am reminded of Newton who claims what goes up must come down – well what goes in the body must come out by exercise. The invisible yet essential fat-muscle ratio can only maintain balance if you do a complete program of exercise along with balanced nutrition. Go and read the Exercise Chapter Six if you have not done that already.

The lack of consistent and effective physical activity is key in gaining weight.

Another phenomenon is excessive exposure and use of the computer. Granted the computer is an amazing tool but should be used efficiently. Hours spent surfing the net can be as hazardous to mental health as TV advertisements. People who spend excessive hours on the computer sometimes refer to themselves as geeks because geeks can perform cunning functions with a computer.

I disagree; if geeks were super-intelligent they would realize that a brain simply does not function well in an unhealthy body. This should inspire them to spend balanced time exercising, eating properly, and even using the internet as a tool to quench curiosity, especially on health websites.

Mens sana in corporae sano—A sound mind in a sound body.

Crash Diets

This phrase refers to any severely limited food intake, both in quantity and quality with the purpose of losing weight. The body physiology is totally altered by being overweight. Logically, rapid weight loss does not alter the severe changes the body sustains when it is overweight. Thus, as soon as the diet is over, the body reverts to its bad habits. It amazes me that anyone would think otherwise but again, the advertising medium is powerfully effective.

This is the reason ninety-eight percent of people regain lost weight after they complete a crash diet. The diet only been a mechanism of weight loss and not a repair of the permanent damage that being overweight causes to a body. As a matter of fact, this yo-yo weight gain and loss adds damage and compounds the obesity problem. Crash diets only satisfy impatience and immediate gratification of weight loss.

Crash diets are extremely damaging to the body for many reasons. *During that starving period, weight is not specifically lost in the fat storage cells, but all of the cells and organs are deprived of proper nutrients.* As a result, weight loss is not only in fat cells, but also in muscles, ligaments, cartilage, organ tissue, the brain and electrolytes systems.

The brain is eighty percent fat. Do you think it is a good idea to lose that fat? Perhaps coming from a medical background, I am baffled *that the public believes only specialized fat storage cells are lost* when the whole body is starved. The offshoot is that when the weight lost on a crash diet is then regained only fat cells return and not muscle and other cells stay with the damage. This not only makes weight loss far more difficult in the future but also has left the body with damaged cells.

A huge number of diets have been patented. A few years ago, I met the head of the U.S. Government Statistics Bureau on a ski hill who told me that there have been about 49,000 diets patented by the U.S. government. There are only a few that are viable. One I believe in is Weight Watchers—and *they advocate a balanced diet with moderation and exercise.*

And, if a particular diet doesn't work, or is challenged, the marketers just immediately package and put another one on the market, and still make their loot. The diet industry is a huge machine that holds the U.S. public hostage with advertising and packaging.

The snack food industry can sell carbohydrates much more easily than other nutrients for several reasons. These snacks generally taste good and quickly satisfy hunger; however, the hunger also returns very quickly so you eat more, creating an addiction. Large food companies package, promote, advertise, distribute and sell high carbohydrate products. They know that if people want to have a snack, they will not get a steak or a glob of butter. Snack companies cannot make huge amounts of money with proteins and fats for snacks, as they are not readily preserved and are not as appealing as the carbs snacks that are better tasting. As a result of this, there is little interest in selling these kinds of snacks. Can you see them selling meat and fish as snack foods? The industry would collapse.

Keep in mind that if dieting is done without exercise, fat tissues will be lost during the diet but so are muscles and every other essential tissue in the body. The end result is that any subsequent weight gain will be only fat—not muscle or other essential tissues. The more these diets are attempted, the worse a dieter's problem becomes.

The damage occurring deep inside the body when it gains and loses weight has far-reaching consequences.

Young people think they can get away with overeating and make it up by dieting later in life. This is an especially damaging misconception, as weight is lost quite easily during younger years when there are more hormones and more muscles to sustain a high metabolic rate to burn more fuel and process fat more efficiently. The truth is that it becomes gradually more difficult to lose weight as the body grows older.

Just remember that the very words "crash diet" mean you lose weight quickly, but invariably you can't wait to return to your "normal eating habits." So you go back and binge, gain more weight, crash diet, gain more weight, and so it goes, on and on.

I strongly believe that you must understand your body, know what it is made of and how it works to feed it appropriately so it works properly and averts breakdowns. Another major hurdle is that *the effects of our dietary decisions are never seen immediately*. They occur only cumulatively, and bit by bit, and it is only later that we realize the harm we did to ourselves.

Hunger
Hunger of course plays a crucial and important role in all this. I remind you to read this important passage on hunger in Chapter Seven on Essential Nutrition on page 171.

In short, the carbohydrate-stimulating high level of insulin is responsible for this hunger. It was the bane of my life until I understood it well.

By the way, people you see shoveling food in their mouths at meals have that extreme hunger and usually are fat.

Habits
A prominent psychological factor is that when eating habits learned as a youth are fraught with a behavior pattern recurrence, the child will get in the habit of performing this behavior. Specific events, sites and people can incite habitual behavior. This trigger mechanism starts the Pavlovian reflexes and creates hunger. The natural treatment is to avoid these trigger events. Take note that I am not talking about addictions

here which actually results from chemical changes in the metabolism. Differently, habits are purely psychological.

Every time I had a beer it had to be with a cigarette and chips. Even when I stopped thirty years ago, this habit re-surfaced in my mind for many years. Certain patterns of behavior trigger the addiction for food like eating before going to sleep, or driving past a McDonald's or Dunkin' Donuts and feeling compelled to drive in to feed an addiction.

Frustration

Many people eat when they are frustrated or need relief from problems. This is a very strong habit. Some people though few, do the reverse and actually stop eating. When people eat more than is necessary for proper body function, they gain weight and then become even more frustrated.

Undereating, or anorexia, is a worse and more damaging disease than obesity. The mortality rate is much higher and in much younger people.

And it is possible to lose weight and then fall into the habit and become fanatically obsessed and thus anorexic. Anorexia is when someone maintains a constant mode of crash dieting which damages all parts of the body *and* the mind, perhaps the reason people lose their common sense and the disease of anorexia is able to control them.

Stress

Stress promotes cortisol hormone secretion.

Stress inevitably becomes part of the damage and the cause of obesity. In fact, stress may come before the weight gain and actually cause overeating. The resultant cortisol causes the fat deposit and hunger.

Body Image

Once weight gain has occurred, people generally feel bad about their appearances. This feeling bad about an unfit body can and often does cause more stress. Their perception of themselves is very poor. This creates constant thoughts of losing weight. This causes more stress and perpetuates the cycle of overeating.

Obesity also causes children to detach from a social circle and their family. This isolation sometimes causes children to eat compulsively for comfort, and thus begins another vicious cycle.

A natural choice for food in this state of mind is anything easy and good tasting so it is likely that bad foods with heavy carbohydrates or fast foods are chosen. Not only does a child become overweight, but the frustration that obesity causes makes children more miserable and they become more demanding, which encourages parents to give in and let them eat improper foods and quantities.

The end result for a child is to become a very unhappy person with compensatory character flaws for the rest of his or her life. I do not mean to fault parents as they do what they also learned or have been brain washed. They often have the same problems and encourage others to be like them so they do not feel inadequate.

Hormone Reduction

It is quite well recognized today that a decrease in hormonal secretion like estrogen, progesterone and testosterone definitely will produce midriff obesity.

Just look at people as they grow older and you will recognize that that the pattern of there obesity changes to skinny legs and arms but the belly and often breast in men become prominent. It is very frustrating but corrected only by specific exercises and hormonal replacement.

So far hormonal replacement has reduced weight, particularly with growth hormone, testosterone and to lesser degree estrogen and progesterone.

All of this is like the saying of recovering addicts that they only had to change *one* thing about their previous lifestyle to get clean—and *that one thing was everything*!

The Damage Obesity Does

Psychological Aspects
- Eliminates ambition   *Nobody will accept me because I am fat.*
- Destroys self confidence   *I can't jump that high.*
- Destroys body Image   *I don't look good in anything.*
- Creates depression   *I am ugly and nobody likes me.*
- Leads to discouragement   *Everyone else runs faster than I do.*
- Creates spiraling ego   *I will never be able to pass that test.*
- Creates lifelong battle to control   *I will eat less tomorrow.*
- Creates/increases stress   *I have to stop thinking about food.*

Physical changes
- *Increases the size of the skin*—and that eventually becomes irreversible. The older you get the more you lose skin elasticity, as witnessed by wrinkles. Even if weight is lost later, the skin still stays the same size and develops severe wrinkling or folding.

- *Increases the stomach size,* which requires more food to satisfy. If weight is lost rapidly, the stomach size usually stays the same. If weight is lost slowly the stomach usually shrinks back to normal but is slower the older we get. The stomach is enlarged each time it has to accept more food than normal Additional food will be required to satisfy the larger stomach size.

- *Reverses muscle-to-fat ratio* where the increase in fat volume creates a vicious cycle. As the fat increases the muscle proportion decreases. In the process the metabolic rate also decreases substantially. There is much less energy expended in the system since the muscle bulk has been reduced and produces less energy to burn off excess fat. It becomes more and more difficult to lose weight especially after dieting occurs. Quite simply, muscle burns calories and fat does not.

- *Requires more storage capacity.* Fat cells never disappear *even if weight is lost.* The more fat or triglycerides stored in these cells, the more the body produces fat cells to accommodate the demand. These cells always demand to be refilled. They cannot be eliminated unless they are excised surgically or by liposuction, another form of excision. So dieting does not help that problem

- *The liver becomes overtaxed* The liver can actually become quite damaged, similar to the damage alcoholism creates by producing a fatty liver ultimately degenerating in cirrhosis.

- *Increases arteriosclerosis in the heart and brain*, creating a much higher chance of a heart attack and strokes. All vessels develop this arteriosclerosis.

- *The blood itself can and does get fat globules* that can result in fatty emboli. There is a higher chance of early demise as a result of all of this. Depending on the severity of the obesity, there is between five and fifteen fewer years of life.

- *The heart has to enlarge to feed the huge* number of vessels that have developed to supply the fat storage. Each pound of fat requires many thousands of miles of extra capillaries and this increases the stress on the heart pump and blood pressure. That leads to congestive cardiac failure.

- *Arteriosclerosis in the young;* Autopsies even in eleven-year-old children who died in accidents show arteriosclerosis in their aortas. Up to thirty percent of fifteen-year-olds in the same situation have similar findings. Admittedly many of these kids smoked and that is also a factor.

- *Responsible for high blood pressure* which leads to an increase in heart size as the heart has to fight against the high pressure and the huge increase of blood vessels. High blood pressure is a silent killer since it has no symptoms but damages the heart and causes strokes by bursting small vessels in the brain.

- *Results in cell resistance, diabetes* and damage to many organs because of the very high levels of insulin caused by high glycemic carbohydrates consumption. Causes type II diabetes, which leads to many major difficulties.
- *Increases the chances of breast cancer* as fat cells secrete estrogen-like compounds that may stimulate estrogen-sensitive breast cancer.

- *Causes sleep apnea,* which is a snoring that renders the airway incapable of adequately bringing oxygen to the lung. This can actually reduce circulating oxygen by 40 percent, which damages tissues. Sleep apnea can lead to a heart attack by itself. Recent research indicates that *sleep deprivation* leads to weight gain. Sleep apnea is caused and aggravated by weight gain. Excessive snoring can become sleep apnea and should be investigated. If you are snoring, get tested. Sleep deprivation and sleep apnea are related and quite dangerous.

- *The human growth hormones,* as endocrine hormones are, mostly secreted during sleep. Sleep deprivation thus becomes a major problem. The less sleep, the less growth hormone production. The higher the level of growth hormone in the body the more fat is lost. The less sleep the tenser and the more cortisol secreted which also depletes growth hormones. Reduces growth hormone production in proportion to the fat gain. The less growth hormone the less muscle develops creating another vicious cycle.

- *Causes shortness of breath* by sheer bulk and by being in poor physical aerobic shape with similar effects as sleep apnea.

- *Causes all manners of skin rashes.*

- *Causes very early osteoporosis.*

- *Causes arthritis from the excess weight* on the joints particularly on weight bearing joints.

- *Causes loss of equilibrium* and awkwardness with resultant injuries.
- *Alters the entire metabolism of insulin and leptin*, which leads to **constant craving** of foods, particularly those high in carbohydrates. The *constant hunger* plus the psychological frustration of denying the pleasure of eating can cause an unhealthy diet pattern.

- *Obesity promotes a chronic inflammatory reaction in the system.* Fat cells contain high levels of bad eiconasoids that promote inflammation. Most overweight people have high levels of C-Reactive proteins, a strong indicator of inflammation. They also reduce mental function by changing the quality of fat necessary for the brain.

- *Men tend to have more muscles* and burn more calories so it is physically easier for them not to become as heavy as women.

- *Smokers tend to gain weight when they stop smoking* unless they take strong steps to avoid the increase in pounds. That weight gain can be another battle to fight for the rest of their lives.

- *Women tend to gain* four to six pounds after each pregnancy.

Vicious Cycles

Let's review some of the material that I have covered already, but look at it from the different perspective of the quagmire or vicious cycles that we have put ourselves into. Unfortunately, we tend to find that out only later in life

You can create vicious cycles in your body that occur very slowly but relentlessly and eventually become nearly impossible to escape. As mentioned, some young people think because it is easy to lose weight they can overeat, eat inappropriately, eat on demand and exercise only sporadically. If the young person chooses and eats them incessantly, high levels of insulin are secreted. The body gradually tires of being over-stimulated with these high levels so its cells go on strike and develop a resistance. They do not respond normally to the effect of the insulin and this is the beginning of Type II diabetes. Also leptin and insulin resistance may develop to continue the hunger cycle, thus a viscous cycle is born.

Insulin is the normal hormone secreted by the pancreas and is the agent responsible for the body's manufacturing process of carbohydrates, and to a much lesser degree fats and proteins. It breaks the carbohydrates down into glucose that is then stored in muscles, liver, fat or brain cells. There is always a high insulin level just after ingesting a high carbohydrate meal. The main function of insulin is storage as it disposes of the glucose circulating in the blood into various storage compartments. That lowered level of glucose creates a great hunger. If the food ingested was carbohydrates, hunger again occurs within two hours after and there is a desire to eat again.

Also, a high level of insulin rids the blood of all glucose and none is left to feed the brain resulting in the classic pre-meal irritability, stress, hunger, weakness, a starving brain that often contributes to making mistakes, bad judgment calls or injury. To function properly brain cells need glucose at all times but not at excessive levels, except during sleep. High carbohydrate diets create very high and very low glucose levels whereas a low carbohydrate diet always maintains a sustained level of glucose available to the brain.

As long as insulin is secreted there is no fat re-absorption from the fat cells. Fat re-absorption occurs only when insulin levels are down and once glucose is out of the blood. This happens at night, while resting and during most lengthy exercise sessions.

The more quantity we eat the hungrier we become. The more a stomach enlarges the higher the volume of food is needed to satisfy this larger space. As long as the stomach is large, it demands a larger food capacity.

Another serious problem is that the heavier people become, the less capable they are of exercising, as it becomes more difficult to carry and move body weight. The heavier a person becomes the more their joints hurt, and the more damage there is to crucial joints like knee joints and the less they want, or can, exercise. One pound of body weight translates to six pounds of pressure on the knee and hip joints. This additional weight results in compression damages to the cartilage and ultimately arthritis. Another vicious downhill cycle begins.

Also the heavier one becomes, the less one wants to be seen. People do not want to look foolish exercising out in public or even at an exercise facility so tend to do this less and less. The heavier people are the more they want to go on crash diets as they perceive these as an easy way to lose weight. However the insulin-leptin cycles, and all the other negative changes that occur in the body are still present and thus another vicious cycle continues they regain any weight they might have lost, their fat cells demanding more fat and thus the cycle continues.

Correcting Obesity

The solution to obesity is all about what you have to do every single day. You must never forget that everyday you accumulate a little grain of sand and that could be a little too much food, pesticides, food preservatives trans-fats etc. There should be NO crash diets. Following such a strict regime does not accomplish your goal of leading a healthy, satisfying lifestyle. Please understand that a crash diet, or any diet, is not beneficial and only a moderate volume balanced nutrition with exercise is required to become successfully healthy. It may be difficult to follow this nice balanced approach elsewhere, like at work, travel or even during mental frustration. You must compensate to not fall too low during these periods by making a real effort to adjust.

Knowledge and curiosity

Curiosity and knowledge are fundamental in your quest for averting overweight. *Consider all advertisements subject them to skepticism.* Read many articles and books. Read more. Read this book and follow through with all the suggested literature that is recommended. You must become an expert of your own body to provide the best possible care so every thing you read thereafter can be inserted in the big picture and make infinitely more sense. You soon will start discriminating between what is good and the nonsense. That fact is very crucial.

There are many reasons why this is a good route to take, and one of them is that you will become more knowledgeable and understand what is wrong and what is right for your body.

Do not let people who do not know what they are talking about sell you a bill of goods. Just listen to people who have researched opinions and can discuss in debt. Be your own final source for information on a healthy longevity. When you have this knowledge, discern what is good for you, and the ability to choose good foods for you will become much easier.

Learn all about food and how it is distributed and used by your body. Once you know the concepts of foods- what they are, what parts of you they feed, what harm and good they do - choosing a healthier diet on a daily basis will be easier. Knowing is important!

You must eat your whole life and that food will make you or break you. You eat more than one thousand meals a year. Why would you not put maximum effort toward the activity that has the most important influence on you and your body? It may be difficult to eat good foods at first because bad foods taste so much better and are easier to access. Feeding a bad food addiction, especially with constant enticement by all media advertisements is easier.

My goal here, as it is throughout this book, is to give you an understanding of what is good and what is bad in food and then it will be easier on a daily basis to select your food intake accordingly.

Also as important is if I can stimulate you to continue reading and researching reliable literature for your specific lifestyle and body so as to find the best way for you to manage your health. That way you can develop a set of guidelines that will work optimally for the rest of your life.

Of course you will fail sometimes, but if you fall get up and start over. Don't be too hard on yourself or you'll get frustrated and not be able to sustain the new lifestyle.

As I keep saying, the most important "car" in the world to you is your body. So learn how it functions, how to drive it well, prevent wear and tear, feed it well, do maintenance to avert further breakdowns, and you will drive it two hundred and fifty thousand miles, that's one hundred years, enjoyably. Nobody else in the world is going to do that for you.

No one else has so much invested in you except yourself. If you expect that somebody else will do that for you, then you will fail miserably, regardless of how important, rich, famous or intelligent you are. None of that has any value if you don't pay primordial attention to the health of Numero Uno.

The first thing to do is establish priorities. Will you continue to accumulate micro-damage to your health, or are you going to establish health patterns that will help you stay well, feel good about yourself and prevent damage and disease that could occur otherwise? When you make the supreme effort that living a healthy lifestyle requires, the rewards are *unlimited.* There are very few situations that cannot be lessened or reversed if you take the bull by the horns. *Nobody else can do this for you.* You can do it, one step at a time, one day at a time.

If you have a mental block only you will be able to surmount it and liberate yourself. *Don't blame anyone else.* That is the "poor me attitude" and it is a useless sentiment that yields absolutely nothing except a downhill course. Your problems are *your* problems. Resolve them. You *can* empower yourself! Just see how magnificent the rewards will be.

Then, as Bob Green suggested in his book *Get with the Program*, you should sign a contract with yourself. That is the most important thing you can do and abide by. Also, when you sign that contract, remember to sign it with your entire life in mind, not with an idealized reality because the ideal life does not exist. Denial of reality can cost you a contract. Make this a persistent, continuous effort and you will stick to it. Instead of hating yourself for breaking a contract you will especially love yourself for keeping *this* contract.

Breaking your contract is not good because the person that you break the contract with is yourself, your first priority in life. It is also important, when you sign that contract to have a clause that says you *will never* return to a weight gain pattern ever again. It's like smoking. If you say *"I'll try to quit"* you will never be successful, you will never quit because you have left the door opened, but if you commit to yourself that *you will never* under any circumstances smoke another cigarette in your life you stand a much higher chance of success. I did that when I finally stopped smoking and it worked. I had tried many times before but in retrospect I had not committed myself so I failed. *Do the same with food. It is a little more complex but very doable and part of the contract.*

You'll have to change both habits and addictions:
Habits are the mental part of our actions and are triggered by familiar things or events that reminded you of eating. Certain places like food stores or fast food restaurants are associated with eating. Some friends and family feed you certain foods or hors d'oeuvres. Bedtime snacks are also habit associations that are developed, you are not necessarily hungry but it is a tradition, a habit.

You must recognize these as bad food associations and either avoid them or learn to brace yourself to change them, or you'll have a tendency to fall back. Often a long time is necessary to erase habits but *you can do it* by willfully, also called will power, tackling the problem. This problem is quite surmountable.

For example, when I travel to third world countries my routine of exercise and eating is totally broken. There is also the long disruptive travel time, cramped airplane rides and jet lag. After these occasions I have to muster up the most intense will power to get back on track with my own exercise and eating regime.

Addiction is different in that it is an absolute alteration of the body's chemical reactions at the nerve junctions, the synapses. As with stopping smoking, the first month is difficult because the body's natural reaction is to reprogram its chemical reactions back to normal. There is an actual feeling of something missing that must be satisfied. But the body readjusts and that discomfort does disappear.

Food addiction is quite real, having to do with carbohydrates stimulating insulin to rise. The good news is that soon after an unhealthy pattern of eating is stopped the addiction goes away. Go and see the insulin curves with and without sugars on page of the chapter on exercises.

Habits last longer but are not as severe. Both have to be recognized and should be contended with seriously. If you do not recurrently fall back into the carbohydrate eating habit, they will have to go through that process only once and it is well worth the effort.

One thing that triggers over-eating is stress. Stress cortisol and adrenalins are circulating which promote obesity. Stress is something that is best dealt with differently than binging on food. Stress is very strong and as a rule will make you do very inappropriate things, particularly involving eating. Some people have the reverse reaction and they become anorexic, however, the majority tends to overeat.

Everyone has up and down cycles in life. During the ups you are very positive and in a *can do* mode. That of course is the easy time because you want to do the right thing and so you do. In the down cycles like in stress we simply revert to bad habits again. These up and down cycles happen to everyone. This also applies to every thing else in life like sickness, operations, pregnancy, severe emotional events and God knows what else.

When these events occur, you must have closure as soon a possible to rid the stress. It is like smoking. If any small reason is used to start smoking again then a smoker may never stop. Smokers must be committed to *never* smoke again, under *any* circumstances. If they slip they should immediately go back to the new healthier routine. Keeping a routine is much easier in a steady, non-stressed life.

You have to believe in yourself and maintain a very positive perspective. Push yourself on a daily basis and read inspiring books by people like Dr. Phil McGraw or Deepak Chopra. Dr. Phil will help you "get with it," as he says. So stop being in denial, start having willpower and follow a good lifestyle with sound health practices.

Oprah Winfrey emphasizes these concepts and informs millions of people around the world on a daily basis as she encourages a no-nonsense life. Just look at the wonderful role model she is to America. Combined with the very difficult hurdles she had to overcome as a child, the mega-star lifestyle she has today also creates stress, although the two are very different kinds of stress. Yet Oprah now adheres faithfully to her contract and maintains her ideal weight, so consider her a great role model.

Curiosity and knowledge are fundamental in your quest for averting overweight. Listen to many outlooks from people you know and a few that you don't know. *Consider all advertisements subject to skepticism.* Read many articles and books. Read more. Read this book and follow through with all the suggested literature that is recommended.

You must become an expert of your own body to provide the best possible care so every thing you have learned will create be inserted in a big picture and make infinitely more sense.

There are many reasons why this is a good route to take, and one of them is that you will become more knowledgeable and understand what is wrong and what is right for your body. Do not let people who do not know what they are talking about sell you a bill of goods. Be your own final source for information on a healthy longevity. When you have this knowledge, discern what is good for you, and the ability to cure any problem will become much easier. Learn all about food and how it is distributed and used by your body. Once you know the concepts of foods- what they are, what parts of you they feed, what harm and good they do - choosing a healthier diet on a daily basis will be easier. Knowing is important!

There is nothing wrong with medium-high cholesterol as long as it is at a moderate level, and not excessively high. For example, eating a low fat diet will indeed lower cholesterol, but at the same time it will harm a multitude of other organs, particularly the brain, along with the cells' membranes and hormone production. Is it worth it?

Everything in life is a compromise and has a gate price. For every balance there is a counterbalance, the yin and the yang, so look at both the good and the bad information so you can judge by yourself. Use your new knowledge to discern the reliable sources of the information you acquire.

When you are fully educated on a subject, and *only* when you are fully educated on that subject, can you make an informed decision. Beware not to fall into the paralysis of analysis mode. Do not let one little occurrence or one exception offset your good judgment. The low fat diet was like that; just to lower cholesterol we damaged the rest of the body in the process.

Stay away from anything that stimulates the appetite. Do not look at food advertisements. Do not linger at food counters in the grocery store and definitely do not shop for groceries when you are hungry. Use resolve when going to restaurants with lush gourmet foods that will be hard to resist.

Take an attitude of gratitude for even being able to enjoy the lovely atmosphere and fine food, and choose to have smaller portions or fewer courses.

Take care not to be stimulated by the Pavlovian reflex through either an appealing appearance or a little psychological bell that indicates incorrectly that you are ready to eat food.

Many times the Pavlovian reflex is an unaware perceived idea in your mind. You may not necessarily be hungry, but then see something appetizing and you suddenly feel like you would like one of those. Obviously, you have to fight these urges and understand that subtle instructions are ever present in advertising and create a very conniving and invasive motivation for overeating.

You must judge if maintaining a healthy weight is good for you with the reward of a strong body, better attitude and pride in your will power. Or are you just as healthy with a slight weight gain, feeding your habits and addictions and loss of your contract? You are the judge.

Remember that calories are a real factor and any eaten must be burned. The more obese you become the less you will burn off because your furnace, the muscles, will not burn these calories. You have to create a balanced intake. If you decide to go with a specific diet, like the Atkins' diet, you can still remain obese by taking in too much fat and protein. You have to understand that moderation is the best and only concept for calories.

A very important concept to realize is that the worst thing in the world to do is lose fat on a crash diet. I know that I belabor this point but it is **so** important. Again, the reason is because crash diets make you lose muscles, fat, and other tissues yet cannot change your body's physiology of altered hormones levels, the large stomach and the fat cell accumulations, especially if you do not exercise.

Lost muscle means losing the wonderful furnace you have that permitted fats to burn. It is very likely—statistically ninety-eight percent—that weight lost from a crash diet will be regained. When weight is regained, there are fewer muscles and more fat since empty fat cells are being refilled, but muscles cannot be regained.

Another damaging cycle is set into motion. The next time weight loss will be much more difficult and so goes the amplification of that vicious cycle.

Obviously crash diets do not work for the long term. This

short-term solution only compounds a problem that will grow the rest of your life. You have to take the bull by the horns and on a daily basis demonstrate willpower, discipline and gradually turn your life around.

Remember that a little bit of willpower each day gradually accumulates. Exercise a little bit more, eat a little less, balance your food a little more and rid of stress. Gradually your body changes and the stomach, fat cells and hormones will revert to normal.

Try not to eat for a few hours before you go to bed. Remember that a little bit of hunger is not going to kill you and as a matter of fact that is when you gradually reabsorb fat from its cells. This is when you are using your storage fat fuel and is really an ideal time to reduce fat. Also remember that perceived hunger, thinking that you are hungry, does not necessarily mean that you are legitimately hungry. It may be, and usually is, only a habit. So fight this routine and start a new healthier one.

Eat slowly as food will taste better and provide better salivation. Chew food well, making digestion easier. Eat a smaller volume which gradually reduces the size of the stomach, and then meals can be more thoroughly enjoyed. This is more satisfying psychologically and can be far better eating at a leisurely and satisfying pace.

When people gain weight in their later years, life is sure to be shortened as older people are already more susceptible to such maladies as heart disease, diabetes, increased blood pressure, strokes, osteoporosis or arthritis. To avoid getting into that stage of life and having to lose weight, start As soon as possible to develop good habits. Take the bull by the horns no matter what stage of life you are in, and go for it. You can do it! You cannot lose weight unless you rid your body of the excess energy fuel. *Calories in Calories out.* The energy comes mostly from glucose and glycogen. Eat fewer carbs so you will not have any excesses that you need to get rid of.

242

You will not be hungry during exercise. You will burn many more calories because muscles are producing much heat requiring calories. It is while you are exercising that the Fat Reabsorbing Hormone will be at work and makes it possible to lose weight. You will feel so good mentally and physically!

Foods

To choose appropriate foods you should understand the insulin concept and know that the lower the insulin, the less hungry you are. High insulin is mostly a result of high glucose or eating carbohydrates. As insulin goes down, because it immediately disposes of the high blood glucose level, hunger returns with a vengeance. If high glycemic index foods such as sugars and pastas are eaten, hunger will continue to constantly recur every two hours.

The quality of food eaten must be changed and improved. Fats, proteins and green vegetables such as broccoli, Brussels sprouts, cabbage or cauliflower, will not raise the insulin very high therefore not create the rollercoaster effect of a sugar or starch diet. A low-fat diet should *not* be followed. An increase in the amount of proteins and fats and a reduction of high glycemic index carbohydrates is required. Very soon hunger will nearly vanish between meals. It is nearly impossible to not be constantly hungry on a low fat diet.

I think most people who criticize a higher fat and meat diet that is a balanced one such as The Atkins Diet have not read the entire book to understand the whole picture. The sustained diet regimen that Dr Atkins suggests is more balanced and more logical than the acute weight loss he suggested at the beginning of the book. It is interesting that Dr. Ornish tempered his philosophy and migrated towards more fats and meats and a balanced diet in moderation. The Atkins group, formed after the death of Dr Atkins, also toned down the overeating of meat, emphasizing a balanced diet characterized by moderation.

Other valuable books to read on diet include *The Zone* by Dr. Barry Sears, *The Carbohydrate Addicts* by Dr. Heller and

Protein Power by Dr. Eades.

Like Dr. Atkins they have followed this concept of a balanced diet and have expanded it by adding more valuable knowledge and insights. In your quest, these books will reverberate for years to come, as you enjoy the newfound health and vitality practices found in them.

Since the Atkins diet tends to produce ketosis, let me explain and dispel any fear of the protein ketosis, which is a high level of ketones, the product of protein breakdown in the body, produced in blood.

First of all, that portion of these diets, the one with high meat and fat intake, is very short in duration, two to three weeks at most or at least should be. If kidneys are abnormal for some reason, ketosis could become a problem and that is more likely if you are a diabetic or have kidney diseases. In general, if mostly meat is consumed constantly, the ketosis level could be very high.

This is the natural way to rid the excess fats accumulating in a body and can be accomplished simply by drinking more water and letting all the ketosis material drain out via the kidneys and sweat. It may be that the body's sweat and urine will smell differently. This is not dangerous to health in short duration with normal kidneys.

Be careful to drink plenty of fluids, mostly water, and ketosis will not be a problem as the kidney will have water to get rid of it. Diabetic ketosis is more complicated and dangerous.

Diabetics should not follow this regimen.

Although I recommend these books, I am not advocating crash diets. All that I am suggesting is that these books contain valuable information to help you understand foods and the physiology for a healthy life style. I am sure there are many other good books on this topic that I have not yet read.

If you are not already following a healthy diet, your pattern of eating should be normalized into a diet of your own. With careful choices about food, your life will be more comfortable and without constant nagging hunger pains. Bad foods, which are mostly processed foods, can create all kinds of abnormalities. Most of these are very high in carbohydrates, preservatives and transfats.

Most are also prepared with oils that have been hydrogenated which are trans-fats that cause a high cholesterol level but also lower high molecular weight lipids, HDL. Most oils, except olive and canola when cooked.

All of these will revert to bad eiconasoids with the problems associated with them. Therefore, the less processed food that you eat, the better off you are. Processed foods also contain many preservatives that I believe are not healthy in the long run. A balanced diet eating varied foods will provide all the necessary ingredients and will also furnish the important vitamins and minerals necessary for your body. Eat moderate amounts if you expect to lose weight. Eat plenty of fish particularly fat fish that contains omega-3s, like salmon, to provide good ecosanoids. There is less chance of weight gain or depression with good ecosanoids.

Drink water reasonably. It is necessary in transporting the byproducts of fat reabsorption, ketosis, through the kidneys and sweat glands. But do not drink too much water, as it can dilute electrolyte levels in the blood.

You *cannot* lose weight without exercise. Start slowly and graduate up until exercise becomes a solid and enjoyed part of your life. This is not going to happen immediately nor will it satisfy any feed-on-demand instincts, but again you are in this for the long haul.

That is a pretty big deal, *to have the opportunity to enhance your entire existence*! So work hard to reach your optimum health weight and continue to follow a suitable exercise and diet regime. Weight gained will be a major load to carry for the rest of your life. Start now!

The more learned you are about a subject, the more you know all the pros and cons, the more objective you will be to evaluate and discuss it.

CHAPTER NINE

Protective Immunity and Healing

Both immunity and healing work closely together as the protective systems of the body in the event of attack by any invaders. Both these systems are symbiotic and complement each other. Without them we probably would not survive babyhood or for that matter any time in our lives particularly at our age due to the constant germs and allergens assaults we consistently have to defend against. These systems are like our bodies' Department of Homeland Security (immunity) and the Maintenance and Repair Departments (healing, or as I will call it *inflammation and repair*).

Now I will use the words *acute inflammation* instead of healing. The reason I do this is the media recently has pictured acute inflammation as a destructive mechanism in our system misleading us to think that acute inflammation is a bad phenomena in the body when actually it is entirely an invaluable one, indeed. It is important that you differentiate between *acute inflammation* and *chronic inflammation*.

Acute inflammation is the healing and repair department in our bodies and is absolutely good and necessary. We cannot do without it.

Conversely, chronic inflammation is also quite necessary but has strong destructive components to it that we must deal with. When the media refers to inflammation or to 'fire in the brain' they really are referring to chronic inflammation and it's destructive by products. It is the one that damages many organs and thus the bad rap it is getting.

Why is this? Because chronic inflammation is the result of two factions; one the invaders that are too tenacious to easily get rid of and, two, the healing process that is also persistent in this endeavor. Both are fighting it out and neither is winning. It is just like Iraq at the present with both factions constantly fighting and none clearly winning. While this is occurring great harm occurs in this ongoing war theater. It is just like any war zone with all the destruction of buildings, electricity, water, communication and so on. Chronic inflammation is a problem without resolution; it is too much of a good thing gone sour as it causes harm to the inner body environment and its organs while attempting to rid that invader

Acute inflammation, on the other hand, acts as the immediate response to an injury or an invader, the immunity is Land Security System that recognizes invaders. They work in very close cooperation. They are the immediate resolve of a problem so the damage has been repaired and gives you a completely restored system and maybe a few scars but life goes on unscathed. . . end of story

The immune system is quite intertwined with the inflammatory system. It deals with invading organisms. It takes over at about the same time the initial assaults are being taken care of by acute inflammation. The body recognizes invaders immediately and responds to quell any threat with all its immune cells and antibodies. Without this wonderful system even the mildest infection would become lethal.

If an infection is so overwhelming that your immune and/or acute inflammatory system cannot handle it, then physicians use the support of antibiotics, surgeries and other additive support mechanisms to fight the insurgents. These cunning organisms can even protect themselves from our antibiotics by developing a resistance to them, so care must be taken carefully and exactly. It is important for that reason to follow the doctor's prescription very closely.

So today when you see mostly lay articles *referring to*

inflammation as harmful, they are referring to inflammation gone haywire, unresolved or chronic inflammation. They often refer to it as the Fire in the Heart or the Fire in the Brain that are causing heart disease and brain disease and they are right:; it is harmful.

So please don't think of inflammation as a bad thing. It is only so when unresolved.

Acute Inflammation or Healing

Together the immediate response of acute inflammation and immunity act to protect and defend our bodies from the moment we are born until all of our systems shut down. When an attack from any forms of invaders or injuries this is what they do:

- Their functions are to prevent, protect, identify and remove the enemy. The attackers are the bacteria, virus, fungi or injuries that come to invade and do physical injury to the body.
- The police department and army reserves: are all of the white cells like leukocytes (acute inflammation), macrophages(the garbage collectors), lymphocytes (immunity) and what they secrete that is the humeral systems (antibodies) that immediately go to the invaders and destroy them. They are the deterrents, the fighting forces forever protecting us. If the invaders are too numerous or too aggressive, they win by destroying part or all the body.
- We need a good road to bring the troops, supplies and ammunitions to the war zone. That's when the blood vessels dilate, enlarge, and increase their circulation to accommodate the new cell traffic.
- Then they fight and kill the enemy and clean up the debris.
- Then the Maintenance Department takes over and repairs or rebuilds the damage: the acute inflammation and repair systems of our body that

deposit repair cells such as fibroblasts that secrete glue called collagen to stick tissues together(scar). Sometimes the repair is by re-growth of cells, called regeneration. This is seen on skin, liver and some nerves.

- We must have a system in place that identifies the enemy and keeps track of their movements. In our country we have the CIA, FBI, and Home Land Security. In the body we have the immune system that tracks the body's own proteins as 'Self Proteins,' instantly recognizing our citizens and sorting out aliens.
- Then we need a boarder patrol, which is our skin, an extraordinary protective physical and immune barrier.
- We also need a whole system that can respond to major attacks such as the army reserves. If we challenge our immune system, it has a way later to *develop huge potential protection on demand.* But it must be challenged by small daily attacks from bacteria or large attacks by controlled vaccinations of serious invaders such for instance polio. This process must start as a child and later in life, at our age, requires maintenance such as revaccinations, called boosters, or the natural daily contacts with bacteria and viruses.
- If the invasions are massive, outside help may be necessary. That is when a physician administers antibiotics as only one example of the many treatments they can do. It will destroy the bulk of the invaders and then the homeland security system, our immune system, can take over and finish the war.
- So if the war goes on and the invaders are not totally controlled, the war theater goes on in a continual basis. That is called chronic inflammation and is very destructive. That is the example of the present war in Iraq.
- If the infectious agents spread throughout your system and this is called septicemia, it can kill the

whole body.
- Antibiotics are specific toxic agents that kill bacteria. They will not kill all of the bacteria but lend a healing hand to the inflammatory system by killing the majority of these bacteria. At this time the white cells take over and destroy the remaining bacteria. So our immune and inflammatory systems are very necessary despite the antibiotics.

Chronic inflammation

If the cellular force is inadequate to handle the infection or the injury, the condition becomes chronic and lasts a long time. It may seem like the infection won. But the win is only partial and the body's healing inflammatory reaction is also a partial win.

For example, in such cases as gingivitis, a leg ulcer or abscesses, repair mechanisms and invaders are constantly battling each other. This is referred to as chronic inflammation or chronic infection as both arc involved in an ongoing destruction/repair mechanism. They are also spewing bacteria and depositing these minor infections all over the body, which starts other inflammatory reactions elsewhere. The goal at that point is to try and stop the invader entirely by putting skin grafts on ulcers, flossing teeth, cleaning wounds vigorously or opening an abscess to rid the bacteria inside and giving appropriate and longer antibiotic treatments and so on.

Other damaging agents like high blood pressure, free-radicals, low potassium, sodium or magnesium, radiation exposure, nitrites, chronic bacterial invasion, can damage the lining of blood vessels or other organs and set up a vicious cycle of chronic inflammatory reaction. Virtually every disease that occurs in a body initiates a reactive inflammation and that inflammation plays a very important role in the whole pathology or disease process of the body.

During any inflammation the, *whole body* is affected as the mobilized the police and maintenance departments are constantly obstructing roads and other areas being repaired or protected. If you get tonsillitis occurring in two very small glands in the throat, you feel absolutely awful during the infection period. Your varied body mechanisms have been mobilized to fight this and you can feel quite totally physically sick. You are tired, do not think well, have aches and pains, fever, just because two small glands are infected.

By the way, bad immunity will *increase* the likelihood of a chronic inflammation presence in our body. It permits bacterial resistance and decreases our fighting powers against these bacteria. It is imperative to keep your immunity as fit as possible.

If this process is ongoing it of course eventually affects the body detrimentally. Chronic inflammation is both a healing endeavor and is an intrinsic cause of disease, or at least a very important part of it. The destructive part of it becomes a huge destructive factor in the heart's coronary vessels, thus directly causing heart attacks.

Inflammation may come from other sources, like constant bacteria in the blood from gingivitis, chronic bladder infection, vaginitis, prostatitis, chronic a viral infection like Lyme's disease, stomach ulcers with H.Pylori, bad eicosanoids, homocysteine, environmental toxins, free-radicals, heavy metals, and the list goes on. Insulin at high levels causes inflammation. Obesity is often associated with chronic systemic inflammation. Cholesterol is an oxidizer thus a free-radical also causing heart disease but only the remaining part after the cholesterol has been used for all its other functions.

Sometimes it is not known where an inflammation is, but an intense search is necessary to find and cure an inflammation. C - reactive protein (CRP) is a blood test that is very reliable *as an inflammation indicator*. More and more physicians now think it is more reliable as a heart disease indicator than cholesterol levels. LDL or low molecular weight cholesterol acts as a free-radical. Fifty percent of people with heart disease have a normal cholesterol level according to Dr. Sinatra.

The strong influence of chronic inflammation in the brain is described in a book titled *The Fire in the Brain* by Dr. David Perlmutter. He describes the fire as chronic inflammation destroying the brain in Alzheimer's, senile dementia and in Parkinson's disease. For instance, in Alzheimer's there is a substance called amyloid which is an inflammation byproduct and likely systematically responsible for the destruction of the brain in these diseases. That substance is secreted by the microglial cells, which are the inflammation cells of the brain.

This recent discovery is of substantial importance. Determining if you have systemic inflammation and ridding your body of it is an essential part of staying healthy.

Immunity

An embryo, and then a young baby, survives invaders by being protected by its mother's immunity transferred through the placenta and retained until about six months of age.

At that time, a body cannot differentiate between its own proteins and that of outside invaders. The mother's immunity must do that for the first six months. During this first six months period, the body labels all its own cells and proteins. That is when the proteins are tagged 'Self *Proteins"*.

Conversely foreign invader cells or proteins become *"Non-Self"* proteins to that young body and for the rest of its life for that matter, and thus immediately incite a rejection mechanism.

By age six months, your system recognizes what are self and non-self tagged proteins. Thus the network of protective responses can now recognize which are our own citizen proteins and which are the invader proteins or *non-self Proteins*.

So the child now can develop his or her own immunity to fight the invaders that it now can now recognize. *Non-self Proteins* are parasites, bacteria, viruses, fungi, pryons, or any other foreign proteins entering the body such as transplanted organs The importance of this is this tagging lasts all our life. It is your passport to security

This protective army in a body will gradually improve as the child ages and as the environment challenges the immune system to grow and become more specific in fighting invaders. Fortunately a healthy immune system can accommodate and readily adapt to the challenges of new invaders by increasing as needed the number of specific cells and proteins to appropriately fight these attackers. The system reacts entirely to stimulus. *If not challenged it will not grow* to meet future more substantial and virulent challenges and will not be able to protect the body adequately. If challenged on a daily basis it will become strong and in constant fighting form thus wards off invaders. It is therefore very important to keep your immune system very healthy.

The entire key to immunity is its ability to ward off attacking organisms. The whole process is the battle of who will win the big wars. The question becomes if the body's police force is strong enough or has specific fighting capabilities to defeat the invaders however virulent they are or is the invader too numerous and aggressive and overcome defenses.

If the invaders win, it becomes an overwhelming infection, a disease that could become fatal. If the immune system armies win, life goes on unscathed. Again if both factions continue in a guerrilla war for a long time, neither winning nor loosing, then it is called *chronic inflammation* as I have described.

It is important to know that if *you must constantly challenge your immune system* with smaller aggressions such as daily contacts with bacteria, viruses, molds etc then the body's responsiveness will be stronger and stronger and ready for greater attacks. There is no reason for that system to grow or be in constant readiness if there is no purpose for it to do so.

As I have said above good immunity will be important to prevent or lower chronic inflammation. The immune system, like any muscle, organ or system, in the body, will atrophy if not used. So when an attacker comes there is no state of preparedness It is too weak to defend the body.

It is thus far better *not* to sterilize everything with all these antiseptics being sold, rather let daily contacts with bacteria naturally occur so the body's immune system is constantly exercised to stays active and fit.

Clean is okay, but sterilizing everything does not challenge the system enough or at all for that matter. Of course, massive exposure to bacteria should be avoided, *but no challenge is by far worse than continual small challenges as your system will not have practice in defense against future attacks.*

We must not be obsessed by sterility.

Today we are overwhelmed with advertisements selling antiseptics for all phases of our life style: hand sanitizers; bathroom sterilizers, wipes and clots and sprays to kill all the "bad bacteria and cold viruses". The media is creating a bad phobia against germs that ultimately will be detrimental to us.

All this is extraordinarily against logic, as you are not developing your immunity, you are using toxic chemicals that by themselves are harmful. And you are developing a false sense of security that will be very detrimental when the serious micro-organism attackers come. These products are developed because big business wants to make huge amounts of money by brainwashing you to think "sterile".

Some attacks against the immune system, such as small pox, whooping cough, poliomyelitis and tetanus, are too virulent (i.e. very aggressive(, thus it's recommended that you prepare for and anticipate an attack by enhancing your immune system with vaccinations. A vaccination is a weakened challenge to a specific disease. Vaccines are the reason we have eradicated these diseases and increased the longevity of society. If the entire population is immunized then no disease will occur and no virus will spread, since there is no disease to spread.

There have been virtually none of these viral diseases since the population has been totally immunized. Nearly all people have had DPTP, small pox and measles vaccinations in their youths. (DPTP stands for Diphtheria, Pertussis [whooping cough] Tetanus and Poliomyelitis.) These diseases are no longer seen in the United States, but there are many instances in third world societies where very few people are immunized. This makes us susceptible when we travel to these places, if we are not vaccinated.

As we grow older and these immunities weaken, so we must re-exercise them by a *booster vaccine*. **All of us senior citizens must do just that—get re-vaccinated (boosted).**

One very interesting fact is that surgery in third world countries maintains nearly the same infection rate as our society. Even though the sterility of US operating rooms is statistically so much better, the post-operative infection rates are nearly the same as ours. Why? Because these third world people are in constant daily contact with germs and develop healthy immunity against them.

In America people are so protective and obsessed by bacteria that they avoid them by sterilizing and putting antiseptics on everything thus do not develop immune systems by daily micro-vaccinations. So Americans become more susceptible to infections instead of averting them with their deliberate and excessive use of antiseptics. It is the obsession of the "Howard Hughes" syndrome and it is very detrimental both for future more involved invasions of germs and for chronic inflammation.

I noticed in my trips to third world communities that I became less and less sick as I went to more countries. I refer mostly to gastroenteritis, colds and flues. I do continue to get colds on these trips as I am trapped in planes for long periods and there are so many cold viruses' species that it is impossible to self –immunize against all for them. But colds are short lasting because of my immunity.

There has been major research indicating our protected civilization has more allergic problems such as asthma, hay fever and allergic skin diseases. There are also very well correlated speculations that Diabetes Type, Crohn's disease, and Multiple Sclerosis also may be the result of the lack of contact with "dirt." Dirt holds bacteria and their endotoxins and exotoxins.

Endotoxins are the bacteria's body material and when destroyed act as a toxin; while exotoxins are a substance secreted by the bacteria similar to snake secreting venom.

Researchers have learned that farmers and children who have contact with dirt in early years have substantially lower levels allergies. We have known this for many years but now it is substantiated by an article in the New England of Medicine titled "Eat Dirt."   [NEJM02; 347; 911.20 and 930]

Auto-immune diseases

The immune system is very powerful. It can protect against a constant flow of attackers and is the reason why humans survive so many years.

Unfortunately, it can also destroy the body with these protective reactions. The constant damage produced by this on going chronic immune reaction is just like in a chronic inflammation that damages many tissues such as joints, muscles heart lungs and eventually many other organs.

But the immune system reacts either to foreign proteins absorbed by the gut or to our own protein that are no longer tagged "Self Proteins" and constantly activated the rejection phenomena.

Rheumatoid Arthritis is a flagrant example of this. Other

such diseases include scleroderma, lupus erythematosus, psoriasis, Crohn's disease, and ulcerative colitis and a few others that each have their own specific methods and site of destruction.

Organs are invaded by many immune cells, in these cases plasma cell that secrete toxic destructive agents. This destruction in turn brings a chronic immune reaction that also is destructive just like the one I described above in chronic inflammation. This creates a double jeopardy that is extremely toxic to these various organs.

We do not know exactly what is the origin of the non-self proteins invading the body. One speculation is that our proteins have been altered, for instance by free-radicals, mutations in the genetic DNA, toxic or radiation damage to proteins that change the faces of these proteins as not recognizable by the body as non-self.

Another point of speculation is that our small intestines become defective (the leaky gut syndrome, discussed in *The Four Pillars of Healing* by Leo Galand MD) and cannot break down the proteins to there smallest versions, the amino acids, which by the way are not subject to the immune reaction when it enters the blood from the gut. Instead it absorbs the proteins in a larger version called peptides and these are immunogenic, thus developing this massive immune reaction against them as they enter the body inappropriately and eventually destroy the body.

Today the standard method of controlling these auto-immune diseases is by preventing the effects of the destructive components like the cytokines, just to name one.

Organ Transplants
If a foreign protein is inserted into the system, such as a transplanted organ, the body will immediately attack this new foreign protein and reject it as a foreign invader, unless of course it is of the same 'type' as our own tissues. This is known

as the Rejection Phenomenon.

If doctors can transplant organs that have a similarity to your own tissue, then the negative reaction will be less or none. For example if I am a blood type "A" and receive a type "A" blood in transfusion, then I will accept the blood as my own. But if a wrong type is transfused, my immune system will reject it completely and it could do great harm to me.

Very recently heart surgeons have started doing heart transplants on very small babies, less than six months of age for that very reason. A child does not have his own immunity before that age so he or she does not reject the donor heart and operations are more successful with no rejection phenomena.

By the way blood, is the most common transplanted organ, and easy to match as it is liquid and cross matching reactions are easy to detect.

Hard tissues such as those in the heart or kidneys, however, do not have that ready capacity for easily detecting incompatible matches as blood. As a result, in transplanting an organ a gross typing is done and the immune system must be tampered down to prevent rejection. The patient then has an impaired immune system so it does not reject the organ, however are more susceptible to infections and cancer.

Quick tips for boosting your immunity

Attitudes
Chronic unrelieved stress is the most severe threat to your immune system. Fear, depression, anxiety, irritability, grief and negative attitude all contribute to releasing chemical changes, neuropeptides-cortisol which greatly reduces the effectiveness of the immune system and sometimes renders it useless.

Strong evidence shows that positive attitude and strong visualization techniques to turn a negative attitude around can improve immunity. The reverse—depression, negative feelings, stress, fear, and bad companions—are great deterrents to healthy immune reactions. One's negative mood can actually reduce the numbers of T.lymphocytes, referred to as *killer lymphocytes*. This fact is well demonstrated in the literature and current research. See the JAMA primer on Allergies and Immunity, December 1997.

Eliminating fear or stress

Visualization is a good defense against alien invaders. A high percentage of cancer patients are immobilized by fear and often this negatively affects their own immune capabilities. Remember in my discussion of brain-body interactions how fear and stress affected the whole system negatively.

A very positive attitude however will greatly improve the productivity of immune cells. This is particularly important in cancer that benefits from the fighting capability of these cells to attack the cancer.

"Eat Dirt"

This is actually the partial name of an article that discusses the protection imparted by the spores in dirt that give natural immunity against allergies. Please do not actually eat dirt as the saying suggests, but remember that the dust or dirt on and around children is a low level contact and is actually quite beneficial. I realize this thought is so opposing and repulsive to the present teachings from most lay sources; however I strongly believe because of my own experience with surgery at home and all over the world, and much reading, that this is the logical, natural way to protect yourself and your children.

Extreme exertion

Remember that activities that necessitate substantial exertion like marathon running or extreme mountain climbing can severely deplete your system and temporarily depress the white blood cells of your immune system. So moderation is in order.

Always stay well hydrated, well nourished, control the heat

and cold carefully, and train well. Also stay focused and use care in the training process. Eat intelligently and *replace electrolytes especially potassium.*

I have a feeling that long airplane travel with its depleted oxygen can weaken your protective system and make you susceptible to colds and flus.

Foods' effect on immunity

Nutritionists know that malnutrition depletes the immune system and those with poor diets, which include crash diets, are more susceptible to poor healing and infections.

Taking the right nutrients, you will create good building blocks for your body, and that is *not* obtained by eating mostly carbohydrates, but by having all the proper amino-acids and essential fatty acids along with the carbohydrates in your diet. This permits the creation and maintenance of healthy humoral globulins, immune cells that fight along with the inflammatory cells against invaders. Stay away from damaging foods and toxins (trans-fats, excess soy, preservatives, and so on). Take anti-oxidant supplements as recommended, as they will neutralize free-radicals from damaging immune cells. There is strong evidence that a vegetarian diet does not procure adequate amounts of essential amino acids to sustain good, strong, and numerous immunity cells. Vegetarian diets are not sufficient and cannot sustain a strong defensive immunity in case of a severe invader. These are provided only by meats, or all amino-acids additives if you insist on keeping a vegetarian diet.

Rapid and excessive weight loss

We all know that attaining and maintaining an appropriate body weight and condition is the first goal in a good exercise regime. Inappropriate diets and long periods of starvation will dramatically reduce the effectiveness of your defense mechanism. They can cause permanent damage to some or all body parts and organs, including your immune system. Your diet should provide the proper nutrients to sustain all your systems and should always be accompanied by an exercise regime.

Surgery and injuries

In post-operative or post-traumatic situations the immune system tends to be depleted due to the mobilization of an intense repair mechanism and trauma to the constitution. Those who take the bull by the horns and fight uphill with a positive attitude and active participation in recuperation do far better and heal much faster. I have seen this time and time again and have encouraged patients to be very involved in the post-operative recuperation with a good positive attitude, exercises that are not immediately detrimental to the surgery and use of the least narcotics possible. Aerobic exercise increases the blood supply to all tissues and accordingly increases the healing capability many folds. There will be less pain and much faster healing to resume your normal life. Your immune system is substantially more functional with a positive experience. Eat the same balanced diet with the same supplements after surgery.

When fighting an illness, use a minimal amount of narcotic pain medication. Don't linger in bed or stay away from work if you can possibly get up and out. Whenever faced with an adverse health situation, be as active and emphatic about your recovery as possible. I am also convinced that narcotics alter immunity, and/or the acute inflammatory reaction. Pain medications interfere with healing and the mental capability that enables you to heal faster. An early and adequate amount of pain medication is quite acceptable, but do not allow extended demand for pain pills to linger into longer recuperations. Protect and stimulate your immune system as much as possible!

Preventions

Vaccines are very effective against viral diseases with the exception of AIDS and so far malaria. They are altered, weakened viruses and do not give the full disease but will stimulate the immunity system when injected. The immune cells have a memory that look at these viral perpetrators and remember them as villains, mostly for the rest of your life. Once they have this memory, they can respond very quickly to an attack and hasten defeat. Rarely is the attacker so overwhelming that the immune system cannot vanquish the culprit once it has captured that memory.

Many diseases in our century have been totally eradicated by vaccines and to deny the enormous benefit for the masses vs. a very minute possibility of complications is what I believe a classic example of the paralysis of analysis that I have written of in previous chapters. I think parents who impose this unbalanced judgment on their sick children should be held responsible for these actions if they cause harm to their children and subsequently to others.

I understand that there is generally no contact with many of these eradicated diseases in our country, but that is not the case in countries around the world and it is inevitable that children will journey afar in the future as travel is easier and more accessible than ever. Many third world immigrants are coming here now and may put us at risk but of course not if we are immunized. These foreign traveler in our country may be carriers of one of theses diseases and could also infect our children if not protected.

You should not adopt any part of the Howard Hughes attitude. Everything around you should *not* be sterile, but instead left to normal levels of contaminants so you will continually challenge and sharpen your immunity's growth. A child who is over-protected from contact with 'dirt' will not have the proper immunity tools to defend against infectious diseases and daily invaders.

I want to re-emphasize the following concept: I believe far too much emphasis has been placed on harmful actions like wiping door handles, not letting a child pick up objects from the floor, using disinfectant soaps, dishes, sterilizing carpets etc. These are actions that deny a wonderful opportunity of developing self protection via the immune system to children. It is the natural form of vaccination.

Question what the media tells you and research everything you are not familiar with regarding your child. I do not suggest that you expose a child to gross contamination but limited exposures, as they occur naturally in the world can actually be more healthy in the long run. If you behave over-cautiously about your child's exposure he/she will suffer the consequences later in life i.e. at our age. Try not being so obsessed about dirt and realize that bacteria are *not* always a predator but normal contacts strengthen our immunity.

There are at least thirteen trillion bacteria in your body, most of which are helpful doing one function or another and living in harmony with your immunity. We cannot live without these bacteria as they are responsible for many functions in the body, the least of which is fighting the unwanted germs assaulting our body. You live with your own environment's bacteria and it is absolutely impossible to not have contact. You should arm yourself against them, and the only way to do this is to immunize yourself by constant contact with these bacteria, thus developing resistance.

When you go to other environments, other countries, use caution since you have not developed the protection you may need for their bacteria. If you go to another country, even a civilized one, the infectious organisms will be different and you will be more prone to get a cold, flue, gastroenteritis, or traveler's diarrhea simply because you have not been in contacts with them. Drink clean water that you have filtered yourself or *sealed* bottled water even though bottled water.

Unsealed bottled water is not always safe as I have very regrettably and personally experienced. Always eat foods that are fully cooked and take care with the vegetables and fruits you are served in salads, as these may have been washed with contaminated water. An illness doesn't necessarily occur because these countries have bad hygiene, but it could happen simply because these bacteria are foreign to your immunity.

Please note that what protection we have developed in our youth will affect us throughout our lives, including and particularly at our age. That is when a strong foundation of immunity cultivated as a youth will come to our rescue when severe germ invasions assault us.

Many adults die of infections because indeed they have not had a good base of immunity and have not challenged or boosted it continually in their life span to keep their fighting capabilities up. This is particularly so in older malnourished, debilitate adults that no longer have a good protective immunity. They have not kept up with it and when they need it most it is no longer there.

Cancer

Cancer is a very complex disease and obviously we do not know all the ramifications. But let me simplify the concepts: cancer cells come from cells gone haywire and that grow totally unregulated. Some form of damage occurred to the original cell that started it. That damage came from an injury altering the DNA-RNA within the cell.

Secondly, if we develop cancer we absolutely need a good immunity as *that is our only mechanism within our body that can fight it*. Chemotherapy, radiation and cancer surgery's function is to rid the majority of bad cells, that is debulk the tumor to permit the body to take over once the large volume of cancer cells are gone. At this point the body's immunity does have a fighting capability.

Chemotherapy destroys cells that are fast-growing. In doing so, it not only destroys the fast-growing cancer cells, but other cells in the body that have a fast rate of growth. Among these are white blood cells including the immunity's and skin cells, particularly hair follicles, to name a few. So there is a period when the body has to recuperate before the immunity takes over, as it has been severely depleted. It is a very fine line to tread. After this, the immune system must take over and destroy any straggler cells.

So your immune system is of crucial importance. This is the time to shore it up since these treatments will create havoc with it.

Just follow the advice below.

How to keep your immune system at high performance

- Keep a positive attitude. We know that our immune cells quantities are elevated with positive attitude and laughter.
- Fear, stress, bad mood, negative attitude are known to seriously depress immunity.
- Having good friends and family as support will boost your fighting capabilities.
- Eat the correct foods in a varied menu with meats and fish. Please remember that proteins and fats are the primary building blocks for immune cells.
- Stay away from toxins including above all smoking. They cause free-radicals that destroy cells including immunity cells. Their free-radical status is known to cause cancer anyway.
- Be very careful not to eat large sustained quantities of soy in any forms.
- Understand that exercise is your strongest advantage though it may not feel like that at first. Excessive exercise can be detrimental.
- Challenge your immune system with normal, daily contact with "dirt." Do so before and after your immunity has recuperated from chemotherapy.
- Make sure you are well immunized with vaccines and get booster vaccines later in life.
- Chronic Inflammation causes a lot of free-radicals that are detrimental to immune cells. So ask your doctor to search for it by doing blood testing (CRP), find the cause

and correct it if it is present.

Do make the decision to take antioxidants, which shore up the good cells, but talk to your oncologist as well, as some feel that they also shore up cancer cells. More and more physicians feel that the cancer cells are defective anyway, so it is best to boost up the immune cells.

Take valuable supplements like those below to boost healing and the immune system. See dosages in the Daily Guide in Chapter Twelve.

- Vitamin C
- Vitamin E (no more than 200mg/day)
- B complex Vitamins
- Co Q-10 (to feed the cell's energy furnaces for better vigor)
- Zinc and selenium: (necessary metals for the formation of immunity cells.) Faster healing occurs in patients after surgery when these metals were added to their regimens.
- Omega-3 fatty acids (to boost good eicosanoids) either as fish in your diet or as pills.

Taking herbal supplements cannot replace proper nutrition, exercise, a positive attitude, and antioxidants. We do not always know what is in them, and some of their unknown ingredients could be noxious. There are many well-meaning healers out there who may convince you to take these herbal supplements. Research your specific situation and weigh this decision very carefully. Remember they have a product to sell.

Also, herbal supplements can have, and often do have, other ingredients in them that could be harmful. Take soy as an example. It has an estrogen-like substance that could be very detrimental to cancer of the breast patients.

Also remember that after you are healed, you must keep a

healthy life style with all the proper foods and supplements. Chemotherapy but particularly radiation by themselves can and could potentially cause cancer twenty or thirty years later, so if you are physically prepared you have a better chance of averting it.

Allergies

Allergic reactions are another form of immunity. Repeated tiny assaults with some form of irritants, especially if done on the mucous membranes of the gastrointestinal track or respiratory membrane, can incite a hypersensitivity reaction like asthma, hay fever, food allergies etc. These are most often seen in children who are not breastfed. There also is a hereditary component.

A great majority of these allergies must be due to proteins. Otherwise they are caused by a chemical hypersensitivity, which is not an allergy.. For example, peanuts have high proteins and will incite allergic reactions called atopic reactions that can be very severe.

An atopic reaction is the vicious response of the allergic system that smothers the body causing very low blood pressure, hives and swelling including the voice box that can obstruct the airway. Obviously very serious, they should be tended to immediately as a dire emergency.

Hypersensitivities tend to develop with repeated contacts with the offending agent. Minute contacts with the mucosa tend to be worse. A flagrant example is the great increase in penicillin allergies in the mid-1940s and '50s.

At that time, all kinds of lozenges and elixirs were produced. They had only small amounts of penicillin in them, but nonetheless hypersensitized many in our population and caused extensive penicillin allergies. I suspect that giving antibiotics to cattle could have the same effect.

Hay Fever

It is a debilitating disease that adversely affects more than twenty percent of all Americans. The offending agents are countless, but common ones include the pollens of grass, trees and weeds, fungi, animal allergens, and dust mites. The symptoms are runny noses, blurred vision, earaches, and grogginess and treatments are focused on antihistamine and decongestants. It is usually a secretion of histamines that causes all the symptoms.

An allergist will often desensitize a patient by multiple, graduated contacts with the allergens. Sinusitis and nasal polyps are closely related to this pathology. Typically, hay fever is worse in childhood, then gradually decreases in intensity with age and generally is gone by the age of fifty or sixty. Allergies to pollens and aromatics usually respond well to anti-histamines. Today there are variations of these that cause less drowsiness.

Asthma

Asthma is a constriction of tiny sphincters, or circular muscles, in the very small bronchi, the smaller tubes in the lungs and when they close the tube, air can get in, but not as easily out. These muscles go into spasm when irritated by an allergen, that is to say the proteins that we are allergic to. This causes wheezing and a longer expiration than inspiration with less air circulating and less oxygen transfer.

Numerous factors will trigger attacks. The onset can occur in infancy, childhood alternatively later in adulthood. Factors can be pollens, viral infections, exposure to irritants, and exercise. Asthma can also occur if you move from one part of the country to another, where different pollens and irritants may exist and you are not resistant to it. The treatment for asthma can be complex, consisting of desensitization where applicable, smooth muscle relaxants such as inhalants, or an anti-inflammatory decongestant. This condition must be monitored closely by you and your physician, and is best treated with such measures as antihistamines, adrenalins like inhalers, and pills.

Food Allergies

Food allergies are like any other allergies in that they are a reaction to a protein to which one is hypersensitive. Approximately five percent of American children fewer than three years of age and one-and-a-half percent of the general population have food allergies. Approximately four to five million Americans are affected. These food allergies are discovered by parents as a child refuses or regurgitates food or get quite sick from it. The treatment is an elimination diet to find the offender; then avoid consuming the identified foods.

Highly allergenic foods like peanuts and sometimes other nuts can be more dangerous as they can cause anaphylactic reactions that could be lethal. A greater occurrence of this anaphylactic reaction has occurred in the last decade. Many foods contain these highly allergenic nuts while some have just contaminants of peanuts that increase the percentage of allergic people and aggravate the severity of reactions. These highly allergic nuts are more often found in convenient and cheap foods processed in vats that have processed peanuts and not been cleaned. Another type of food allergy are the Sprew syndromes, where people become quite sick without knowing why and then discover that they are allergic to something like glutens or lactose. Again the treatment is avoidance but that can be quite difficult and demand much research and knowledge to determine the problem.

Overall, we are meant to look after ourselves. It is certain each has to eat for himself, digest for himself, and in general care for his own dear life and see to his own preservation. Nature's intentions, in most things uncertain, in this are decisive.

Arthur Clough

When resting in safety, do not forget that danger may come.
Confucius

CHAPTER TEN

Antioxidants

Vitamins

Vitamins are facilitators of various chemical reactions in the body called catalysts or enzymes whose function is to facilitate chemical reactions in cells and neutralize free-radicals and excessively *oxidized* molecules, thus the term *antioxidants*.

There are many types of vitamins and each has a specific function. Some vitamins are fabricated by the body such as vitamin D. Most, however, come from outside sources such as diet or supplements. Vitamin C is not produced by the human body at all except during pregnancy.

If you maintain a balanced diet, you are likely to obtain all the ingredients required necessary for the facilitation of these chemical reactions but you may have to eat large quantities of unnecessary other ingredients. If you want to make sure you have enough in your diet then take additive vitamins. Sometimes your body cannot absorb vitamins, like in the instance of antibiotics that may destroy the bacteria that facilitate the absorption of vitamin K. Another example is the lack of the 'intrinsic factor' in the stomach that is necessary to absorb vitamin B12, and that is lost as aging occurs or stomach acid blockers are taken. This is more likely to occur as we age so it is best to have more intake of vitamins to overcome these deficiencies.

Many Americans over age sixty are quite deficient in vitamins *C, E, A and folic acid* even by minimum standards, according to a Tufts research. Although being deficient in vitamins at any point in life is undesirable, these years are especially dangerous. The body is in a natural breakdown phase already and requires all the vitamins possible to stay healthy. Many diseases are attributed to the higher demand of vitamins and the lower supply of these vitamins to the body. Accelerated aging is demonstrated by heart disease, cancers, diabetes, brain diseases, cataracts, arthritis or osteoporosis. Simple increased dosages of vitamins may avert these debilitating diseases.

Taking antioxidants during youth may slow down the cumulative damage by oxidation and free-radicals could become more harmful in older years as the body deteriorates. I believe taking antioxidants may even maintain higher strength of constitution for much longer.

Proper kinds and dosages of vitamins are crucial supplements for pregnant women as developing little human beings need exactly the right ingredients for proper development. These additional vitamins regulate and promote healthy growth for the extraordinary miracle called the embryo. Early development from two cells to a full fetus is so intricate that every step requires exact amounts of all the micronutrients and enzymes necessary for each individual step.

One example I have had much experience with is a cleft lip. If not hereditary, as in twenty-three percent of the cases, this condition is caused by a lack of fusion of the cell at the lip edges of a six week old embryo. A lack of a vitamin or damage by free-radicals caused by pollution such as smog, smoking, viruses and radon are the cause the cells do not fuse at that lip edge leaving a cleft of the lip and/or palate.

The lack of folic acid during the development period, pregnancy, for instance results in brain or spinal cord abnormalities, such as Spina Bifida, an opening in the spinal cord and other brain and spinal defects. This is mostly preventable by taking folic acid. There are very serious consequences for the lack of folic acid, especially considering that preventions are simple. Every woman in the world should take folic acid during pregnancy to avert that dreaded defect.

In aging, the cumulative damage of free-radicals is far greater than it was during our younger years. See Chapter five for more about free-radicals.

In our youth, vitamins stay in the body longer, but as we age these vitamins do not linger in the body as long. Therefore, they must be replaced constantly. This is why you need to take more vitamins as you age. So equip yourself well, protect what you have, and you will have a far better chance of surviving without diseases.

Interesting studies have recently shown that older adults taking vitamins and supplements have fewer diseases with less cost to Medicare, to the tune of a few billions annually. Get on the vitamin band wagon now!

In her book, *Stop Aging Now*, Jean Carper includes the following concepts:

- A natural part of aging is mineral and vitamin loss and deficiency.
- Mega doses of antioxidant vitamins and minerals are better to give the body a choice of what it needs. The body will use what is needed and eliminates any excess. One exception to this involves oil soluble vitamins such as A, D, and E. Be careful not to take too much of these as they accumulate and can reach toxic levels.
  Dr. Linus Pauling believed that taking mega doses of vitamins permits cells to perform at their peak genetic efficiency and will consequently slow aging and disease.
- Do not believe that food provides all the vitamins required. Processed foods have lost so many original vitamins that they are unreliable as a vitamin source.
- Vitamins do stave off diseases such as scurvy and rickets but also have an important and major role in

fighting chronic diseases like cancer or heart disease. They keep other functions healthy.

- Government sanctioned doses are the very minimum vitamins required to prevent specific ailments such as scurvy. They hardly help the very demanding aging deterioration in their recommended doses, let alone reverse this deterioration.
- The main function of vitamins is to increase antioxidants that battle free-radicals.
- Vitamins and minerals are relatively safe in mega doses. A few exceptions are mentioned later.
- Vitamins, minerals and supplements are cheap considering the cost of treatment for diseases they can prevent.
- Vitamins work in unison to protect you, enhancing and complementing each other. For instance vitamin E (lipid soluble) works on the cell membrane, which is a lipoprotein(fat and protein), while vitamin C (water soluble) works mostly on the cytoplasm (the inside structures) of the cell. They need each other to satisfy the whole cell.
- People who take large doses of vitamins, especially C and E appear to live longer and healthier.
- Heart disease victims have comparatively low blood and tissue levels of these antioxidants.
- Statistics show that large doses of vitamins decrease the incidence of heart disease, cancer, cataracts, and strokes and greatly improve immunity to fight infections.
- Although antioxidants are present in food, obtaining the high dosages that are now believed to be required is simply not possible from food. Because the quantities of antioxidants in foods ingested in a normal diet are much lower than recommended dosages, large volumes of foods would have to be eaten in order to receive the appropriate amount of vitamins. For example, in one eight ounce glass of orange juice there are only 30 mg of vitamin C and but 30 mg of sugar. If you wanted to provide even 500mg of vitamin C, you would need to

absorb about 510 mg of sugar, or 2,040 calories. Most doctors and dietitians usually recommend about 1,000 to 2,000 mg of vitamin C per day. These requirements are not met using only food as a provider of vitamins so supplementing vitamins in wise.

- Cooking also denatures many vitamins during food processing. For instance, most cereal companies add vitamins since processing often has destroyed them.

Christopher Columbus and his sailors on the Pinta, Niña and Santa Maria developed severe cases of scurvy. The problem could have been solved immediately by eating oranges. Obviously, each person could not eat hundreds of oranges, but even a few would have improved their health. The small amount of vitamin C was enough to cure scurvy, but not the free-radicals. Oranges did solve the scurvy problem but their life expectancy remained at thirty-six to thirty-eight years.

Although researchers do not know exactly how many vitamins the body needs, *the body ultimately makes the decision* on what vitamins are kept and used in the body and then discards any unused vitamins through urination. *I feel much safer letting my body make the choice*. And if taking supplemental vitamins reduces disease, it will be exponentially much less expensive in the long run.

This is not an area to pinch pennies. You would never even consider not putting oil in your car. Taking supplemental vitamins should be viewed as an investment, not a cost.

There has been much controversy on the subject of supplemental vitamins. As studies are analyzed, some researchers determine the results on inadequate doses and conclude that this or that vitamin is not effective for the reduction of disease. I believe that if there is no risk or problems in taking higher doses, and there is a possible large benefit, then taking supplemental vitamins is the safest course of action for preventative health. We see the benefits only years later.

Supplements are specific foods that accentuate levels of a certain protein or enzyme to make sure parts of the body are nourished well. For example, glucosamine is a basic food for the cartilages while Luteins improve eye health. Minerals are usually trace elements necessary in the biological functions of the body. Potassium is important for the inner function of the cell, particularly the very active muscle cell. Calcium phosphate and magnesium keep bone healthy with exercise.

Antioxidants

Antioxidants are agents that destroy free-radicals in the body. In various ways, they attack the various types of free-radicals and neutralize them. Numerous antioxidants such as vitamin C, E, A and coenzyme Q-10 tend to protect the body against harmful oxidative processes. Many others do the same in different sectors of the body.

Very important to remember is that vitamins are not solely antioxidants but that each has its own functions of safeguarding the development and normal functioning of a specific part of the body. Thiamine and folic acid work with brain and nerve tissues, vitamin D works with calcium, and so on. Also there are many antioxidants that are not vitamins such as Melatonin and Co-Q-10.

Following is a review of the various, more important, vitamins, supplements and minerals that the body requires. Remember that there are many more of these, but for the sake of simplicity only the important ones are covered here.

Vitamin A

Vitamin A is fat soluble, called *retino,* which is derived from a larger molecule of the type called *carotinoids.* The most important one is b-carotene, which is crucial to vision.

A deficiency of b-carotene is the leading cause of blindness in children. The eye retinas are rods for night vision and cones for color vision. The rods need to replace rhodopsin depleted during night vision, and retinol is required for this regeneration.

Zinc deficiency and alcoholism impair the release of rhodopsin from the liver.

Vitamin A attributes:

- Night blindness is the earliest symptom caused by deficiency.
- Maintaining the *epithelium* of various parts of the body. In the eyes this deficiency can cause corneal ulcers, blurry vision or dry eye. This deficiency also affects the lung lining, sweat glands, the whole mucosa of the bowel and a loss of taste.
- Considering that the small bowel is lined underneath mucosa with the greatest amount of lymph glands in the body, a deficiency in vitamin A damages the mucosa, indirectly the lymph glands and then the immunity system.
- Decreasing the mortality rate for children in Third World countries due to viral diseases at the rate of seventy-seven percent, and thirty-six percent of diarrhea. B Carotene would avert most of these mortalities. That also applies to American children although not that high of a percentage die in the United States.
- Boosting immunity to prevent or reduce skin and bowel problems for AIDS patients, Vitamin A in high doses, 15,000 to 20,000 IU has been effective.
- Alleviating skin problems substantially, including acne. There is strong evidence that new growths of cancers such as basal cells and squamous cells are arrested by a vitamin A supplementation of 30,000 IU per day.
- Improving diseases such as emphysema and chronic obstructive pulmonary disease.
- Aiding in prevention of cancers of the epithelium such as basal cells and squamous cells of the skin, prostate cancer and lung cancer. Protection is derived in part by taking 30,000 IU of vitamin A per day.
- Helping heal wounds like sunburns or incisions when treatment with vitamin A significantly speeds up the healing process.

- Helping blood sugar disorders as it adds stability to metabolizing glucose
- Vitamin C enhances its function.

Some studies indicate that *excess retinols* can increase the possibility of bone fractures in animals. A study in Sweden showed an increase of two-and-a-half times the number of hip fractures in older people with excess retinols, so do not exceed recommended dosages. The study does *not* indicate over dosage. Remember, it is a fat soluble vitamin and excesses can cause problems.

Vitamin A is found in cod liver oil and liver and to a lesser degree in butter, milk, cream and egg yolks. Dosage should be 10,000 to 30,000 IU per day.

Carotenoids
It is a derivative or a synthetic vitamin A and a commercial product of Vitamin A.

Lutein
Lutein is an important carotinoid and as a result is probably the best agent to prevent free radical formation in the eyes. There has been an increase in suggestions to take Lutein as an important antioxidant for the eye. Some studies show that it can prevent the formation of cataracts and also cuts the risk of macular degeneration by over fifty percent.

Dosage should be 10 to 20 mg per day. If vitamin A is taken to replenish part of the carotinoids, adding Lutein to the diet probably will not be necessary.

Lycopenes
Lycopenes are among the strongest vitamin A components. There was a wonderful study done in Italy of nearly fifty thousand men that showed a substantial thirty-five percent reduction of prostate cancer when participants ate two servings per day of foods containing tomatoes. Remember that

Lycopenes is a fat soluble vitamin and needs to be taken with somewhat of an oily or fat diet.

Dosage should be 10 to 30 mg per day.

B Vitamins

The B vitamins are a whole group that share, with some variations, the same general functions of deriving energy by extracting it from carbohydrates, fats and proteins to become useful for cells. They all work in cooperation with each other.

B1 or thiamine

B1 or thiamine's major function is to provide energy for nerve cells, particularly for initiating the nerve conduction in the peripheral neurons.

Deficiency can cause peripheral neuropathies with pain, tingling in hands and feet and weakness of muscles. Heart weakness called beriberi, heart disease, irritability, anorexia, headaches and weight loss are also results of B1 deficiency. Severe cases can cause brain disease with memory loss and confabulation, learning disabilities, emotional disturbances, mental impairment, emotional disturbances or Alzheimer's.

B1 is very important in promoting learning capabilities for both children and adults.

This is known to help diabetic neuropathies if given in therapeutic doses.

High doses have been known to ease painful headaches for many patients and are known to counteract lead poisoning.
Dosage should be 50 to 100 mg per day.

B2 Riboflavin

This B is not a major player, but like all members of a team, necessary as part of the B squad. Pure lack will mostly cause the following symptoms: Mouth irritation with burning and soreness, tongue inflammation, itching and burning of the eyes, anemia, personality disorders, night vision deterioration. B2 is also a natural tranquilizer and is necessary for the production of glutathione. It is also an important antioxidant. People with no cataracts have no deficiency in Riboflavin. Dosage should be 20 to 30 mg per day.

B3 Niacin

The symptoms of B3 deficiency are those of a gradual sensitive mouth, particularly tongue sores.

Confusion, disorientation, apathy, or outright dementias are other possible symptoms. Alcoholics have deficiencies in B3 because of their poor absorption and dementia may occur as a result.

Niacin is known to reduce LDL cholesterol levels substantially, up to twenty percent, and is used for that reason. One needs to take extremely high doses to do this and usually is monitored by a physician. Niacin appears to reverse schizophrenia at higher dosages.

Niacinamide is a B3 but has different functions. does not reduce cholesterol but is helpful for diabetics who require less insulin with it. It also protects the pancreas, reduces joint pain and improves mobility in osteoarthritis.

Niacinamide is found primarily in poultry meats, seafood, nuts and seeds. Dosage should be 20 to 30 mg per day. However, if used for cholesterol reduction up to three grams a day can be prescribed but treatment should be followed closely by a physician. This may elevate blood glucose in diabetics so careful monitoring is important.

Vitamin B6 Pyridoxine

Pyridoxine is an essential vitamin of the B complex and is involved in many important biochemical reactions:

- *Heart* Pyridoxine dilates vessels, opens bronchial passages, and is indispensable for producing prostaglandins, which are produced by platelets with pyridoxine, and are among other things, vasodilators. A mild diuretic, it increases urination to rid excess fluid in the body.

- *Diabetes* Pyridoxine decreases damage high blood sugar causes, preserves red blood cells, and lowers blood sugar thus helping reduce vision loss.
- *Immune system* The lack of Pyridoxine reduces the number of T-lymphocytes which protect the body from infections.
- *Hormone* Estradiol is a form of estrogen in women and is the likely carcinogenic estrogen.
- *Pregnancy..* depletes the body of pyridoxine, which aids with nausea, and alleviating depression.
- *Kidney stones…* Pyridoxine cuts down the formation of oxalate stone along with magnesium.
- *Brain and nerve problems…* Pyridoxine improves autism, epilepsy, attention deficit and depression. This is actually an important factor in producing epinephrine, serotonin necessary for normal brain function. Older people have better scores on memory tests when the Pyridoxine level is healthy.

Dosage should be 50 mg per day. At least 30 mg per day during pregnancy is recommended, and much higher doses in autism, depression, and epilepsy cases, up to 100 to 200 mg per day.

Folic acid

Folic acid has been known to have the following attributes:
:
- Being one of the most important B complex vitamins.
- Preventing ¾ of cases of the terrible birth defect called Spina Bifida and some other brain deformities when given to women during pregnancy.
- Getting rid of homocysteine, which has been known to cause heart disease, brain diseases such as

Alzheimer's, strokes and some cancers. It prevents and cures a certain anemia when combined with B12. Today we know that more people have homocysteine genetic defects that we know and since the clinical demonstration occurs only later in life it is wise to take this vitamin early. There is no harm in taking it and may save you life or quality of life substantially.

- Helping in osteoporosis.
- Helping in hormone therapy.
- Helping intestinal disorders like Crohn's colitis with large doses.
- Aiding in epilepsy, depression and schizophrenia in large doses.
- Alleviating peripheral neuropathy.
- Reducing cancer of the colon by seventy-five percent, according to a twenty-one-year study at Brigham Young University.

Found naturally mostly in foods like liver or kidney, this can also be obtained in smaller doses in kale, broccoli, beef, turnips, corn or beets. Cooking destroys ninety percent of the folic acid in the food.

Dosage should be 20 mg per day for average supplement., 20 mg per day is recommended for heart disease patients and 20 to 60 mg per day for menopause, colitis or depression. This is a safe supplement to take even in high doses. During pregnancy, consult with a physician but make sure folic acid is included in the diet.

B12 Cobalamine

Cobalamine is an important B vitamin and necessary for red blood cell formation and sustaining brain function. Present in all animal foods, Cobalamine is manufactured by bacteria in the bowel. Food needs an intrinsic factor in the stomach to permit absorption into the blood stream. As aging occurs, that factor is decreased and makes the body susceptible to B12 deficiencies thus the need for B12 injections.

Anti-ulcer drugs impair B12 absorption. Examples of these drugs include Prilosec, Aciphex, Prevacid and Nexium. An increase in B12 intake is then necessary and is best given by injection, although now a sublingual form seems as effective.

The main function of this vitamin is its involvement in the formation of myelin. Myelin is the envelope or insulator of most nerves in the brain and body. Various neurological problems will occur if the body is deficient in Cobalamine.

Cobalamine is important for:

- Improving mental functions for emotional, cognitive or memory confusion capabilities. Dementia can occur in older people, which is not surprising since they have less intrinsic factor and absorb less B12.
- Relieving nerve pain like diabetic neuropathy and shingles often abate after B12 injections.
- Relieving sleep disorders. Insomnia is often overcome as B12 contributes to the formation of melatonin.
- Ringing in the ears is a common symptom of B12 deficiencies. It is often demonstrated as earring loss since the ringing or a din constantly heard in the ears renders hearing difficult especially in older people . B12 injections are called for t=in these cases.
- Heightening homocysteine levels for Multiple Sclerosis patients. This is a demyelinating disease and B12 contributes to the formation of myelin.
- Some of these include viral hepatitis, low blood pressure, dizziness or lightheadedness when standing up.

As aging occurs, B12 shots may be necessary. Injections of 1 to 10 mg per day have profoundly changed patients with chronic fatigue, depression or brain fog. Oral supplements can be taken either as cyanocobalamine or as hydroxicobalamine. Hydroxicobalamine keeps levels higher for longer periods of time. Dosage should be 100 mg by mouth per day; 200 mg is recommended if over fifty years old. Much higher doses should be given to Multiple Sclerosis patients. No toxicity has been apparent at higher levels.

Vitamin C

Vitamin C is ascorbic acid and is a water soluble substance. This vitamin is found in many citrus fruits in high doses. It can also be found in fruits and vegetables like asparagus, avocadoes, beet greens, broccoli, green peas, mangos, papayas, onions, spinach, strawberries, sweet peppers, tomatoes, turnips and watercress. A very high diet of these vegetables and fruits is necessary to attain the recommended levels of 1,000 to 2,000 mg per day so supplementation is usually advisable. However, supplementation done with *ascorbic acid* tends to be very irritating to the esophagus and stomach, often causing heartburn. Because of this, many people stop taking vitamin C or eating citrus fruits, fearful of the heartburn and indigestion created.

Some people with severe reflux esophagitis (heartburn) can develop vitamin C deficiency (scurvy) today with bleeding gums and chronic fatigue. Years ago, a good friend and excellent surgeon, Dr. Clem Hiebert, told me that he believed many Americans with heartburn did not eat citrus fruits because they aggravated their symptoms. As a result many suffered from bleeding gums and fatigue.

I myself had been experiencing some heart burn and was indeed doing just that—avoiding those foods because they aggravated the symptoms. I was tired and thought it was because of my very busy schedule. I also had bleeding gums. When I started taking Vitamin C as ascorbate at Clem's advice, my bleeding gums and tiredness went away. I had scurvy and did not realize it! Sometime it *is* just that easy!

Another form of vitamin C is an ascorbate, also called *esther-C,* a salt that effectively unites ascorbic acid with a metal such as calcium, selenium or magnesium to provide the benefit of simultaneously absorbing the useful metal.

The great advantage is that it is much more user-friendly for the stomach causing little or no heartburn so is taken easier and more consistently.

The major function of vitamin C is to work on water-soluble areas such as the cell's cytoplasm, which is a water base where the mitochondria and various cell organelles are located. This enhances the function of mitochondria, which is the energy center of the cell where the cell furnaces ATP and ADP energy systems are produced. Therefore, enhancing the function of the cell and the breakdown of the enzymes that permit a normal metabolism of the cell is essential.

Although some authors question this, vitamin C has been known to help heart disease by enhancing the function of the cardiac muscle cells, and skeletal muscles. Brain cells also have high energy and benefit from it. Actually, all cells benefit from vitamin C.

Foods that have been processed, heated, stored, chemically treated, or cooked have greatly reduced or destroyed their ascorbic acid.

Remember that Vitamin C is created by most animals except the human being and guinea pigs. Humans produce this only by females during pregnancy. Animals produce about 15 mg of ascorbic acid per pound of their body weight. Based on this animal profile, a person who weighed one hundred and fifty pounds would produce about 2,000 mg of vitamin C per day. So if humans did produce vitamin C, the calculation of 1,000 to 2,000 mg requirement a day would be about the daily requirement of our body.

Vitamin C:

- Improves immunity to fight infections from viruses, bacteria, fungi or cancer.
- Speeds healing of wounds from surgery, trauma or burns.

- Plays a major role in the formation of collagen, the substance the body uses in healing a wound that acts like glue.
- Reduces the genetic damage of DNA by free-radicals that cause cancers. Also repairs free radical damage caused by carcinogens, toxic agents that cause changes in DNA.
- Slows cancer progression in some cases.
- Enhances immunity thus helps fight cancer and infections like colds and flu.
- Reduces the odds of chronic bronchitis and asthma.
- Acidifies the urine so there is less chance of bladder infections.
- Reduces the formation of a cataract at doses above 500 mg per day.
- Reduces gingivitis by preventing scurvy and riding the gums of free radical damage.
- Decreases cholesterol in the blood.
- Lowers the incidence of blood clots in the veins.
- Lowers the incidence of heart disease and arteriosclerosis.
- Helps keep lungs healthy and may help smokers.
- Lowers stress.
- Helps weight loss at high doses.
- Delays the formation of gall stones by three hundred percent.
- Restores energy in the long run.
- Reduces clogging of the arteries by platelets.
- Cancels the deleterious effects of nitrosamines, the carcinogenic compounds in the stomach.

Dosage should be 1,000 to 2,000 mg per day but try to divide the dose into two installments. Use *Esther C*, which is an ascorbate instead of an acid, with food in your stomach. Drink a decent amount of water immediately afterwards to flush any unneeded excess through your kidneys. Excessive doses potentially cause kidney stones but that is usually the case only with very high dosages, above 5,000 mg per day. Large doses should be ingested only for short periods of time. Individuals who have gout seem more prone to develop kidney stones in association with large doses of vitamin C.

Vitamin D

Vitamin D deficiency is one of the important deficiencies in **light affective disorder,** which is the depression--minor or major--that affects people mostly in the northern climes. These people have little sun exposure especially in the winter and become depressed. Those in the southern regions do get out and get exposure to the sun. Vitamin D is produced by the skin when exposed to the sun. It is wise for northern people to take vitamin D to prevent this syndrome.

Osteoporosis. If you are not reading this book in consecutive chapters you may want to read that section now as it is important to this chapter. Vitamin D affects many parts of the body. See Chapter Six , Exercise, on page 130.

Vitamin D:

- Helps the major agent controlling *calcium absorption in bone*, coagulation, arthritis and high blood pressure.
- Helps small bowel ailments such as Crohn's and muscle contraction.
- Facilitates nerve conduction in the brain.
- Activates lymphocytes to enhance immunity.
- Controls calcium at the synapses of brain cells and other nerve cells and because of this is a major neurotransmission player.
- Regulates calcium around the muscles for proper electrolyte activity.

The exact incidence of osteoporosis in vegetarians is unknown, but since these dietary practices lead to lower vitamin D intake, such individuals may become predisposed to bone deficiency diseases. Meat and dietary products are the principal sources of phosphates, and vegetarians who exclude them from their diets can also experience phosphate deficiencies with resultant osteoporosis. Vitamin D is an important mediator of this calcium phosphate crystallization on the bone matrix. Refer to the osteoporosis section in chapter five.

Remember you can provide all the vitamin D required simply by being in the sun for one-half hour a day for at least six months of a year. So if your food intake is deficient in vitamin D then at least sun exposure (not burning!) will alleviate the deficiency. In some instances, such as Crohn's disease, 400 IU per day may be helpful, but use caution as excess can easily accumulate and cause severe deposits of calcium in many tissues such as arteries or tendonitis areas with tennis elbows.

Vitamin E
Vitamin E is a lipid soluble vitamin and dilutes only in oil or fat so fat-based structures benefit from its antioxidant qualities. In the cell vitamin E's membrane is made of lipoproteins, which are fat, and proteins. The membrane will not absorb water-soluble antioxidants like vitamin C but will readily absorb vitamin E. The combination of vitamin C and vitamin E covers the inside of the cell and its very important membrane that regulates the entry and exit of all nutrients, minerals and enzymes into the cell. This combination of vitamins also permits the docking of hormones on the membrane's exterior surface. Studies have shown that vitamin E has two main purposes. One is in the nervous system where it prevents deterioration and the other is in the immune system by keeping the spleen's lymphocytes healthy.

Vitamin E:

- Lowers cholesterol (LDL) up to thirty to forty percent, lowers triglycerides and increases HDL.
- Lowers the incidence of heart disease up to seventy-seven percent (two Harvard studies) by keeping the heart muscle in good condition and reducing clogging in

the coronary arteries. But that is *providing you do not take about the suggested amount.*

- Improves circulation in vessels and keeps the artery walls from deterioration caused by free-radicals.
- Lowers the stickiness of platelets and acts as a natural blood thinner thus preventing clogging in the arteries. Studies show decreased incidences of TIAs when vitamin E and aspirin are taken together.
- Prevents cancer by permitting more nutrients into the cell to fight budding cancers and lowers carcinogens that may initially cause the cancer. Vitamin E neutralizes nitrites found in smokers, apnea patients and preservatives used in pickled foods and nearly all prepared meats like sausages, bacons, meat loaves and pâtés. Nitrites are transformed into nitrosamines, which are carcinogenic.
- This protects the nervous tissue membranes that are in many instances covered with myelin, a fat. It has been beneficial to Parkinson's disease patients by fighting free-radicals produced by L-dopa, a treatment drug. At 2,000 mg per day vitamin E helps Alzheimer's patients, along with present treatment medications for these diseases.
- Eases menstrual symptoms by *releasing estrogen from fat cells* thus providing a natural, mini form of estrogen replacement therapy.
- Enhances immunity especially in older people to prevent cancer and infections.

Vitamin E should not be taken for two weeks before surgery as it thins the blood and could increase intra-operative or post-operative bleeding.

Dosage should be 200 to 400 mg per day. Excessive dosages may increase blood pressure in some cases so dosage should not exceed the recommended amount unless there is a special reason for this and it is monitored. Just always remember that it is a fat soluble vitamin and that a lot of the bad things said about this vitamin are most likely due to over dosage. When large quantities are indicated it is important not to do it for long periods of time.

Vitamin K
Vitamin K creates the capacity for calcium-binding to certain proteins so these proteins can use calcium in their functions. There are two major functions.

Coagulation needs calcium-binding proteins to use the calcium in four of its steps. If vitamin K is low or absent, uncontrollable bleeding may occur.

These same proteins are used in the mineralization of bone, or osteocalcin. If there is only a partial deficiency, osteoporosis may result.

Vitamin K occurs naturally from two sources. The first source includes green leafy vegetables such as broccoli, turnips, Brussels sprouts, lettuce and spinach.

To a lesser degree, vitamin K can be derived from liver, bacon, cheese, butter and coffee. The second source is by production of vitamin K by the normal bowel flora, or bacteria.

Dosage should be 5 mg per day, as menadione, the form of Vitamin K that can be taken by mouth.

Coenzyme Q-10 (CoQ-10)
The major function of CoQ-10 is as a facilitator of a very important chemical reaction in the mitochondria, the furnaces of the cells. It recharges the furnace catalyst to reproduce usable energy, converting ADP to ATP. The net result of this is increased energy and better muscle performance as the furnace is working at full capacity. CoQ-10 also happens to be a great antioxidant.

Due to its capacity to increase the energy output in all cells, CoQ-10 can boost the immune system, slow the aging process, decrease gum disease, prevent oxidative damage to the brain such as in Parkinson's disease by reducing the loss of dopamine, improve memory or brain fog, lower blood pressure and prevent cancer by providing better immunity.

CoQ-10 makes such dramatic improvement that it may be difficult to stop taking it once experiencing the wonderful feeling of well-being and energy provided.

CoQ-10 is obtained from foods such as peanuts, sardines, liver or heart, but is not well absorbed by the body in this form.

Dosage: 25 to 100 mg per day. Do not take in late afternoon or at night as this inhibits sleep.

DHEA

DHEA (dihydroepiandrosterone) is a hormone precursor that, like melatonin, can possibly retard aging. Normally this is secreted by the ovaries and adrenal glands and is best supplemented as aging occurs.

DHEA will metabolize into some of the hormones missed as aging progresses, namely estrogen and testosterone. A summary statement is that DHEA increases immunity by decreasing cortisol and reducing stress, enhancing brain function, memory, deeper sleep, cardiac strength, muscle strength, sex hormones, insulin function, and increasing glutathione levels.

DHEA could potentially increase the incidence of breast cancer although there is probably very little chance of this occurring. The possibility for this supposition is based on the fact that it will some times increase estrogen levels.

Occasionally, it has been known to cause impotence or a condition known as gynecomastis, which is the development of breasts in males. If either of these symptoms develop, stop taking it. DHEA may also increase liver damage in predisposed patients. Dosage: 50 to 100 mg per day for men and 25 to 50 mg per day for women. The dosage should increase as aging occurs.

Supplements

There is a large variety of supplements available and obviously not all of them will be covered here. You could actually live by just taking supplements but if you only used supplements you would have to use so many that there would be no space for food! Also, remember that a balanced diet does provide most, if not all, the nutrients required through most of life.

In certain instances, you may want to ensure proper coverage of a particular additive to improve one particular function. Certain athletes, such as weight lifters, may want to provide specific proteins that permit them to feed muscles that are enlarging. These athletes may need to push cartilage re-growth and take glucosamine and chondroitin. A calcium supplement for bone growth may be desired, and so on.

I believe that certain foods are not obtainable strictly through diet in a high enough quantity. These should be supplemented and suggestions are as follows:

Glucosamine and Chondroitin

Dr. Theodosakis wrote a book called *The Arthritis Cure* in which he emphasized these two components. He had excellent results and a much lower surgery rate with his hip and knee joint patients who used this supplement.

Soon after he wrote this I started recommending Glucosamine and Chondroitin to my patients for a year or two with similar results. I treated osteoarthritis of the thumb base and did quite a few surgeries that helped some patients.

But many times I felt that surgery was too drastic of a treatment for some early, albeit very painful, cases. I started suggesting Glucosamine and Chondroitin to alleviate the pain. Soon these patients were reporting back to me with much less pain and later evidences of regenerating cartilages. My surgery rate on these patients went down about eighty percent.

What these two compounds do together:
- *Glucosamine* directly feeds the cartilage of proteins specific to their growth. It softens and makes cartilages more elastic and they are less likely to crumble under the stress of the weight and the grinding imposed on them, especially during certain high-impact sports like running.

- *Chondroitin* enhances the formation of synovial fluid in and around joints to lubricate them. There is less wear and tear to cartilages because of improved lubrication.

Cartilages cannot naturally receive the blood supply as the compression of body weight on the cartilage would cut it off constantly so feeding must occur by diffusion. By over-saturating with higher levels of those proteins, the feeding value is improved and cartilage stays healthier and even re-grows in some instances.

Glucosamine and Chondroitin sulfate are specific amino acids that are originally derived from some animal cartilage, such as shark. They are now being produced synthetically.

My strong belief is that everyone over age forty should take these supplements, since that is when hormones and reserves start to deplete and the damage with micro damage starts to accumulate. That is when joints start aching and the cartilage crumbles.

In reality it is around this age that the joint cartilages start deteriorating. Even if there are no symptoms or problems in this area, a preventive maintenance is wise at this point is best done now rather than playing catch-up later.

This age is also when the type of sport you do everyday should become more user friendly. Cease doing any pounding or destructive moves on the joints, running in particular. Use common sense and realize that you, like everyone, have indeed a human body. Performing more gentle exercises like biking will keep you going much longer and you will be much healthier.

You will have better joints, and if deterioration ever should occur, it will happen later in your life with this prevention. Think of your car and its maintenance. You practice prevention to your car by oiling and greasing the joints every three to five thousand miles because you know that it will prevent wear and tear and prolong the smooth-running of the automobile. It is also better for your car to drive on smooth roads and be less damaging to the entire car. These same principles apply to your body.

Another point that Dr. Theodosakis made that I also experienced in my practice is that many over-the-counter products are not good quality. Thus results are not the best they can be, sometimes not even satisfactory. Because of this experience, I find it best to get these supplements through reputable vitamin providers such as Puritan or GNC.

I am sure many other reputable stores are in your neighborhood, and there are many mail order providers but make sure you research them. If you use a product and it does not work despite proper dosage, go to another source. Steer clear from any stores that have neither track record nor a good reputation to uphold. Large mail order companies rely on a solid reputation to sustain their huge business and should provide high quality products. That reasoning did prove itself true in my practice.

There are very few adverse reactions occurring and to my knowledge there are no adverse interactions with other medications. When the source of these compounds was only shark cartilage, there were a few allergic reactions reported but that rarely occurs now that the substance is being produced synthetically. Occasionally some people get tired a few hours after taking it. Take it at night. Note that it will take three to four months before results are seen, pain is diminished and at least one year before cartilage is re-grown. This should be taken for the rest of your life. You may not be able to tell a difference because the supplement is slowly doing its job. Without this, you would start getting wear and tear arthritis. Think of this as maintenance for you, just like the car is maintained with regular oil changes.

Sometimes Glucosamine and Chondroitin are combined with MSM as a pain reliever and that is probably satisfactory but should not be used for extended periods of time. My experience is limited with this added MSM. Dosages: should be 1,000 to 1,500 mg per day of glucosamine sulfate and 500 to 1,000 mg per day of chondroitin sulfate.

Hyaluronic acid

Hyaluronic acid is another supplement to fortify the joint cartilage and permit regrowth of its proteins. Many support structures are made of hyaluronic acid such as tendons ,ligaments fascias, the dermis in skin and of course cartilage. It has the added advantage of greatly reducing pain and swelling not only in joints but in these many ligaments and tendons that are injured or inflamed.

Dosage; Take 50 to 150 mg/day

Carnitines

Carnitines are amino acids that are mostly present in meats, beef particularly, but also lesser quantities in chicken, fish, eggs and milk. Grains and vegetables can contain very minor amounts of carnitines. There are two carnitines: L-carnitine that feeds mostly the muscle energy system and acetyl-carnitine that feeds mostly the brain's.

In essence, the carnitines are the food necessary in the furnace of the cell, or mitochondria. With the help of Coenzyme Q-10 they are able to change ADP to ATP and reconstruct a depleted energy. Coenzyme Q-10 is the enzyme that facilitates this chemical reaction. Carnitines are the building blocks that reconstitute ATP and glucose is the fuel. The food that is necessary is carnitines made of lysine and methionine. These are two of the essential amino acids not present in anything but meat, and again, vegetarians do not have this in their diet.

L-Carnitine

L-Carnitine is activated by exercise and also feeds the mitochondria of the muscles. Particularly helpful for people who exercise, the muscle energy system is then very well fed. L-Carnitine also strengthens the heart muscles and is particularly helpful in many heart weakness situations such as heart attacks, rhythm disturbances and chronic cardiac failure.

Along with coenzyme Q-10, L-Carnitine can be a very effective strengthener of the heart making recuperation from problems much faster. These two compounds are amino acids and therefore can be taken in conjunction with other medications.

During exercise, L-Carnitine will enhance endurance in the muscle and facilitate the use of muscle for longer periods of time by increasing the energy storage. It also reduces the amount of lactic acid formation caused by heavier exercises and may also maintain muscle bulk and prevent muscle loss in some debilitating diseases. Dosage is 1 to 2 gm per day, as the bulk of muscle in the body is very large and the need is a little bit higher than the acetyl-Carnitine.

Acetyl-Carnitine

Acetyl-Carnitine is beneficial in energizing the brain because energy production is increased in the mitochondria of the neurons.

Restoring memory and often eliminating brain fog, it can also improve mood and intellectual energy and will keep the brain cell healthier for longer periods of time. Acetyl-carnitine is being more accepted, since it is now an intrinsic part of Alzheimer's and Parkinson disease therapy.

Carnitine, for example, is one of the important amino acids for the function of muscle. It permits fatty acid penetration into the mitochondria the battery of the cell, thus providing a strong source of energy. Carnitine is also important for the heart muscle. Dr. Steve Sinatra cures chronic cardiac failure patients with very weak heart muscles using carnitine along with B12 and CoQ-10. These patients were not getting carnitine in their diets. Carnitine is synthesized from lysine and methionine and only found in meats.

It provides two-thirds of the energy in the heart muscle and allows fat and glucose to be used by the mitochondria. Carnitine lowers triglycerides and elevates HDL in the blood. Sources are beef, chicken, fish, eggs and milk.

Acetyl-Carnitine is the super carnitine that provides energy consumption to nerve cells, decreases Alzheimer's symptoms, improves mood, increases melatonin secretion in the brain, helps immunity and speeds recovery of stroke patients. Both Carnitine and acetyl-Carnitine can be taken as supplements at one or two grams a day.

Dr. R. Atkins states in his book *Vita Nutrient Solution* that he would not go a day without taking L-Carnitines and Acetyl-Carnitines because of the energy he derived from them. I feel the same way. He wrote an extensive study about these two supplements. As brain facilitators, both help in Alzheimer's disease, stroke recovery, and immune disturbances. Exercise activates the carnitines. Taking the supplement by itself is not enough, as exercise is an important stimulator of these two components.

Dosage: about 1 gm per day.

Melatonin

Melatonin, one of the hormones secreted by the brain, is the major orchestrator of the hormonal system and a super anti-oxidant. There is a great decrease in melatonin as aging occurs but this can be easily replaced orally.

Do not take melatonin early in the day as it is a natural sleeping pill for the body. Take this one half hour before bedtime. This will boost antioxidant capabilities and will also permit you to sleep better which in turn does even more wonderful things for the body. Melatonin is also discussed in Chapter Four, beginning on page 47.

The older you get the less melatonin you secrete, and the less you sleep. Take melatonin just before bed otherwise you may sleep all day. One milligram will last only four hours so take a sustained release tab that will liberate half the dose four hours later (SR).

Dosage should be:

Age: 40-60	2mg SR
Age: 60-70	4mg SR
Age: 70-80	6mg SR

Glutathione

Glutathione is known as one of the better antioxidants in the body particularly the brain and is manufactured by many amino acids, particularly cysteine. In many instances a genetic defect prevents its fabrication.

Glutathione is very helpful in situations where there is generalized disease. Reducing the risk of heart disease, arthritis, diabetes, improving the blood pressure, body fat and cholesterol ratio and brain diseases are some examples. Glutathione has also been very helpful in increasing the T-killer cells in AIDS patients. Immunity-wise, it has been very helpful and also aids in detoxification, or can permit the liver to function more normally when it has been damaged by acetaminophen, Tylenol, poisoning.

Heart diseases are aided as there is less muscle damage than in the case of a cardiac infarct. It also reduces blood pressure and complements vitamin C to be helpful to colitis and breathing problems.

Glutathione also reduces or prevents hair loss in woman though not in men because a woman's hair loss is caused by a sulfur deficiency. In general nothing needs to be added to diets for glutathione is amply available in vegetables, fresh fruits and meats. A balanced diet will usually provide all that is required.

In cases where supplementation is absolutely necessary, the N-acetyl cysteine is the supplement given that will transform itself into glutathione in the blood. Dosage should be 150 mg a day.

Minerals

Calcium

Calcium is probably the most voluminous mineral in the body forming all of the bones. Calcium levels are very important to feed bones appropriately. If bones are not used, the calcium leaches out of the bone and is eventually eliminated through the kidney.

Calcium also has an important role in immunity as its cells need it. It is important in blood coagulation as three or four of its mechanisms require calcium for coagulation. Calcium is also important for formation of some hormones. It is known to block high blood pressure. All its functions are regulated by the parathyroid hormone and by vitamin D.

Calcium inhibits cancer as people who have a normal intake of calcium have a reduced amount of colon cancer and this may also apply to some other common cancers like breast and prostate cancer.

Studies have shown decreases in the percentage of cancers that are seen when there is an intake of fairly high doses of calcium, about 1,500 to 2,000 mg per day.

There are various forms that can be taken like calcium chloride, calcium gluconate or calcium carbonate. Calcium carbonate seems to be the more efficient one of the supplements for this purpose. It is important to realize that taking calcium *should be combined with phosphates* as the calcium deposited on bone is calcium phosphate. Also, it must be accompanied by proper levels of magnesium as the structure onto which the calcium is deposited is made of cells that have to stay healthy with specific amounts of magnesium.

Dosage: is 500 to 1000 mg a day. It is better if taken with phosphates and magnesium.

Magnesium

Magnesium and potassium are the most regulatory electrolytes that exist in the cell as they are very involved with all the intrinsic chemical and Ph functions of the cell. The most active cell, the muscle cell, has the highest percentage of magnesium. Approximately twenty-seven percent of the magnesium in the body is in the muscle cells. It is also an intrinsic part of the bone matrix cells and is necessary for their health.

Magnesium should be in constant equilibrium with the calcium outside the cell, just like potassium is with sodium. For example, calcium excites the nerve conduction and magnesium relaxes the nerve conduction. Calcium is necessary for muscle contraction and magnesium is necessary for muscle relaxation. Calcium is necessary for blood clotting and magnesium prevents overactive clotting to keep a free flow of blood.

Low cardiac muscle cell magnesium levels can cause arrhythmia and tachycardia as it and the potassium are extruded from the cells showing abnormal electrical activities in electrocardiograms. Magnesium relaxes muscle contractions and also will relieve high blood pressure. High blood pressure is the result of tense muscles in the blood vessels.

Arteriosclerosis even in children, vascular spasms, increase in blood pressure, angina syndrome (a spasm in the coronary arteries), infarct or acute coronary spasm can be caused by a magnesium deficiency. Thus magnesium deficiency can cause sudden death because of infarcts or arrhythmia, blood clots or insulin resistance. Thought to be the cause of metabolic syndrome X, which is a diabetic syndrome, it can create over-activity to stress hormones, adrenaline and cortisol. It will permit calcium entry into the cells thus changing the metabolism of contracting muscle cells and will increase free-radicals, or oxidative stress.

A superb book called *The Magnesium Factor* written by Andrea Rosanoff, PhD, covers this subject in great detail and is wonderfully done.

Magnesium obtained through diet is usually adequate. However, one of the easiest ways to get magnesium is in hard water that has a higher level of magnesium and people who drink this have less heart disease. When the amount of magnesium in the heart muscle is analyzed, considerably more magnesium exists in the heart muscle cells of a person who drinks hard water than there is for one who does not. If you drink bottled water it is likely that there is very little or no magnesium in it.

If you do drink coffee, tea, soups, reconstituted juices or any food cooked with water, and if you take that water from the tap, then the likelihood is that you are going to get enough magnesium. Again, if you use distilled or filtered water for any of these purposes you will not get magnesium. Some bottled waters do contain magnesium and you can choose these.

Foods that have the highest amount of magnesium are soy beans, wheat flour, black-eyed peas, cashews, Brazilian nuts, pecans, peanuts and shredded wheat. Although to a much lower degree, potatoes and oatmeal also provide magnesium.

Dosage should be about 200 to 500 mg per day as a sustaining amount of magnesium, although you may not ever have too much magnesium. Your body will excrete the excess not necessary. If, however, you have heart problems or any form of spasms or muscle cramps, intestines, etc. you are probably low in magnesium and the dosage could be increased to between 400 and 700 mg per day. You are probably much better off in this instance to have a physician monitor this situation.

Electrolytes

Potassium, sodium, bicarbonates and chlorides are the electrolytes of the blood and the inner environment of the cells. Their function is to keep the acid and base balanced at the normal 7.4 Ph level. If that balance is offset, blood becomes more or less acidic and then all kinds of chemical reactions are not produced, or produced very inadequately.

Blood pressure is also regulated by the sodium and potassium balance between the cell and its environment of extra cellular fluids. If the equilibrium is disrupted, all kinds of chemical and osmotic imbalances occur and many chemical activities will not happen appropriately. If this imbalance occurs the whole body becomes drastically sick very quickly.

Potassium

Potassium is the electrolytes of the inner cell and absolutely necessary for proper function of the cell. If there is a deficiency, then various processes are lost, even normal heart and skeletal muscle performance.

Potassium is mostly in the cell and controls the concentration of magnesium, which is important for regulating many chemical activities.

It also controls the inner cell equilibrium and the electric activity, particularly in muscles and nerves. As long as there is the correct amount of potassium inside, the cell will function very well. Exercise causes a large loss of potassium from the muscle cell into the outside fluid called interstitial tissue and from there into the blood. When potassium leaches out of the cell, the blood concentration increases substantially. As the exercise continues, or even after it stops, the potassium should reenter the cell to reestablish its normal potassium-magnesium balance for proper performance. When the potassium blood level is very high and one sweats profusely potassium is lost from the blood through the sweat and no longer available to reenter into the muscle. The muscle then has a deficiency and becomes weak and/or has cramps. This phenomenon occurs as much in the heart muscle as it does in the skeletal muscle.

This leaching produces an abnormal electrical activity that makes muscles, nerves function inappropriately. People who suffer severe vomiting, diarrhea or heavy perspiration lose much potassium. Injuries or severe traumas also seriously lower the blood potassium level. People who are on diuretics for high blood pressure or heart failure have very low levels of potassium. Interestingly, *beta blockers and blood pressure ACE inhibitors also impair the blood potassium levels by lowering it*. You can imagine the intense damage that occurs in hyperthermia when most of the cell is deficient in potassium.

There are a few articles that claim the inner part of blood vessels, the endothelium, is damaged by low potassium, and probably low magnesium. The cells of this lining will be damaged without their proper inner environment. The more potassium levels in the body were analyzed, the more it was realized that low potassium can be quite damaging, and very often is a silent very destructive agent. It is crucial to survival for normal levels of these two ingredients to be maintained.

Regarding heart disease, potassium deficiency is known to create life-threatening arrhythmias or heart fibrillations. As mentioned, the electric potential of cells is offset therefore no normal conduction mechanisms are able to occur. One problem is that food is processed with very low levels of potassium while factories add too much sodium. This changes the balance of sodium potassium in blood and cells and creates major shortages of potassium.

Cultures that have normal potassium levels in their food combined with normal levels of sodium have much less heart disease and cancer.

Sometimes young people who run many miles daily suddenly die of a heart attack. What likely happened was an arrhythmia or fibrillation because of low potassium. The original assumption was that these people died of atherosclerotic blockage of the artery that killed the heart muscle; however, now we know that the arrhythmia indirectly causes the blocking of the artery by abnormal blood circulation in the coronary arteries causing eddies, forming clots thus blocking the arteries thereby causing the heart attack. That arrhythmia is caused by very low potassium, and this is another good reason to take a potassium supplementation during intense exercises.

High blood pressure carries the same risks. In an attempt to restrict the amount of sodium, people are told to eat less salt however that also creates an imbalance and increases blood pressure. The reduction of salt simply lowers blood pressure very minimally by a few points, but taking a potassium supplement, which incidentally salt substitute is, would help so much more, especially if a person is on drugs such as diuretics or ACE inhibitors.

The potassium loss in runners, exercisers and hard physical workers is exacerbated by low-calorie dieters who are particularly susceptible to this. As suggested, taking 200 to 1000 mg of potassium depending on the amount of exercise and sweating.

Potassium comes in many vegetables and drinks. Popular sports drinks contain about 30 mg but this is not enough. Some other drinks have more, but you may be taking in more calories or carbohydrates in the process. Instead, drink liquids like V-8, which has 800 or 900 mg of magnesium in a small can. Emer'gen-C has 200 mg and one, two or three sachets on an exercise day, or hot day, are recommended.

Using a salt substitute like potassium chloride instead of sodium chloride will provide a diet higher in potassium that will be more balanced. A very high level of potassium can be as dangerous to the cardiac muscle as a reverse mechanism of low potassium. On the other hand a person who has normal kidney function and drinks water while running, will regulate the excessive amount of potassium. If you do have kidney problems, then take care not to overload yourself with potassium. You should always have an adequate amount of water intake to prevent over saturation.

Replacing potassium is recommended in situations where there is heavy exercise with sweating or if the weather is very warm and you are borderline or outright hyperthermic or have high blood pressure. I would not use potassium as a daily supplement. High potassium can be a problem in people who cannot eliminate it such as in kidney failure.

It is very important especially for the athlete to understand the whole concept of potassium's function during exercise as it could prevent cramping or heart fibrillation or death. More on potassium can be found on page 160.

Dosage should be 200-1,000 mg per day, depending on the amount of sweating, the exercise and the heat environment. There has also been great improvement in people who have cramps after exercise, because this is very often caused by potassium depletion that can be immediately corrected.

Sodium

Sodium is a very important part of the diet and is taken as table salt or sodium chloride. It adds a good taste to food. Found in many products, in fact probably nearly everything, it is also a very important part of the electrolyte balance of the body.

As previously explained, sodium is important but sometimes a problem occurs with exercise caused by low sodium called hyponatremia. In general, hyponatremia is related to very severe heat climates, or mountain climbing such as in the Grand Canyon or biking in heavy heat. The hyponatremia occurs first by some loss of sodium, often in our times by drinking too much water so the body expels it quickly either by sweat or urination. Sodium as potassium will leach out with this water and levels are depleted. This can be life threatening.

Excessive water intake definitely lowers sodium and creates this problem. To advocate excess water consumption is to promote these dangerous electrolyte imbalances. If moderate amounts of water are good, then more is not better. If you need large amounts of water such as in extreme heat or during exercise, you must supplement with potassium and sodium. Excessive water will make you retain water and swell-up. The Brain is particularly susceptible to the swelling and this phenomena can become very dangerous and life threatening. This is seen in marathon runners etc. that drink excessively without electrolyte replacement.

The problem that occurs is not only low sodium but also a dangerous part of this is low potassium. Many times low sodium is mentioned but it is more likely that low potassium is also dangerous. The replacement should not be just salt pills but some potassium also, or appropriate foods should be added.

For example, eating potato chips to replace potassium is not adequate as there is only sodium present in them, no potassium. I am not trying to minimize the damage that low sodium can do as it is also very dangerous. Excess sodium on the other hand can also be a cause of hypertension as it is retained in the system, water is also retained which creates swelling and weight gain along with increasing the work of the heart. So one must be aware of this and avoid excessive salt consumption.

Iron

Iron is very important for blood as it nourishes the red blood cells, or hemoglobin, which transports oxygen. Oxygen going into the lung is carried by the iron molecule and hemoglobin and then propelled into the cell. The iron then goes back to the lung and repeats this course over and over again. Hemoglobin is not formed without iron and if you are low in iron then you will become anemic.

Conversely, excessive amounts of iron can pile up if the body does not have a mechanism to get it expelled. So once all your red blood cells are produced and have stored a reasonable amount of iron, do not try to stock pile huge amounts of iron. If you bleed, such as women during the menstrual phase, then do replace the iron .Otherwise, do so very gingerly or not at all.

Accumulated storages of iron are called ferritin (*fer* in French means iron). A Finnish researcher J. Salonen, M.D. learned that cholesterol, the LDL portion, will not deposit in arteries unless it is damaged. He further noted that cholesterol will not deposit unless it has been oxidized. Men with high concentrations of ferritin have a much higher oxidation process of LDL and that is one of the reasons cholesterol is deposited.

The only way iron is ever depleted, except for very minute amounts rid by the body's own chelation, is if you bleed. In general, a man never loses iron. Because of this, taking huge amounts of iron becomes very damaging due to higher oxidation and free radical formation, plus a higher chance for arteriosclerosis.

Women who menstruate bleed and lose red cells and their iron regularly so this keeps their storage of ferritin fairly low. Oxidization of the cholesterol and damage to the vessel will not occur with so much frequency. Women traditionally have less heart disease than men, except later in life after menopause. Now women seem to have added stress in their lives and have moved towards the same statistics for heart disease as men. A pregnant woman also requires more iron to nourish a healthy growing embryo.

As menopause occurs, iron starts accumulating, especially if a woman takes large dosages of iron replacement as many feel that iron replacement is paramount to energy and a robust constitution. The percentages for heart disease start increasing after menopause for that very reason.

Iron supply demands a delicate balance. If you have low iron, then you become anemic and you will not oxygenate well and this vicious cycle occurs and continues. Conversely, if you have too much iron and too much oxidative damage occurs, the dreaded free-radicals happen.

Iron can be supplemented by a healthy diet including red meat, chicken and fish. You can absorb only 2 mg of iron per day with such a diet. This generally creates a normal balance that prevents over-accumulation and creates an appropriate level of iron in the body.

Supplements are good if iron levels are low and if there is anemia, but are very bad if you are just supplementing to stay healthy.

I want to emphasize that iron is essential and a certain level is required to keep the hemoglobin transporting oxygen well. However, it is an oxidizer and excessive oxidizers can become very damaging as free-radicals. In specific points in life that damage has to be prevented and corrected. This can be done by simply not taking excessive iron. If you want to know for sure if taking supplemental iron would be beneficial or detrimental to your health, have a ferritin test done. With the results from this test a doctor will be able to find out how much reserve you have and whether that amount is excessive or not. Hemoglobin and hematocrit blood tests will show whether there is anemia or an excess of iron.

Dosage: No daily supplementation should be taken unless suggested by a doctor.

Zinc

Zinc is also a metal that is very useful in many enzyme functions. The main function is to permit certain cells to grow and certain chemical reactions to occur.

Zinc is beneficial in healing wounds. During long surgical experiences people who are given zinc before and after surgery, in acceptable doses to elevate their body level of zinc to normal levels, will heal substantially faster. Another example is chronic wounds such as lingering leg ulcers that improve substantially when treated with zinc. Infections and injuries will tend to track zinc and eliminate it through the urine therefore the levels become low. Replacement can be very beneficial. Calamine lotions improve healing on wounds. This is also true for acne cases.

Zinc has been known to have the following attributes:

- Infection and Immunity – An appropriate level of zinc will increase the T-lymphocytes and white cells and improve immunity. Zinc prevents or improves acne for that reason. During colds, zinc reduces the amount of sick days. There is promising evidence that it may also be a cooperative agent in cancer prevention.
- Night Vision - People who have lost night vision and are given a fairly high dosage of zinc for two weeks (100 to 200 mg) may regain their night vision because of this treatment. Zinc functions here to convert vitamin A to an active form that then improves night vision.
- Prostate and Fertility - Taking zinc can increase sperm count and decrease benign prostate hypertrophy. It also decreases infections and therefore there is less prostatitis. It may also be a factor in benign prostatic hypertrophy. Pregnant women are less inclined to have toxemia and delivery is smoother, even using small doses like 22 mg of zinc per day.
- Neurologically - In some instances various psychosis and schizophrenias are helped with zinc. Alzheimer's patients are said to improve when zinc is added to their regime.

An interesting taste test can be done for zinc. If you ingest a solution known as zinc sulfate hepta hydrate and you experience a bitter taste, then you have an adequate amount of zinc.

If, however, you do not experience that bitter taste, then zinc levels are too low.

Dosage is 10 to 15 mg per day as normal maintenance. Increasing this dosage to 150 mg per day should be done only for short periods of time.

Selenium

Selenium is an excellent immune cell implement and is known to increase T-lymphocytes and white cells.

An anti-viral agent, selenium acts like zinc as a cooperative agent to block cancer. It also decreases heart disease because of decreased vasospasm so there is less of an opportunity to experience a spasm in the coronary arteries. The likelihood of stickiness of platelets is also less.

Selenium relieves anxiety, decreases the possibility of strokes and is a good antioxidant.

Dosage is 100 mg per day.

Chromium

Chromium is mostly a sugar control. It has been known to have the following attributes:

- Permits the formation of glucose and then transfers glucose into cells.
- Eliminates chromium from the blood and lowers the insulin rises that glucose incites.
- Lowers the chance of adult onset diabetes.
- Reduces fat deposits and increases lean body mass.
- Lowers triglycerides.
- Lowers fatigue and chronic urination.

- Lessens weight gain as high levels of glucose are not present in the blood, therefore not stimulating high insulin levels that usually cause hunger.

Dosage should be approximately 200 mg per day. There is no known toxicity for chromium.

Herbal Medicines

I am very harsh and skeptical about herbal medicines. While I do recognize there are many effective herbal products, I personally implore you to purchase and use these supplements with great caution. Do your research and use these products based on your *own* knowledge, not the marketing efforts of some manufacturers. Do not take claims of *natural* or *safer* products for absolute truth unless you have personally researched these products. I believe herbal medicines may not be the best choices for many reasons.

Companies are dealing with medication whose origins and circumstances are not always known. For millenniums, herbal medicines have been used when there was no alternative. Manufactured medicines are often derived from herbs, by extracting a specific amount of the valuable chemical in that herb.

In this instance the specific medication that we are seeking is not mixed with other, possibly undesirable chemicals. Herbs grow in different climates, environments and soils. They are tended in different manners. One specific plant may have more of the compound being sought, but because there was a drought, or a flood, or less natural fertilizer, these amounts may have changed dramatically in that individual herb plant.

Growing in one type of soil versus another type will create a different plant and may contain different chemicals that can be dangerous in different soils.

Huge quantities of these herbal medicines are now consumed so they are cultivated in large quantities. Herbicides and preservatives are sometimes used, thus compounding the situation.

Another important factor is that many herbal crops are protected with herbicides and are not washed before consumption. Most herbicides are neurotoxins that can become very dangerous. Because of all these reasons, and some interesting articles written expressing the uncomfortable feeling of ingesting these products, I have chosen to use and recommend only pharmaceutical supplements.

There is no control whatsoever of the quality or safety of herbal medicines as controlled by the FDA. With herbal medicines, little is known about harmful interactions that may occur with other medicines taken. Studies in California in 1998 showed that natural products often contained prescription medication. Some also contained toxic lead, mercury, arsenic and contaminants. This is almost to be expected when there is no controlling sanction for the safety of these herbal medications.

Another point is that the people who sell these drugs do so in very high volumes, sometimes with no control over the quantities and qualities of their product. I doubt there is any way they can consistently provide a product that is safe.

Another important factor that fascinates me is that there is a one billon dollar annual market for herbal medicines, when *natural* products are sometimes far more of a gamble than regulated drugs that are known and tested. The usual belief from users is that herbal supplements are milder and safer than regular vitamins. And it is the case that hundreds of compounds have good things in the—like bioflavonoids, flavones, lactones, glycoside, polysaccharides, essential oils, terpines, lycopenes, Luteins, and so on.

But problems occur because these compounds are not present in exact amounts, but instead the supplements contain uncontrolled and varying quantities. Pharmaceutical drugs are usually a single compound, and if they are presented with another compound they have been tested and are known not to be self-negating. It seems more logical to take lutein pills, for example, that have had the appropriate dosage extracted. The quantity is controlled and there are no unknown compounds or incompatible qualities.

I understand that many of these herbal remedies have been used for centuries, but nobody mentions the complications or severe side effects that may have occurred because of them. Also, the argument that certain cultures have used something for centuries does not mean it is good. You do not know if that population had good health or longevity.

Today's population lives twenty to thirty years longer than did people in centuries past. Longevity is far better in the current world of medicine than it was in the olden days. And just because something has always been done one way does not mean that is the best way.

Changing to more modern medicines may be in your best interest. Change is almost always good, albeit rarely comfortable.

An ounce of prevention is worth a pound of cure.
Author Unknown

CHAPTER ELEVEN

Medical Growth in the Future

What do we see in the future of this aging science or of standard medicine as they grow together? When we consider how far we have progressed in the last thirty years, imagine where we can go if we stay on this trajectory!

I started my residency in plastic surgery in 1967. My chief of plastic surgery, Dr Fred Woolhouse, said to me "Jean, thirty years from now, you will know one hundred times what I know today."

I thought he knew everything, but now I have seen thirty-eight years of development in my science and do firmly believe that he was absolutely right. Let me enumerate just a few developments I have witnessed during these years:

- Silicone breast prostheses had just come out and we were experimenting with them.

- We were doing many innovative flaps including the beginnings of transfers of muscle flaps for breast reconstruction, for radiation damage, bone infections, open joint and tendon injuries, etc.

- We were at the inception of microscopic surgery, but the extremely fine sutures were not available. They became commercially available in 1971. At that time, I took a microscopy course from two well known experts, Dr Klienert and Dr Harry Bunke. From then on, we saw an explosion of microsurgery for reimplantation of fingers, hands, even penises. Our imaginations permitted us to transfer free flaps from any part of the body to any other part.

- In 1975 I did the first triple muscle flap closure of heart surgery infected chest wounds. In essence these muscle closures were the only ones to cure the infection in the breast bone. These turned out to be great life savers as these infections had a forty-five percent mortality rate and we reduced it to five percent.

- During this time, hand surgery soared into more precise surgery with better sutures, microscopic reattachments, tendon and nerve grafts with better results, better plates and screws for fractures, a better understanding of the function of the intricacies of the hand. We took basic principles laid down by Sterling Bunnel and went way beyond his original concepts. Hand surgery is so much more refined today.

- Cleft lips and palates that were done so elementarily became a fine science and our kids no longer looked like they had been born with severe defects.

- Face lifts and other cosmetic surgeries were more and more in demand and exploded in refinement and marketing. It was and is propelled by our population that does not want to age and money as a fuel to cosmetic plastic surgeons.

- Breast reconstruction surgery, mostly for cancer, attained a high level of refinement using silicone or also transferring tissue from the back and abdomen in all manners and shapes to attain very good results. We learned to make them bigger and smaller, and we learned to do the surgery in our surgery centers rather than in hospitals, which in many cases is the preferred way to do surgery.

•

I have discussed this mostly so you would understand the great growth in our medicine and to make you realize that at this rate the future is nearly infinitive. That was only the beginning, only the tip of the iceberg! And that was only in my field of plastic surgery. Now I will try to project the future and what we need to do so and what the objectives are.

There are **four important factors** that are responsible for the extraordinary brain storming and development presently occurring in our country and in many other countries like ours.

- **One** is the influx **of immigration in America**. People from all over the world came here for the opportunity to grow, develop, get their educations or conduct research, and this entrepreneurial country provides those opportunities for them. These people had great imagination and initiatives to put into action. Then they empowered their children to be entrepreneurs, and so does the geometric progression continue. As growth goes on, science and medicine are naturally a part of the progression. And that growth includes the growth of our understanding of aging and how to slow it down.

- **Two:** Have you heard about the **Massive Brain Theory?** In a free world, a world of total freedom of expression, in which science is free from government repression, researchers and innovators of all sorts will likely and willfully communicate their research to each other. They have nothing to hide from the government. One innovator learns the techniques of the others, this learning grows exponentially. *It is as though one big brain is constantly intercommunicating and brain storming.* That is why this country and those who have the same philosophy have the benefit of the massively growing club the explosion of science other knowledge.

Without this extraordinary freedom of speech factor, none of this would occur.

-
- **Three:** Of course, **computers** are an important tool for the massive brain theory as they permit easy and instant communication and interaction between parties, permit immediate access to massive amounts of information and the computations to support it. They are also excellent at calculating and figuring theorems and problems encountered in research. The new order of sophisticated digital wares now can outline and see cells, the shape of molecules and their interactive chemistry, understand of their functions and repair them if defective with new appropriately designed drugs. They can also see the various effects it has on other parts of the body and predict complications. This is where a computer or an actuarial calculation can tell what percentage of a population will actually have good results from a new drug and who gets complications. The analysis of the genome has profiled the population and now we know what the normal DNA is, permitting individualized correction of the defects. That would be totally impossible without these computers that had to store five billion pieces of data to be compiled and analyzed. Also the computer has become a dictionary and reference for this genome to be easily accessible for research. The more we progress in all sciences and literature the more sophisticated, user friendly and accessible computers become.

- **Four**: The motivation **of financial incentive** is both good and bad, as we all know so well. Neither individual corporate research or government sponsorship of research and development would exist without monetary investment and financial incentive. Unfortunately, greed is an addiction and exaggerations have taken place and are responsible in part for the high cost of medicine today. So you see that on the one hand corporate support is quite necessary and promotes growth for a much better future for us. On the other hand, human greed could destroy our health care by making it too expensive and unavailable. Some politicians would go to a government system that would destroy all incentive and competitive edge and actually would cost more.

•

What will permit exponential growth of medicine that will keep us living well and longer? It is not a single factor, and just like the musical instruments in an orchestra, all are necessary to attain the melody of good health.

Education at large is key to the ultimate growth of health care for the individual and society.

Of Individuals

The more people know about themselves and the available medicine, the less they will be controlled by their environment, by the media and by physicians and especially pseudo–medical personnel. We must personally arrive at a point where we know enough to question what is wrong with us and indicate to the doctor that we are aware and have done some internet research or other readings.

The more clues you give the physician the more he/she will focus on problems. I used to love having patients quote articles, books and the web because I knew these people were on the ball and it gave me more fuel to have intelligent discussions with them.

Remember, curiosity is your best ally.

So the higher the percentage of the population managing their own health, using physicians as their guides, the better the ultimate health of the population. The greater their understanding of their bodies the less they will be dupes to the constant brainwashing of infomercials and the more we understand how to do proper prevention to avert disease and stay happy.

Of Physicians

A new breed of physicians is being educated and much better able to detect diseases using new sophisticated knowledge and equipment. The Art-Science of a physician is that of a well trained detective who can find all the clues necessary to detect disease using ever more sophisticated tools available to help in this endeavor.

They need more patient–physician time since that is where the real precise diagnoses are made. Right now, physicians have their hands tied behind their back by not only *managed care* but by the forever looming sword of Damocles *of malpractice.*

One of the great challenges of the future will be to solve these two problems by reducing the cost of exorbitant medical drugs, supplies and equipment and by removing the immoral contingency reimbursement of the tort lawyers, all of which greatly increase the cost of medical care and insurance. As for lawyers removing their contingency fee (a percentage of the settlement), it would reduce their remuneration to that of other country's reasonable levels. We are the only major country that has a contingency fee structure, to my knowledge.

One other problem physicians encounter is they are *harassed by the drug representatives' lobbying and the media's advertising of drugs.* One day, hopefully this will be forbidden. Already there are proper monthly information leaflets published by the state's medical society that are analytical and unbiased and these will give proper knowledge of the drugs without the bias of financial gains.

Of the Media

The media is responsible for an unusually large portion of the knowledge and culture of this country. In the mix of all the cross section of programs is a constant and repeated subliminal and actual brain washing by all the commercials and when it comes to health foods and prescription drugs most of it is inappropriately biases or outright lies to sell products.

A lot of concepts are advertised to cater to the population's beliefs and fancies so they buy the product.

Somehow the trend has to be reversed, because we are being harmed. Worse still is the fact that often a good TV program that is succeeding in teaching good concepts of living will be interrupted by many advertisements sending precisely the wrong message. The net effect is that the bad influence of the commercials can destroy the good influence the program might otherwise have.

A few examples of the bad:
The fat free craze that ended up causing the obesity epidemic: (see chapter seven, Essential Nutrition). It pervaded our entire infrastructure—all the restaurants, food markets, and health industry preached it. The population believed in it and the vendors took advantage of it.

The media of all sorts must be a strong factor in educating and inciting the public to know and self direct their own care. The media has the responsibility to report *trends* in medicine that are useful to the patients, *not merely splashes* that are reported by inadequate, uneducated medical reporters.

There are exceptions such as Newsweek and Time Magazine have high quality special reports. There are many others. It is best not to get your health advice from single 'philosophy' magazines.

Beware of magic pills, diets and exercises. Don't believe extreme articles that totally denigrate a subject such as genetically engineered crops, dirty details about our produce and such. Beware of any article written with a clear bias or one that comes from a vendor. There are so many misconceptions and all for the sake of commercial greed.

One of many examples is the 'sterility frenzy' that has everybody wash and sterilize everything. That is fueled by the companies that sell all the antiseptic hand washes counter top and toilet cleaners; even for door handles for God's sake. They are creating a population with inadequate immune responses, and that will seriously haunt us in the future by decreasing our fighting capabilities against chronic inflammation, increasing bacterial resistance and decreasing our fighting powers against germs.

Is that not a major step backwards in the effort to improve the quality of health care in the future?

Imagine how much better you would be if you truly knew what you need to prevent to keep infection away, not based on the greed of drug companies We need to set this as a goal for the future of our health as a country and to keep progressing in our fight to slow aging.

Early detection of disease
The earlier we find diseases, the earlier we treat and cure them and the more chance we have of averting massive and expensive medical care.

There is no question that lab tests are getting more specific. That pin prick that started out as just analyzing hemoglobin years and years ago, can now detect the whole profile of DNA analysis derived from the Genome.

We have progressed to knowing levels of homocysteine, oxidative stress, PSA for prostate cancer, screening hereditary types of breast cancers, cholesterol levels, and a million other factors. Now x–rays no longer are just that, but we must get tomograms, sophisticated cat scans, and MRIs and MRAs. Some of these diagnostic tools will prevent countless surgeries or pinpoint where and when to intervene

Clearly, all of this will lead eventually to a very sophisticated little machine like in Star Trek's, Dr Mc Coy opening his little hand held scanner to know where all the problems in the body were they are and how to cure them. But the key is still awareness: the physician's, the patient's and it all comes down to true unadulterated education and knowledge.

New agents that will affect or cure diseases

Replacement drugs

Insulin that supplements a defective pancreas; stem cells that would replace the absent or deficient islets that produce it, cholesterol-lowering drugs that effectively control high blood levels, hormonal replacement therapy when we stop secreting hormones, and so many others yet to be discovered.

Vaccines

The present vaccines have changed the whole profile of disease in our society and refusing them endangers this society. In the future, we need vaccines against AIDS, vaccines to bypass or neutralize proteins that enter the body and cause rheumatoid arthritis, vaccines against the severe allergens caused by gluten and lactose allergies, cause of Wagener's granulomatosis, Crohn's disease, ulcerative colitis, and on and on.

New Treatment Technologies

Surgeries

Prostheses such as heart valves and pacemakers, joint implants and artificial tendons all over the body, muscles transposition, microsurgery permitting movement of tissues all over the body and coronary transplants. Now they are doing robotic surgery at a distance and crumbling kidney stones with ultrasound.

Invasive X-ray Technologies performed by radiologists doing Endovascular Stints in the heart aorta and other coronary vessels

Endoscopic surgery, or minimally invasive surgeries done by endoscopes (like a periscopes) for such things as gall bladders, nearly all intra-abdominal organs, carpal tunnels, most joints, hearts. These techniques are also used for going down into the gut to see or prevent disease of the stomach and colon, or for repairing such problems as gallstones and repairing the stomach from regurgitating into the esophagus.

There are so many innovative surgeries that it is difficult to keep up with advances. I can just imagine the future growth in these fields. We are limited only by our imagination.

Objectives for research

Prevention

We already have learned to prevent many diseases simply with *education*. On striking example is the AIDS epidemic that has been mostly thwarted in this country by educating people about the disease and how to avoid it. Elsewhere, the epidemic is rampant—mostly as a result of populations that are unaware and uneducated in these matters.

Another example is vaccines that have literally eradicated many viral diseases and more are coming. We had to educate people to get them. Now we have to educate the population that there is a vaccine for cancer of the cervix. a. As I write this book a vaccine to prevent cancer of the cervix (HPV or Human papillo-virus). If we could extend this knowledge to all preventable diseases, and I believe it is quite feasible, then we would cure or prevent many afflictions. It is simply a question of spending time in health prevention education so that people can understand the major importance of the vaccination versus the minimal chances of complications.

Why, for one thing, isn't everyone taught CPR (cardio-pulmonary resuscitation)? Why doesn't everybody know the fundamentals of first aid?

With this knowledge in place, everyone would have a solid foundation to take care of themselves and their friends and neighbors in emergency situations. Imagine how many lives we would save!

Find the origin of disease

The key to so many diseases is to find the causes producing the malfunctions in our system, what causes the micro-cumulative damage that ultimately produces disease. If we simply could eliminate the sources of cellular damage we could eliminate diseases.

For example there are many diseases of which we have found the etiology, such as cancer of the lung that was directly attributed to smoking, melanoma of the skin caused by sun exposure, prostate cancer caused by lack of testosterone, asbestos that causes lung consolidation and the list goes on. We are eliminating the causes thus will eliminate the diseases…if everyone knows about it and cooperates.

The key to future prevention is to find the offending agents, which seems easy but actually is actually quite complex. Just think for example how to sort out which of five thousand food preservatives approved by the FDA will cause cancer, let's say of the stomach or colon, especially when the irritation has occurred over ten, twenty or thirty years.

The FDA has tested all of these preservatives, but they do so over a period of two or three years and one food preservative at a time. The cumulative damage occurs only much later, so it makes it difficult if not impossible to sort out which substance is the culprit and which one interacts detrimentally with the others.

It is difficult to find the offending agents due to years of micro-accumulation and to onslaught of so many toxins together. Which one was it that caused lymphomas, leukemias, cancer of the breast or of the pancreas? What agent has accumulated over so many years to cause the dreaded Alzheimer's and other brain diseases? What bacteria or viruses are involved?

Think of the heavy metals, a lot of which like lead and mercury we know. But there are also the slew of others we don't know. Think of the industrial emissions and how they affect us and how many have been corrected but how many are still present.

Many pesticides are neurotoxins that will destroy the insect's brain. How do we know it does not do the same to us, simply because we don't see any effects immediately? The dosages we get when we spray a pesticide are minute. But in the long run they, too, are cumulative. Look at bottled water that releases dioxins in the water it contains when it is frozen. Dioxin is a known carcinogen.

By far the greatest stride for the future of our health will be to sort out all the toxins in our lives and get rid of them. It is not a minor task, but it is a major factor in our well-being. Just think of all the cancers that cause us to say to ourselves "what caused it?" To find the cause of disease is a major goal, albeit a very difficult one to achieve. But we have made great strides so far. It will not stop here.

Specific foods

I was in Papua, New Guinea, years ago, after the days of cannibalism. But when it had still been practiced thirty years earlier, I learned, when its practitioners killed an opponent in battle, they would eat only the legs of a fast runner, or the heart of a brave man, or the brain of an intelligent chief, so they would gain the best traits of their victims.

"You are what you eat." It sounds so simplistic, yet was it not for the selectivity of our absorption mechanism of the gut and liver; we would not be able to produce the nutrients so necessary for the growth and maintenance of our so complicated organism with its even more sophisticated computer. Humans take eating as a recreation and a gratification rather than a body-sustaining activity.

The goal is to research and develop foods that are nutritious, yet pleasant, non-addictive and effective in promoting the health of various organs.

Some people need specialized foods.

A few examples:
The athlete who requires a certain blend of proteins-fats and carbohydrates at given time. Ask Lance Armstrong what made him perform so well.

Also consider these people and circumstances:

- The type II diabetic who needs micro-carbohydrates to alter the docking stations of the receptor cells and to lower carbohydrate levels.

- The obese person who needs to change the pathway of triglycerides.

- The pregnant mother watching her personal health and nutrition to grow a healthy embryo all the while staying healthy to feed it better once born.
- The various blood types, and more specifically genome types, that each require a different profile of foods for growth and development. There are so many different types of being of all shapes, sizes, color, cultures with different physical and brain capabilities, why should we expect one food to feed all. We must research and find the individual specific foods to satisfy the genome, blood, type, and race.

As it is, our eating habits are based on cultural tradition (childhood habits), as well as smell, taste, appearance, appeal, gratification, and, of course, advertising (the drooling that it entices, called the Pavlovian reflex). But how can this haphazard feeding satisfy the specific, individual needs of our cells?

We have no clue as to what effect food has on our constitution, or which may cause disease. Why does the small bowel develop "the leaky gut syndrome" and begin absorbing large proteins, thereby potentially causing rheumatoid arthritis?

326

Why does our body form abnormally high cholesterol? It could be genetic, but it also simply could be caused the improper combination of foods we eat. What causes us to develop chronic inflammation that affects the brain, the heart, obesity and diabetes?

One example is the research the Dr Barry Sears (*The Zone*) has done to find and define the eiconasoids in the cell environment. There are good and bad eiconasoids, and they are apparently strictly regulated by the types of foods specifically the types of fats we ingest. I think more research of this type is mandatory.

The whole profile of food should and will be researched, and when we know and apply this knowledge, our health will improve substantially. It will also be a giant step toward better health. But we must ignore or outlaw the food advertisements to be successful.

Genetically Improved Crops

One of the potential ways to alter foods will be by designer engineered foods that will fit the needs of individual physiologies. It will require many years of trial to arrive at very sophisticated engineered foods to fill specific needs. There will be a period of trials and tribulations, and it is not for us trying to undermine the search out of a fear of what we do not know.

Meanwhile, genetically-modified crops make it possible to feed massive populations that otherwise would starve. Of course they are not prefect, but they sure fill a huge void. *The "bad" side effects are few when weighed against the millions of lives they will save.*

There is a lot of future in this genetically engineered food. Right now, we are at the very beginning of the research on this development that promises to be a massive provider of not only food in general, but foods nourishment that is specialized to meet the needs of particular populations or categories of people.

We were not very sophisticated when we first tried antibiotics like penicillin and sulfas in the later 1940s, as an example, but look at the mass of specialized antibiotics today. The same will be true with all fields of research, where our knowledge may be elementary today but will be quite advanced tomorrow. We tend to be afraid of these new developments mostly because we don't know much about them, but they evolve with time.

If they are not good, they disappear, but if they are good, they add much to our lives. That industry is rising to the challenge, but there is much more to do before we are perfect. Meanwhile, we are able to feed or provide drugs to millions.

Hormones

There is no question that hormone replacement therapy will be, and should be, a major source of research in the future. The hormonal system is a highly influential system in our body and it controls aging. Researchers are fearful of HRT, as the media and the general public are scared of it due to the cancers of the breast and prostate.

As we speak, they are doing intensive studies on gonadotropins as the instigator of Alzheimer's. If that study is right it will prevent and maybe cure that disease.

On the other hand, if we had the right bio-chemical replacement hormones, everyone would be taking them and living happily ever after. That is entirely possible.

The Genome

In 2003, we completed the mapping of and essentially identified the whole structure of human DNA, which projected us into a new era of understanding human genetics. In combination with IBM's master computer, called the Grid System, with its massive brain power, many technicians and biologists from around the world combined in the effort to map the Human Genome and develop an understanding of how to use it.

With this knowledge, science will be able to analyze the entire human, in general and in particular, and find ways to replace damaged or genetically altered DNA proteins (target therapy) causing disease anywhere in the body.

Then we have to identify the disease ("target"), find where it is on the chromosome that causes it, and find a neutralizer DNA or a drug, which would block the defect. That is where most of the causes of hereditary or mutation diseases will be identified. We would recognize the gene source of damage to the individual cells causing the disease. With this information, we could find the cure, whether it is to block, remove, replace, or duplicate it.

From this point on, it will require massive, sophisticated computers—and the geeks to drive them—as well as a whole team to brainstorm the issues. It will also take about $50 billion a year for all the searching involved.

In 2004, thirty-eight drugs were approved by the FDA. Some examples are a drug called Imitanib (Gleevec) that blocks the enzyme on the single gene that causes myelogenous leukemia (a blood cancer) in children and cures it. Another one is Norvir that blocks the replication of the virus in HIV. Yet another is Allegra that functions as an antihistamine. Another is Remicade that blocks damage responsible for Rheumatoid Arthritis, Crohn's disease, and so on.

With a method called recombinant DNA technology, we managed to use bacteria and yeast to fabricate various drugs that would block disease at the "target" site on the DNA molecule. One example that will make a huge difference in aging is "*Muscle Doping*." At the same time, it could change the whole face of athletic competition and the Olympics.

In essence, our muscles have multiple nuclei with repair mechanisms. DNA immediately repairs a muscle that is injured by overstraining,, and as it does so it makes the muscle fiber grow bigger, thus the hypertrophy that occurs after exercising.

There also is a factor called myostatin that prevents this excessive growth. We can use outside stem cells to transport a portion of the DNA into the muscle fiber itself, thus letting the muscle grow normally. In a disease called muscular dystrophy (too much myostatin, which is produced by the abnormal gene and prevents muscle growth.)

This method could change the whole profile of the aging person that has the same problem with myostatin. It would add more strength, more stability and equilibrium to aging people. The technology is about ten years away, but what a bonus it would be for older folks.

National Geographic, in a system called Genographics, now has developed an ingenious concept of tracing the migrations of the human race through the eons and finding who our ancestors were, how we got here, and age-old questions of that sort just by doing your personal chromosome analysis. Eventually we will find medical traits of our ancestors and correct those that have been genetically transmitted to us. For more on this, visit:

www3.nationalgeographic.com/genographic/snptest.html

Well, this is but a glimpse at the potential of this newfound knowledge. It is greater than any sciences in any fields in the whole world's knowledge. The human organism is by far the most complex mechanism ever, and it has replicated itself to the tune of six billion humans in the world. It is hard for me not to acknowledge intelligent master orchestrators overseeing this complexity.

So the future is definitely optimistic. All of this is not science fiction. It is real, it exists, it is going on in giant steps, as we speak.

Stem cells
Stem cells are *the basic building blocks of all cells*, because originally all cells "stem" from them. They are present in the

330

very early stages of an embryo and from them grows or blooms a beautiful human being. That is, all its cells originate from the stem cells. But they will remain active throughout life, busy replacing all blood cells. They are very involved in repair or regeneration of damaged tissues, inflammation, immunity and even in cancer growth as we found out recently. They age like any other cells by having a shortening telomere (the regeneration portion of a DNA molecule). As they grow older, the telomere shortens and the replication slows down. That is the reason why researchers want embryo cells that are very young, thus more vigorous and lasting longer. Now they are harvesting them from skin in young babies. We used to take them from early embryos.

We can take the stem cells and alter them to become and replace any specialized cells in the body. Stem cells' growth can produce bone, tendons, skin, muscle, brain and even cancer cells. The ones taken from children younger than six months have few or no "self-tags," the system to identify them as "nonself," and therefore are not rejected by the immune system.

We already have used twenty thousand stem cell skin grafts that are commercially available, primarily for burn patients, made countless ear cartilages for reconstruction, and applied numerous bone grafts to injuries. We have bypassed the embryonic donors, so controversial (the President Bush veto), by using other types of stem cells (babies' skin). That, in fact, was the ultimate result of the president's veto, as it has sent the human mind searching for other alternatives that will be far more usable.

There are countless uses for this technology but it is not the answer to every problem.

Right now we are working at creating isolated donor organs like hearts and kidneys that will facilitate transplants but also will have little or no rejection, a great benefit. That is done by cloning just a part of a human being, preferably the one that needs the organ transplant, to fabricate the appropriate organ. Cloning is duplicating another animal or human. It does not have to be the whole being, we can do only parts of it, such as an organ or skin or bone or cartilage or probably any part of the body needed.

Just imagine what the present stem cell research will yield in the future! They are helpful, although to a limited degree, in regenerating blood cells destroyed in chemotherapy. We are working on the replacement of damaged or dead parts of the brain as in Alzheimer's, Parkinson's or severed spines from accident cases and God knows what else.

Please understand that this stem cell development is only one part of the big picture in the future of medicine. It is not the cure-all, but it will be an intrinsic part of it. It is but another limb on the tree of life.

Tissue transplant

Today, with the newer tissue typing and cross matching, we can identify the proper tissues to go to the proper person with less tissue rejection.

The first tissue transplant ever was a blood transfusion. Imagine how many people died at the beginning when we did not know blood typing. But now we are transfusing millions of people a years and countless lives are saved. It was but a stepping stone to all the organs we transplant today.

I remember when Christian Barnard transplanted the first human heart in another human being in South Africa, and just how revolutionary that was. We, the human race, talked about the ethics of doing so and how wrong it was to "fiddle around with God's Creation." We did that when Banting and Best discovered Insulin, and we are still doing that with stem cells, the human genome and genetically altered crops. The time will come soon when these discoveries will be mainstream and the ethical questions will have been forgotten. The professor types and religious types who talk about ethics forget that **God** created our brain and its extraordinary creativity and imagination, and he did this for a reason.

Today we do many transplants of hearts, lungs, kidneys, livers, heart-lung units and the list will go on and on add infinitum. We are now working on better anti-rejection drugs, we are triaging organs to be more compatible, and we are *building new organs* using stem cells—organs of the proper size and shape, and tissue types, so as not incite tissue rejection phenomena, and that will live longer due to short telomeres. Heart surgeons recently started doing heart transplants in babies younger than six months. so the body does not reject the new heart. So the future is very encouraging in this field also.

Nanotechnology

The prefix *nano* means extremely small. Remember the movie called "The Fantastic Voyage?" A "spacecraft" twice the size of a red blood cell was injected into the blood stream with the mission of dissolving a clot in the brain.

We are doing exactly that by fashioning molecules to target various organs for repair, such as is done with stem cells or medication, by coating certain cancer medications to enable them to attain their objective and be more effectual, or coating the inside of vessels, plugging holes in them, and even coating the inside of stents so they will not thrombose and obstruct later on. Nanotechnology will do two things: it will develop certain proteins to mimic the ones we need to replace, cure, and so on. Then it will be a specialized transport through the blood or lymphatic system to the very site where the pathology needs it. We already transport healthy chromosomes to replace genetically defective ones.

Angiogenesis

Angio means blood vessels and *genesis* the beginning of growth. So angiogenesis means promoting vessel growth in areas that have lost it. Now we have developed *angiogenesis inhibitors* that will do the reverse and stop blood supply to, let's say, a cancer. It in turn starves its blood and it will regress. It is a technology that will open many branches of treatment.

Finance and affordability

It is absolutely impossible to do all this development without huge amounts of money, and the incentive to make money in the process. Unfortunately, the downside of it is greed that is one of the biggest weights that will drag our medical system down the drain. Why? Because it is a fat cow, an endless well of money into which anybody can dip the ladle.

Of course, our government wants to protect private enterprise, but it does so at the cost of much suffering and many lives that cannot afford it. Fortunately, there are many doctors and clinics that provide free medicine, but it is not the norm. Just think of the exorbitant costs of medicines, surgical equipment, supplies and even garbage disposal. All professionals touching medicine—including accountants, lawyers and management consultants—jack their fees up "because doctors make a lot of money." But think of malpractice insurance premiums and, far more so, the hidden cost of practicing defensive medicine, a concern that takes the form of ordering excessive lab, x-rays, maintaining excessive records and all the computer needs that it has brought about.

Corporate greed also plays a role. Drug companies only research drugs that will make big money. Medical supply companies develop equipment of borderline usefulness and charge huge fees for it, but soon this equipment is set aside to be replaced by new "state of the art equipment."

What fuels all this is the fact that the businesses are on the stock market and have to show huge profits often to satisfy the stock owners, at the expense of the patients. Conversely without this huge amount of financing there would be no research and breakthroughs in such areas as stem cells, genomics, drugs, equipment or education. It is a Catch 22 that is presently very difficult to resolve. But it *can* be corrected and the future will see that done.

Medical reimbursement

Private insurance vs. government

Private insurances seem to charge exorbitant fees, but that is due to the great expense of all aspects of medicine, as I have discussed above. Nevertheless, the monthly health insurance premiums are usually less than the cost of owning and operating your car for the month. And they are far cheaper than the increase in taxes that a government managed care would bring with it. Private insurance is managed by highly motivated people with financial incentives, and therefore well managed. Meanwhile, you are getting the best quality medical care in the world.

Government insurances (Medicare and Medicaid) on the other hand are poorly managed by people who have no direct incentive, so spending money does not affect them directly. The cost is triple that of private insurance. You think that it does not cost you anything because "it is free," but just look at the elevated income taxes of countries that have universal care.

Canada has one of the highest income taxes in the world and about one third of that revenue is to pay the medical bill. On top of that, they must cut down the number of employees including doctors, nurses, and paramedical personnel. They must close hospitals and they often have cut-off ages for certain procedures. In our spoiled nation, this type of coverage and quality of medicine would look like mediocrity to you. I practiced for two years in that system and could not stand becoming a vassal to government employees who did not care for high medical quality. None of you want to wait two days in an emergency room or a mandatory fifteen months for an open heart operation.

By the way, it would be impossible in this country with lawyers on contingency fees to have such poor quality medicine as this socialized medicine. They would have a field day or we would have to cut the exorbitant remuneration of tort lawyers. Canada manages to snuff out malpractice cases, often leaving the poor patient hanging. Besides, in Canada, the mean life expectancies went down five years in the time since the inception of universal care thirty-six years ago. If you expect things to be done for you, which is totally against all that is good for your aging welfare, expect to lose quality and growth of your great American medicine.

.

Conclusions

These are the keys:

- Finding the *causes* of diseases.
- Finding *the body's specific foods* that will fit the individual's genome and not starve it or damage it.
- Developing *new sources of therapy* by continuing the existing and exiting research.
- Preventing the great danger of losing it by government via *socialized medicine* controls. These are political maneuverings to gain notoriety and votes that would be destructive to the ongoing growth of our research. There are very few socialized medicine systems in the whole world that are progressive, prompt, intense, proactive, and focused on the teaching of their medical personnel and the promotion of intensive research like the ones going on with stem cells, genome, and so on.
- *Educating the population* to behave preventatively by *knowing* and that means controlling the uneducated teachers like the some of the media, many self appointed magazines etc.
- Making *medicine affordable* by controlling excess greed interwoven with politics. Financial incentive is very important, but it does not have to be based in greed. The future challenge is to control the balance between excess profit of those who take advantage of the golden goose in the health system on the one hand and keeping the exorbitant cost at bay to permit everyone to have access.

- We have the *greatest and the highest quality* medicine in the world. We just have to smooth out the wrinkles, but at all costs we must keep it. We must put our biases aside as we would all benefit from this.

-

May I remind you that in 1900 the mean survival was forty-six years of age. One century later, it is around seventy-eight to eighty. If you are fifty, sixty or seventy, your chances of healthy, vigorous self-reliant survival to one hundred are very good if you apply yourself. **Only you that can do it.** And every year it will get better.

The doctor of the Future will give no medicines, but will interest his patients in the Care of the Human frame, in diet and in the causes and prevention of diseases.
Thomas Edison

CHAPTER TWELVE

The Ten Commandments for a Daily Guide

What I hope you took from this book is the message that when we "retire" we have the opportunity to recycle ourselves to a new exiting life of positive attitude with health and vigor.

This is the time for new hobbies or perhaps that non-stress part time job that you always wanted, for spending time with spouses, grandchildren, and many good friends.

With this positive outlook you may live longer. Every day you must strive to attain these ultimate goals by ordering your *priorities*.

So you must control your own health and behavior. You must get to know as much as possible about how your systems functions and act accordingly. *Nobody else will do it for you,* since there is only one very strong motivator to keep your body and mind healthy and alert as *you*.

No one else has so much invested in you and has so much to gain or lose as you do. You cannot blame someone else for your problems and you cannot rely on anyone to do it for you.

Sure, people will help you, but never in every detail as you will.

So what I am saying is you need to do prevention and preparation, and this book gave you a lot of advice towards this. You also must do maintenance, so if something goes wrong you must soon repair it so as to keep all systems in functioning order.

Ten Commandments

- *1-Aging is a preventable and curable disease* and it can be enhanced by knowledge and positive maintenance of the problems.

- *2-Attitude.* The whole motivator is your mind and if it is negative nothing happens. *If it is positive the entire orchestration of the symphony is magnificent, including its finale.*

- *3-Aging is the result of gradual damages* caused by daily tiny accumulated assaults over years and years. We *do not see the changes since they occur in minute increments* every day. Our bodies do not deteriorate one organ at a time, but all together, bit by bit, and the interactions among the thirteen trillion cells are so interwoven that eventually, as more cells are destroyed, the systems start crumbling, ultimately ending up with a massive collapse called senescence That is the only time we finally see the accumulated damage, and that is called aging

- *4-We are mostly responsible for the accumulated damage through* our ignorance, apathy, denial and lack of priorities.

- *5-The most intense damage is the lack of physical exercise.* If we don't use it, we lose it. Every day!

- *6-Mental exercises.* The brain needs exercise as much as the muscles and the heart; otherwise it deteriorates.

- *7-Nutrition.* We have to provide the right building blocks to keep our cells healthy and well maintained. Food's primary function is not to satisfy our taste. That means we require a *balanced diet with all the ingredients in it.* There are *no magic pills, diets or alternative medicines.*

- 8-There are *so many injurious agents.* We cannot avoid all of them, but at least as much as possible we can reduce the amount of contact we have with toxins that wreck our cells and our lives.

- *9-Hormones are the most important orchestra leader.* They must be present in all stages of our lives, including aging

- *10-Immunity* and acute inflammation are our protective armies. Our immunities must at all costs be kept healthy and prepared, with good attitude, vaccinations, *no* Howard Hughes behavior (i.e. sterilizing everything around us). This will protect us until the end.

What is a perfect day to the age aware person?

- *Attitude*; willfully change your mood if it is bad. Don't bite your mate, friends, neighbor, etc., as that only creates a vicious cycle that will stress you, a no-no.

- Denial is the biggest killer.

- Mental block is a paralysis. "I don't take pills." "Smoking does not cause cancer." "That is your opinion; I read an article and it said different." "Aging is inevitable and we can't do anything about it."

- Laugh every day.

- Empower yourself. "I can do that."

- *Exercise your brain*; read for recreation but also for learning. Take courses and go to symphonies and plays. It is your brain that will grow-up..
- Do not retire, recycle.

- Curiosity is your best ally.

- Hormones are necessary.

- Smoking is a bad, destructive drug.

- Avoid toxins such as industrial agents like turpentine, benzenes, and pesticides and drugs like Larium, Statins when allergic etc.

- Stress with cortisol and adrenalins create havoc with your brain.

- Make sure you test for Homocysteine and glutathione.

- Take antioxidants.

- *Exercise;* it is the primordial necessity for health and vigor in your aging period.

- Know all about electrolytes and hyperthermia.

- You will feel so good once you start. *There is no more important priority* for you. You should exercise diligently thirty to sixty minutes a day, five times a week. Make sure you replace potassium. Running will eventually kill your knees and stop you from exercising.

- Exercise is the most significant thing you will do for your health and satisfaction in your aging years, and they will last much longer. If not I'll give you your money back.

- Get rid of *inflammation*. Find infections and do not procrastinate to treat them—gingivitis, boils, vaginal infections, etc. You will be less likely to have them if your immune system is healthy.

- Be aware of all *toxins* that you have contact with on a daily basis and try to eliminate as many as possible.

- *Food*: *try three meals* a day and not many snacks in between. If you eat good meals, you will be less hungry, or not hungry at all. These meals must not be mostly carbs, but have proteins and fats. Example:

- Breakfast, Two eggs with whole fruits and grain bread and butter or Smart Balance.
- The other two meals should have red or white meats. Trim the excess fats and don't be afraid of fat in meats.

- Fish has a lot of good fats in them and forms good Eiconasoids. You should eat one to three meals of fish a week. Salmon is the best for that reason.

- Lots of vegetables mostly colored that are fresh and that have all the good supplements in them. White vegetables should be eaten sparingly as they are starches. Wheat and other grains like oats and barley are starches also, and should be consumed gingerly.

- Fresh whole fruits are good, but remember they are carbs.

- Eat a variety of foods, i.e. all foods, but don't exaggerate saturated fats (animal fats), and emphasize good eiconasoids, the omega-3s. Eat eggs, but the ones with omega-3. Instead of msrgarine, use Smart Balance.

- Sugars and pastas are the causes of obesity, diabetes, and constant hunger. These are the high glycemic index carbs. You must minimize them, but not get rid of them.

- If you must binge or splurge on bad foods, do so only once a month. It is the daily accumulations that will kill you.

- Do not crash diet; it is harmful and totally unproductive. A   crash diet will reduce fat, but also reduce all cells in your body particularly in your brain (eighty percent fat).

- Obesity occurs a little bit every day and is very difficult or impossible to get rid of it.

- Drink water, but *not* eight glasses a day as it will dilute your electrolytes. Stay at three or four glasses a day, more in hot weather or with exercise. Drink little or no coffee, which makes you secrete stress hormones. Same with soft drinks. Keep wine or liquor to only one a day, or four or five a week.

- Sleep is a recuperative time when you replace all your hormones and heal some of the micro damaged cells. When we are young we think we are 'macho' to sleep only a few hours. But we are not helping ourselves by doing this.

- Later in life we lose melatonin secretion and thus sleep. It is incumbent on us to replace the missing melatonin.

- Know and avoid all the toxins we have talked about.

- Don't be afraid of your genetics. You do not know if you have longevity, and can't assume that you have bad genes. Just be positive and investigate.

- Keep your immunity and healing systems in good order

- A little bit of damage occurs every day, and don't ever let that concept out of your mind.

Daily guide to supplements and vitamins

I take all of these:
Vitamins
Vit. C 500 to 2000 mg/day. Take the Esther form.
Vit. E 200 I.U. /day (no more) or 400 I.U. every other
       day.
Folic acid; 400 to 800 mcg/day.
Vit. Bs complex (150) one a day.

Vit. A 10,000 units (no more) every three days.

Co Enzyme Q -10; 50 to 150 mg/day.

DHEA; 50 –100 mg/day [men] 25-50 mg/day [women]

Selenium; 100 mcg every two days

Glucosamine sulfate; 1000-1500 mg/day and take it for the rest of your life

Chondroitin sulfate; 500 mg/day. Same as above

Hyaluronic acid 50 to 150 mg/day

Glutathione; 150 mg/day if you have brain fog or a known genetic deficiency.

A multi-vitamin, one/day

> The best one I have analyzed and like is Centrum Silver without iron. It has many good supplements and vitamins. It is also very easy to digest. If you are menstruating then take iron.

One half hour of sunlight every day for vitamin D (you can take too much Vit. D). But if you are not sure you are producing enough, take 400 I.U. (No more).

Sometime skip all your vitamins for a day or two or three to relax your system. In other words, it is not bad to forget a day or two here and there. If you have trouble taking all of these, separate them into two or three sessions a day.

In the case of **Vitamin C,** do take the *Esther form* as it is much less irritating to your stomach. Often it is combined with calcium, selenium, potassium or magnesium, which also are useful supplements. In the case of women, the calcium is particularly helpful. DO NOT take too much vitamin C, as there are some reports of kidney stones (e.g. 2 gm or more). Calcium supplements should always be accompanied by magnesium, either in the same pill or with a good balanced diet with meat, which has a lot of magnesium in it.

Vitamin E is a lipid (fat) soluble vitamin, and the excesses will not be secreted easily by the kidney, so accumulation *can occur. That can be harmful.* Stick to 400-I.U./day maximum.

Folic acid, along with other Vitamin Bs, is vital for the nervous system (mostly the brain). It reduces homocysteine, which greatly increases the chance of heart disease and brain disease. A fairly large number (ten to twenty percent) of people are born with a very damaging elevation of homocysteine. It is lowered by folic acid.

Co Q-10 is an energy enhancer. Best not to take it at night, it may prevent you from sleeping. It will take a week or two to have an effect .It enhances the mitochondrial function, which is the furnace of the cell, by accelerating the chemical reactions and renewing the energy cycle.

Selenium and Zinc (in Centrum) enhances the immune system and thus is helpful in fighting colds and other infections (and maybe cancer). It relieves anxiety and reduces vasospasm thus less heart attacks and strokes.

DHEA is a precursor of other hormones. Rarely does it cause gynecomastia (breasts) in men. (Usually that complication is dose dependant, e.g. the more you use, the more likelihood it will happen). Of course, it does not have that effect on women.

EVERYBODY who is older than forty-five years old should take **Glucosamine, Chondroitin and Hyaluronic acid** to protect joint cartilage against future destruction. These render the cartilage less brittle and more elastic, and thus less prone to break down from exercise. They permit the cartilage cells to regrow when damaged and thus keep the cartilage healthy.

I repeat, be very careful not to take excessive lipid soluble vitamins as they can be harmful to you. These are Vitamins A, D, and E. I know people who feel tired and lousy overall, and on questioning it turns out they are taking more and more vitamins to feel good. They are likely overdosing. If you start getting tired on vitamins, stop all of them and wait a couple of weeks. Then re-start one at a time. Make sure you are not taking excess lipid soluble vitamins.

Other supplements (that you may want to add)

- **Saw Palmetto** one or two capsules a day to relieve prostate problems for men

- **Garlic** is a super- anti oxidant and is known to reduce cholesterol.

- **Acetyl-carnitines** (1 gm a day) Are foods that specifically feed the furnace of the nerve and brain cells [mitochondria].

- **L-carnitines** (1 or 2 gm a day) Same but for muscle cells [both heart and skeletal muscles].

- **Lycopenes** daily have been showed to substantially reduce prostate cancer. Eating tomatoes in any forms five or six times daily will do it. Centrum Silver has added it along with Lutein. Blueberries, interestingly enough, are shown to contain a supplement [Lycopenes] that reduces cancers and heart disease.

- **Lutein** prevents eye problems, particularly macular degeneration.

- **Melatonin** 2mg TR (time release) 1, 2, or 3 depending on your age, one half hour before bedtime. Plain melatonin lasts only four hours. It is the natural sleeping pill and helps regulate jet lag.

All of this is covered more extensively in Chapter Ten, so please refer to it.

The new concepts dictate that we all should take essential fatty acids, especially Omega-3 fatty acids, in the form of a capsule daily. **EFA's** feed the cell membrane and are **very** necessary for all brain cells' function. You could have fatty fish (mostly freshwater fish) three to four times a day to replace this however.

Two peptides that are derived from meat are **Acetyl L Carnitines** [take1-2gm/day] that is very important in brain cell mitochondria's function, thus contributing to more mental energy and improved mood. **L-Carnitines** also is a major food for the muscle cells, especially the heart muscle. [Take 1- 2 gm/day]. Both also help reinforce the immune system. They both supplement the mitochondria, in the brain and in muscles.

Hormonal Replacement Therapy I believe that after menopause men and women need some form of hormonal replacement. Each individual is unique and requires a physician to titrate the amounts .according to your blood levels etc. You must see a physician who understands this such as an anti-aging M.D. It is difficult to suggest a specific dosage or type of hormone as each individual's metabolism is different. Although mild as a replacement DHEA is an alternative.

I warn you it will not be easy. You will have to get off your duff mentally, emotionally and physically. You will have to break long lasting habits. "I can't stop smoking." "I love my coffee." I can't exercise, I have back problems." I'll be damned if I go without my butter, sugar, etc.." "I am too busy to exercise, too busy to eat well ..." (What's wrong with your priorities!?)

You can have coffee, but keep it to one cup a day.

Merely taking vitamins is not the whole answer, nor is exercising once a week. Get the Picture!

If you feel tired or don't feel good

- *Not enough sleep*; No chance of recuperation. You cannot do without sleep. Don't exercise at night before bed. Don't drink coffee or tea or soft drinks especially Mountain Dew. Take Melatonin. You must sleep in a quiet and dark room. Bananas, chocolates and cheese haves an excitant (monamine oxidase inhibitors)

- *Too much exercise,* like running six to eight miles, will just get you tired, but also you overdose on brain hormones that charge you up and prevent you from a good sleep. Too much exercise will also depress your white blood cells and change your fighting capabilities. *Not enough* and your body is not strong enough to sustain daily activities. See Exercise on page 130.

- *Review foods* You may be tired after meals because you are getting too many carbohydrates, which elevate insulin. In the case of food allergies, some develop after many years; Glutens, Lactose intolerance, peanuts, preservatives like sulfites in wines, nitrites in meats etc. Tea and toast diets will cause exhaustion. Anorexia is malnutrition. Vegetarians often will become very tired after ten to fifteen years of the diet and as soon as they revert to balanced diets they feel better. You do not see the damage immediately, only years later when it has accumulated and surfaces. See Essential Nutrition on page 172.

- *Light affective disorder;* Lack of sun and /or vitamin D will cause some people to feel tired and depressed. See Antioxidants, vitamin D on page 287.

- *Review vitamins and supplements*; If you take too much it will concentrate, much of it in your blood, and offset the balance for a while. So divide the doses in two or three times a day. Glucosamine and Chondroitin will sometimes tire you during the day so take then at night.

- *Analyze your pills*; stop them and restart one at a time to identify which makes you tired. Take these pills at night.

- *Electrolyte imbalance*; Sodium and potassium and

water. See page 160.

- *Too much water;* that is a very common cause of lack of energy and you dilute your blood, and then you will urinate or sweat the excess and have electrolytes deficiencies. Also discussed beginning on page 160..

- *Too much caffeine;* coffee, tea, chocolate. Caffeine will stress you all day and you will have trouble sleeping well thus tired he next day and so goes the vicious cycle.

- *Too many soft drinks;* acid, sugar and caffeine. Acid will acidify your blood and create isotonicity imbalance. Sugar raises your insulin.

- *Some toxins;* Mercury, lead, house, air and water, lots of industrial agents. All described in Chapter Five beginning on page 72.

- *Chronic mold and mildew contact.* See page 99.

- *Chronic inflammation in your body;* Chronic arthritis particularly neck pain and back pain will tire you.

- Any forms of low grade bacterial or viral infections creating a constant battle in your body. See Chapter Nine, beginning on page 247.

- Obesity

- *Depression;* Will often make you tired.

- *Mental energy;* You are without energy either because you are mentally apathetic or plain lazy to do anything. Only you can be the doctor to cure that problem. But you are the best doctor, so your chances are good to get out of that slump.

Then, of course, many if not all diseases will tire you and sap your energy. That is when you must see a doctor to rule out major problems. If you are still tired after taking these steps, get tested for Chronic Fatigue Syndrome, Lyme's disease, Hepatitis, Encephalitis, cancer. Don't wait too long. If it is one of these, the longer you wait the less curable it will be. You must not do the denial bit. Disease of the heart, lung, kidney or other organs will all tire you. It is imperative that you have a physician assess you, because procrastination could mean the difference between cure and too late to cure.

Take a risk except when you are sick. Not taking a risk is the biggest risk of all. You stand to lose much more if you do not take hormone replacement therapy, or exercise or eat well. Be flexible with change and stay on top of your situation at all times.

Doing nothing is going downhill. You have only two choices: to grow and climb the hill to satisfaction and vigor, or to do nothing and wither away downhill to ultimate deterioration.

You do not see the damage on a daily basis but it become apparent only years later when the massive accumulated damage called senescence surfaces.

Are you so ingrained in your habits and prejudiced in your thoughts not to hear the message?

BIBLIOGRAPHY

Healthy Aging, Andrew Weil M.D., Knopf 2005

YOU, The Owner's Manual, Michael Roizen, MD and Mehmet Oz MD

The Nation's Health, Philip R Lee, Carroll L Estes, Jones and Bartlett 1994

Interpreting and Teaching American History, William H Cartwright and Richard L Watson, Jr. 1961

Heal Your Headache, David Buchholz, MD, Workman Publishing 2002

Ten Weeks to A Younger You, Ronald M Klatz, MD 1999

Real Age, Michael F Roizen MD, Harper Collins 1999

Dear Meg Tells You, Meg Whitcomb, Warner Books 1986

Heart at Work, Jack Canfield & Jacqueline Miller, McGraw-Hill 1998

The Longevity Factor, Richard A Passwater PhD, Keats 1993

Why Am I So Tired?, Sherry Rogers MD, Phillips Publishing 1997

Drugs: The Worst Offenders the Best Alternatives, Sherry Rogers MD, Phillips 1997

Choosing the Right Long-Term Care Insurance, J K Lasser John Wiley & Sons 2002

Merchants of Immortality, Stephen S Hall, Houghton Mifflin Company 2003

How to Feel Younger Longer, Jane Kinderlehrer, Rodale Press, Inc. 1974

Fit For Life, Harvey and Marilyn Diamond, Warner Books, Inc. 1985

Bypassing Bypass, Elmer Cranton, MD, Medex Publishers, Inc. 1997

The Lives to Come, Philip Kitcher, Simon & Schuster 1996

The Heart of the Soul, Gary Zukav and Linda Francis, Simon & Schuster Source 2001
Body for Life, Bill Phillips and Michael D'Orso, Harper Collins 1999
Coagulation: the Essentials, David P. Fischbach, MD, & Richard P. Fogdall, MD, Williams & Wilkins 1981
Group Psychology and the Analysis of the Ego, Sigmund Freud, Bantam Books 1960
Forty Something Forever, Harold and Arline Brecher, Healthsavers Press 1992
Right Brain Sex, Carol G Wells, Avon Books 1989
When Old Men Die, Bill Crider, Walker 1994
Younger Next Year, Chris Crowley and Henry S Lodge, MD, Workman 2004
Power Aging, Gary Null, PhD, New American Library 2003
Grow Young with HGH, Dr. Ronald Klatz, HarperCollins 1997
Textbook of Medical Physiology, Arthur C Guyton, W B Saunders Company 1986
Cecil Textbook of Medicine, James B. Wyngaarden, MD, and Lloyd H Smith Jr., MD, W B Saunders Company 1988

2-Mind over Matter
The Cortisol Connection, Shawn Talbott, PhD, Hunter House 2002
*The Blessing, Gary Smalley & John Trent, PhD, Simon & Schuster 1986
*Virus of the Mind, Richard Brodie, Integral Press 1996
Self Matters, Phillip C McGraw, PhD, Simon & Schuster Source 2001. Dr Phil
*Beyond Relaxation Response, Herbert Benson, MD, William Morrow & Co. 1975
Minding the Body, Mending the Mind, Joan Borysenko, PhD, Addison Wesley 1987
Don't Sweat the Small Stuff, Richard Carlson, PhD, Hyperion 1997
Ageless Body, Timeless Mind, Deepak Chopra, MD, Three Rivers Press 1993

3-Aging is a Disease & Curable
How and Why We Age, Leonard Hayflick, PhD,. Cell Associates, Inc 1996

4- Hormones
*The Testosterone Effect, Ed Shippen, M.D.
*The Schwartzbein Principle Dr Schwartzbein
*The Wisdom of Menopause, Northrup
The Cortisol Connection, Shawn Talbott, PhD, Hunter House 2002
*The 30-Day Natural Hormone Plan, Erika Schwartz, MD, Warner Books 2004
*Hormones of Youth, Ronald M Klatz, MD, 1999
*DHEA Breakthrough, Stephen Cherniske, MS, Ballantine Books 1996
Grow Young with HGH, Ronald Klatz, MD, HarperCollins 1997

5 -Micro damage
The Yeast Connection, William G Crook MD, Vintage 1986
Dust, Joseph A Amato, University of California Press 2000
*Migraine: The Complete Guide, The American Council on Headache Education with Lynne M Constantine & Suzanne Scott, Dell Publishing Group, Inc 1994
*The Four Pillars of Healing, Leo Galand
*Manifesto For a New Medicine, James S Gordon, MD, Addison Wesley 1996
*Beyond Relaxation Response, Herbert Benson, MD, William Morrow& Co 1975

6-Exercise
Biomarkers, William Evans, PhD, and Irwin H Rosenberg, MD, Simon & Schuster 1991
Make the Connection, Bob Greene and Oprah Winfrey, Hyperion 1996

7 -Nutrition
*The Zone, Barry Sears, PhD, Harper Collins 1995
Omega RX Zone, Barry Sears, PhD, Regan Books 2003
The NutriBase Guide to Protein, Carbohydrates, & Fat, Avery, 2001
*Love & Survival, Dean Ornish, MD, Harper Collins 1997
*Dr Atkins' Diet Revolution, Robert C Atkins, MD, Bantam Books 1972
*Good Fat vs. Bad Fat, Maggie Greenwood-Robinson, PhD, Berkley Books 2002
*Protein Power, Michael R Eades, MD, Mary Dan Eades, MD, Bantam 1999

8- Obesity
Enhance Your Weight Loss Results, Shawn M Talbott, PhD,
Make the Connection, Bob Greene and Oprah Winfrey, Hyperion 1996
Death by Diet, Robert R Barefoot, Triad Marketing 2002

9-Immunity
The Immune Advantage, Ellen Mazo and Keith Berndtson, MD, Rodale 2002

10-Antioxidants
The Magnesium Factor, Mildred S Seelig, MD, Andrea Rosanoff, PHD, Avery 2003
The Calcium Factor, Robert R Barefoot and Carl J Reich, MD, 2002
Isoflavones and the New Concentrated Soy Supplements, Phillip N Steinberg, Healing Wisdom Publications 1996

INTERNET QUICK REFERENCES

American Association of Retired Persons (AARP):
http://research.aarp.org
Demographics and references

American Academy of Anti-Aging Medicine (A4M):
www.worldhealth.net
Multiple articles are discussed on new development in anti-aging and health issues and in good health in general.

American Medical Association (AMA): www.ama-assn.org
Quality patient info from the JAMA information files.

Bandolier: www.jr2.ox.ac.uk/bandolier
An excellent monthly review of prominent subjects like organic manure. claudication, painful menstruations, etc.

Center for Disease control and Prevention (CDC);
www.cdc.gov
It provides searchable patient info for hundreds of topics like air bags, aids, yellow fever, parasites, etc here and abroad.

Dr, Duke's Phytochemical & Ethnobotanical Database;
www.ars.grin/duke
Research and data on plant s as medicines.

Environmental test kits; www.testproducts.com
Many test kits for the home including Radon, CO, Air quality in the house,

Health Finder: www.healthfinder.gov
U.S. Department of Health and Human services.

Intelihealth; www.intelihealth.com

It is a joint venture between Aetna and John Hopkins University that provides general health advice, drugs and the index of the contents supplied by the NIH and the National Health Council.

The Journal of the American Medical Association (JAMA): http://jama.ama.org/
A good physician reference journal

Mayo Clinic: www.mayohealth.org
A team of doctors discuss diseases in lay terms .they have a monthly publication. You can e-mail questions.

Medscape from WebMD: www.medscape.com
www.webmd.com
Excellent up to date data on all of medicine in internal medicine and surgery. Access to Medline

Mercury Amalgams Homepage: www.altcorp.com
A review of literature by dentist and physicians of the effects and damage of mercury. Lot's of info.

National Academy on an Aging Society:
www.agingsociety.org

National Institute of Health (NIH) : www.nih.gov
U.S.A.'s best research organization for all that is related to health.

National Institute of Neurological disorders and Stroke:
www.ninds.nih.gov/disordres/parkinsons-disease
The nation's leading supporter of biomedical research of the brain and nervous system

National Center for Health Statistics (CDC):
www.cdc.gov/nchs

The New England Journal of Medicine:
http://content.nejm.org/

The ultimate journal for physicians the keep up with the development of standard medicine.

PubMed: www.hcbi.nlm.nih.gov/pubmed
It gives access to Medline, a data base of abstracts from NIH National Library of Medicine (over 9 million articles from 38000 medical journals)

Quackwatch; www.quackwatch.org
Your guide to quackery, health fraud and intelligent decisions

Environmental Test Kits for the Hazards of your Home: www.testproducts.com
Such as radon testing canisters.

Water Quality Association:
Go to Google and search "Water Quality" and press 'I feel lucky'

Search Englne; www.google.com or www.ask jeeves.com
You can find a million things here.

Fun and Useful Websites

How Stuff Works: www.howstuffworks.com
Good curiosity satisfier on everything and then some.

Maps; http://maps.expedia.com/

Modem Speed Test:
www.computer4sure.com//speep.asp?

Newspapers: www.onlinenewspapers.com

Search by Streets: http://peoplesearch.whitepages.com/

Search for people: www.infospace.com

U.S. Legal Information: www.inter-law.com

U.S. Census: WWW.census.gov/cgi-bin/popclock

WebCams: www.earthcam.com

Worldwide Time cams: www.guesswatches.com

Zip Codes: www.usps.gov:/ncsc/

The Best Site
Interplast: http://interplast.blogs.com
A thirty six year old non profit charitable high quality organization that does surgery on third world patients, teaches the local physicians reconstructive and hand surgery, and encourages consults with us in the United States.

Index

Stretching, 143-145
Stroke, 90, 134, 137, 150, 297, 356
Sugar, 66, 115, 148, 162, 173-176,176, 187-189,
192, 194, 197, 198, 203, 206, 207,
214, 227, 243, 274, 310, 342, 347, 349
Suicidal thoughts,
and depression, 30
Supplements, 14, 128, `46, 191, 206, 261, 267,
268, 271, 273, 274, 276, 283, 292,
294, 297, 306, 308, 311, 312, 322,
342, 344, 346, 348
Support system, 17
Surgery
endoscopic, 253
injury, 231
invasive x-ray technologies, 253
microscopic, 245
open heart, 335
and postoperative patients, 256, 262, 289
Sympathetic Nervous System (SNS)

T
Tendons, 141-144, 146, 151, 168, 295, 322, 331
Testosterone
Deficiency, 54, 60-61
Replacement, 54
Theodosakis, Dr., 292, 294
Third World, 7, 34, 124, 131, 237, 256, 263, 277,
358
deformities in, 46
Thyroid 66, 67, 107, 129
Thyroid Stimulating Hormone, 56, 299
Tissue destruction, 41, 86, 87, 194, 204, 207, 224,
230, 241, 257, 288, 331
Toxins, 44, 57, 84, 85, 87, 88, 99, 100, 125, 129,
202, 252, 261, 266, 324, 325, 340,
341, 343, 344
Trans-fat, 44, 121, 184-186, 190, 205, 207, 245
Transplantation surgery,
In tissues, 262
Truth
In relationships, 16
TV, watching, 21, 221-222, 320

V
Vaccines, 126, 128, 255-256, 262-263, 266, 322-
323
Viagra, 119
Virus, 101, 110,202, 249, 250, 253,-257, 262,
272, 285, 323, 324, 329

Vitamins, 178, 181, 187, 191, 200, 245, 267, 271,
272, 273, 274, 276, 281, 288, 312,
343, 344, 345, 347, 348
Volunteering
in retirement, 29, 33, 34, 36

W
Walking, 37, 133, 136, 150, 156-158, 216
Water, 25, 44, 73, 74, 96, 97, 102, 112, 115, 116,
120, 158-163, 166, 178, 191, 244, 245,
286, 301, 305, 306, 343, 349
and contamination, 78, 79, 88, 95, 98, 103-105,
109, 110, 111, 123, 125, 126, 264, 325
drinking
Weight gain, 54, 61, 67, 94, 147, 209, 210, 212,
218, 223, 224, 226, 230, 232, 236,
241, 245, 246, 306, 311
Weight Watchers, 208, 224
Woolhouse, Dr. Fred, 314
Work
attitude toward, 10, 12

Y
Yoga, 21, 37, 143, 145, 154, 156

Z
Zinc, 108, 111, 267, 277, 308-310, 345